AMERICAN VICTORIANA

AMERICAN

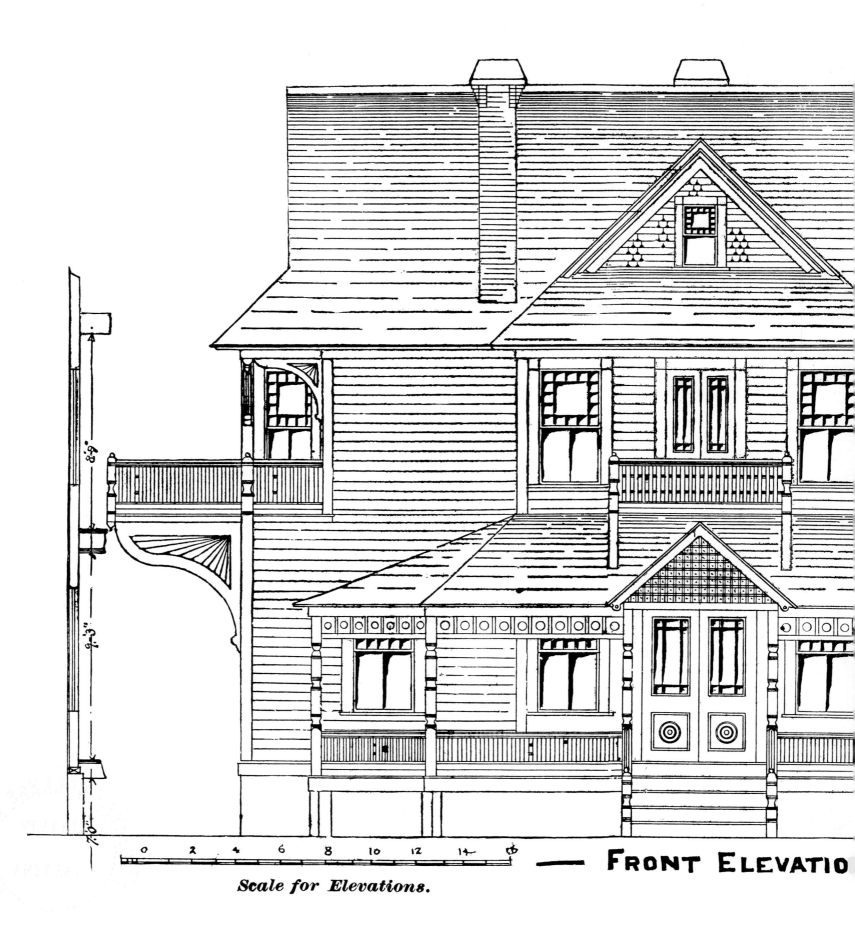

Scale for Elevations.

FRONT ELEVATIO

VICTORIANA

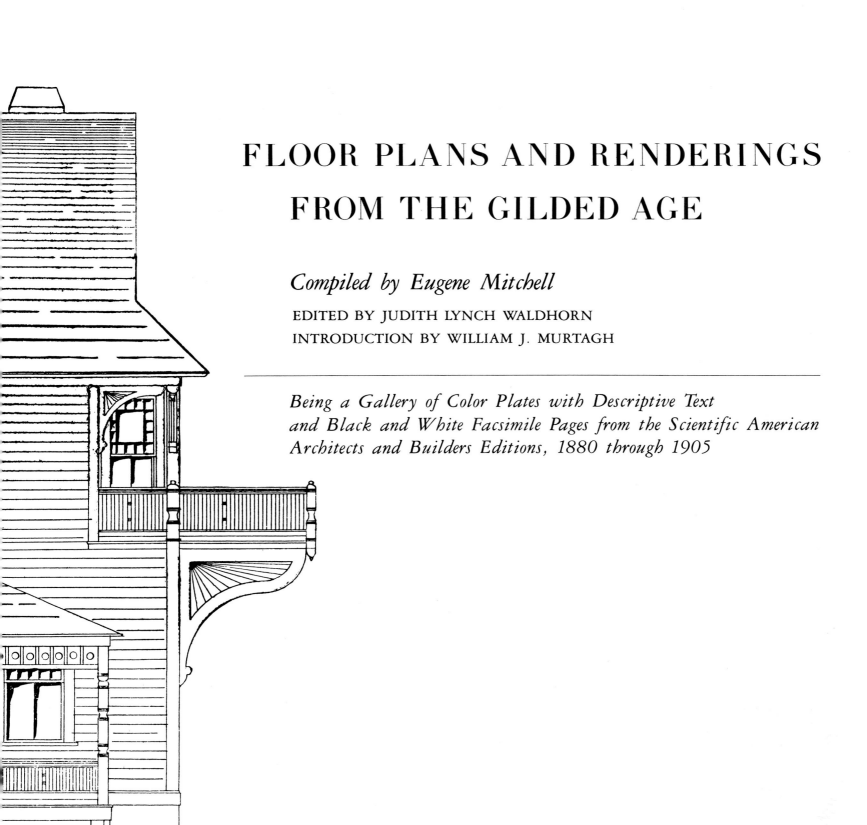

FLOOR PLANS AND RENDERINGS
FROM THE GILDED AGE

Compiled by Eugene Mitchell

EDITED BY JUDITH LYNCH WALDHORN
INTRODUCTION BY WILLIAM J. MURTAGH

*Being a Gallery of Color Plates with Descriptive Text
and Black and White Facsimile Pages from the Scientific American
Architects and Builders Editions, 1880 through 1905*

VNR **VAN NOSTRAND REINHOLD COMPANY**

NEW YORK   CINCINNATI   TORONTO   LONDON   MELBOURNE

First published in paperback in 1983
Copyright © 1979 by Eugene Mitchell
Library of Congress Catalog Card Number 82-25924
ISBN 0-442-26393-7

Printed in the United States of America
Designed by Wendy Cunkle Calmenson

Van Nostrand Reinhold Company Inc.
135 West 50th Street
New York, New York 10020

Van Nostrand Reinhold Company Limited
Molly Millars Lane
Wokingham, Berkshire, RG11 2PY England

Van Nostrand Reinhold
480 Latrobe Street
Melbourne, Victoria 3000, Australia

Macmillan of Canada
Division of Gage Publishing Limited
164 Commander Boulevard
Agincourt, Ontario M1S 3C7 Canada

Cloth edition published 1980 by Chronicle Books

16 15 14 13 12 11 10 9 8 7 6 5 4 3 2 1

Library of Congress Cataloging in Publication Data
Main entry under title:

American Victoriana.

   Reprint. Originally published: San Francisco:
Chronicle Books, c1979.
   Includes index.
   1. Architecture, Domestic—United States.
2. Architecture, Victorian—United States. I. Mitchell,
Eugene Frank. II. Waldhorn, Judith Lynch.
[NA7207.A67 1983]   728.3'7'0973   82-25924
ISBN 0-442-26393-7 (pbk.)

PREFACE

IF ONE were to choose a single word to describe the *Scientific American Architects and Builders Edition*, the word would be practical. Filled with articles on constructing homes to stand the test of time, this architects' and builders' magazine was written for the general public. Its principal aim was education—how to distinguish between a well-constructed home and a poorly constructed one, and how to decorate it once you'd bought or built it. In this context, the magazine is as useful today as it was then.

Scientific American Architects and Builders Edition was first published in the 1880s by its parent magazine, *Scientific American*, when straightforward, reliable advice was desperately needed by America's new home buyers.

Scientific American is one of the oldest continuous publications in the United States. It was founded in 1845 by Rufus Porter, a Yankee artist credited with over one hundred successful inventions. The new publication was only eight weeks old when the printing house was destroyed by fire. Porter sold his interest to Alfred Beach, son of Moses Beach, editor of *The New York Sun* and well-known inventor, and Alfred Beach's school friend, Orson Munn.

On July 23, 1846, the new firm of Munn & Company published their first issue of *Scientific American*. It became the most influential magazine devoted to science in the history of the United States. Inventors themselves, Munn and Beach nurtured other inventors and soon opened a patent agency. By 1866, theirs was the largest patent agency in the world.

Novice and famed inventors alike constantly conferred with *Scientific American*'s staff of editors. This constant exchange of information also provided stories for the magazine. It was not uncommon to see inventors such as Elias Howe, Samuel Morse, Dr. R. Gatling, and Thomas Edison in the magazine office. In fact, the first article on Thomas Edison's new talking machine appeared in the *Scientific American* in 1877. By then, circulation of the magazine was up to 40,000 copies a week, an impressive figure at the time. The publishers always maintained their ideals of giving value to subscribers, exchanging information within the magazine and through personally answered letters to the editor. This personal attention to readers was standard *Scientific American* practice at a time when high ideals and reliability were rare.

The booming building market in the 1880s was rife with opportunity and opportunists. The industrial revolution after the Civil War resulted in mass production. The rapid expansion of railroads across America made manufacturing and distribution on a large scale profitable and possible for the first time. Goods and services were available in plenty—but frequently the goods and services were of poor quality. The business philosophy was "Caveat Emptor," or "Let the buyer beware."

Hundreds of thousands of people were sold unsafe, poorly constructed homes. Families sometimes discovered that their sales contract had a hidden clause that could have them turned out overnight for one late payment. Building codes enacted to set minimum standards for health and safety, opened fertile fields for the dishonest. A builder could bribe an inspector to swear that a structure met code standards, when both knew the certificate was a sham.

In this atmosphere of hucksterism and fraud, the *Scientific American* stood as a monument to honesty. In the 1880s, several professional publications were published for the nation's fewer than 4000 architects. The new *Scientific American Architects and Builders Edition* tread the path between irresponsible construction hucksterism and theoretical architecture. Its purpose was to educate the customer of both the architect and the builder. Specifications, plans, and up-to-date articles on the latest products and proper methods of construction and decoration filled the pages, highlighted by splendid illustrations of attractive buildings readers could afford.

For 25 cents a month, editors introduced potential home buyers to the work of honest architects and contractors. If the magazine could not directly halt abuses in the building trades or corruption of public officials, it could teach its readers to understand plans and specifications, to make sure their homes were well built and that sales procedures were fair. The editors of the *Scientific American Architects and Builders Edition* felt that readers deserved good value for their money, whether they bought a cottage for $1,000 or a mansion for $10,000.

Advertisements for new products and notices of new inventions continued Munn & Company's original plan for exchanging information. If a reader had a better type of paint, another method of laying floors or a device to revolutionize the wood-working industry, the editors

v

wanted to know it—and they wanted their readers to know it.

Aside from its philosophy of presenting the most innovative techniques and merchandise available, the *Scientific American Architects and Builders Edition* had a unique feature: color plates with complete specifications for two buildings were published in each issue. Other periodicals of the era used black and white woodcuts or engravings which failed to do justice to the building illustrated. But the color plates captured the exciting contrasts of light and shadow, the projections and recesses, the colors and composition that were the most appealing qualities of Victorian dwellings.

By enticing readers with color illustrations of new dwellings, the editors felt their publication would also benefit the home-building industry: "The beneficial influence of this method is very great, very practical, and is sensibly felt by architects and builders in all parts of the country. Their services are in greater demand because their customers, no longer satisfied with cheap and ordinary buildings, now ask for the latest, the newest, the best designs, such as the *Scientific American* brings to them."

Within a few years, the *Scientific American Architects and Builders Edition* claimed the largest circulation of any builders' magazine in the world. Although professional architects still favored the *American Architect and Building News*, most of the houses built in the United States during the Victorian times were designed and constructed by and for people like the subscribers of the *Scientific American Architects and Builders Edition*.

As a result, the architectural "styles" were a marvelous conglomerate, as diverse as the American public. Interior arrangements were as varied and personal as exterior detail. Some homes had libraries, others did not. One would have a pantry, a sewing room and a smoking parlor; the house next door might have none of these features—but it might have a greenhouse.

The *Scientific American Architects and Builders Edition* ceased publication in 1905, near the end of the Victorian Era, when it underwent a change in content and reappeared under the title *American Homes and Gardens*. But its original purpose, to educate the clients of the architect and the builder, continues in this publication of AMERICAN VICTORIANA.

AMERICAN VICTORIANA is divided into two sections. First is a selection of twenty-two color plates from *Scientific American Architects and Builders Edition*, followed by excerpts from the specifications for each building. To help the twentieth century reader trace two decades of the evolution of architectural style, interior features, and exterior paint fashions, the renderings are arranged in chronological order. The second section is a selection of facsimile pages, also in chronological order. These articles, plans, and advertisements were chosen to give the reader insight into the world of the *Scientific American Architects and Builders Edition*—a glimpse of the new products recommended by the editors and the latest fashions in gardening, decorating and furnishing. The index will guide the reader to specific topics.

Think of AMERICAN VICTORIANA as a primer, a first step toward understanding the history of construction, design and decoration of homes in the late nineteenth century. For those with a strong interest in the history of the Victorian era, the book provides an introduction through the eyes of one of the most influential periodicals. The *Scientific American Architects and Builders Edition*—which had the serious purpose of improving the quality of American homes—is also delightful reading. AMERICAN VICTORIANA proves that the art and science of domestic architecture can be fascinating, down-to-earth, and filled with undeniable charm.

Eugene F. Mitchell

ACKNOWLEDGMENTS

When a book is finished and about to be published, one must pause and reflect, then bring to the publics' attention the names of the important people behind the scenes. These are people often known only to the Author or Editor.

I will start by thanking my literary agent, Elizabeth Pomada, for the time she devoted to this project. I learned a lot from her. The same type of feeling is again expressed for my other agent, Michael Larsen. In addition, my thanks goes out to Janet Murphy for her generosity in loaning me certain achitectural materials. My good friend, Larry Scholl is due a special acknowledgment for allowing me to use his home while I was in San Francisco working on this project, for some last minute typing and for putting up with my ambitions. A note of thanks to Bob Ray and Ben Nussbaumer for their help. And then we come to Mr. Steve Thomas, of Thomas Fine Arts of San Francisco. It is important to note that a number of these very interesting color plates may be found in his establishment on Clement Street. Steve has always been a constant source of encouragement. And lastly, I want to thank my wife Kathleen and children for allowing me to be absent from home, when this project demanded my immediate attention in San Francisco.

INTRODUCTION

WITH THE exception of pockets of earlier buildings in coastal areas, America's built environment dates from the nineteenth century—that diversified era of burgeoning development and expansion to which a British Queen gave her name. Inventiveness and diversity are the keystones of the era. While the eighteenth century imprinted on our nation such abstracts of democracy as freedom of speech and freedom of religion, the nineteenth century's bombastic enthusiasm for itself and its products created a veritible parade of structures across our land, secure in their own aesthetic inventiveness.

The wealth of wood to use as the basic building material in many parts of the country lent itself in a submissive way to the workings of the jig-saw—an invention which expanded the carpenter's ability to express himself. Those fanciful designs proposed earlier in stone or brick in the seminal writings of such tastemakers as A. J. Downing, Calvert Vaux and others were translated *en masse* into wood. Out of this marriage of invention and materials came the confections of the second half of the century, of which we are only now beginning to take cognizance.

Every aesthetic movement appears to have to go through a seventy-five year period of disregard. To a child playing in the attic, mother's dresses are funny, grandmother's are interesting, and great grandmother's are fascinating. The further one progresses through time, the more acceptable become the aesthetic efforts of the proceeding era. Finally, distance allows subsequent generations the perspective which time and time alone can give.

As we enter the last two decades of the twentieth century, this new perspective is affecting our perception of what the nineteenth century produced here. In the halls of academia, its creations may have been ridiculed in the 1950s, but at least it was talked and thought about in selected art history courses. The late Frances Lichton's book, *Decorative Arts in of Victoria's Era*, was an early twentieth century treatise for popular consumption. Interest in the nineteenth century has escalated in the last twenty-five years. One indicator is the increased prices asked for nineteenth century artifacts and furniture. They have moved from "junk shops" to "junque shoppes" to "antique shops"—a chronicle of acceptance *par excellence*!

Sir Nikolaus Pevsner, dean of British architectural historians, became chairman of the newly formed Victorian Society in Great Britian in 1954. The Victorian Society in America was created in 1966—to study the nineteenth century and to make its achievements more widely understood and appreciated by the American public. This private membership nonprofit organization is headquartered in Philadelphia in the Athenaeum—the earliest Renaissance Revival building in the United States. Its membership has grown by thousands, and its local chapters have proliferated to thirty-five in the last several years. Its magazine, *19th Century*, is acclaimed for its content and quality; its workshops assist the house restorer and inform the specialist, and its summer training schools in Boston and London unite its efforts with its British parent.

A second major ingredient in the recognition of the achievements of the nineteenth century was the establishment of the National Register of Historic Places in 1966 under the auspices of the Secretary of the Interior. This official list of the cultural property of the American people not only concerns itself with pivotal national landmarks, but it has broadened in scope to consider evidence of state and local significance, not only for single structures, but also for groups, where we find the surviving examples of the vernacular products of the nineteenth century mass builders.

Long unheralded and unheeded by the layman, the nineteenth century has finally "arrived." Rediscoveries such as *American Victoriana* will find a new appreciation and understanding of how creatively our forebears interpreted the free spirit of the industrial revolution. Publications such as this help us chart what's ahead by giving us a better insight into that which went before.

William J. Murtagh
President, the Victorian Society in America
Director, Historic Preservation Program,
Graduate School of Architecture and
Planning, Columbia University
Former Keeper of the National Register of Historic Places

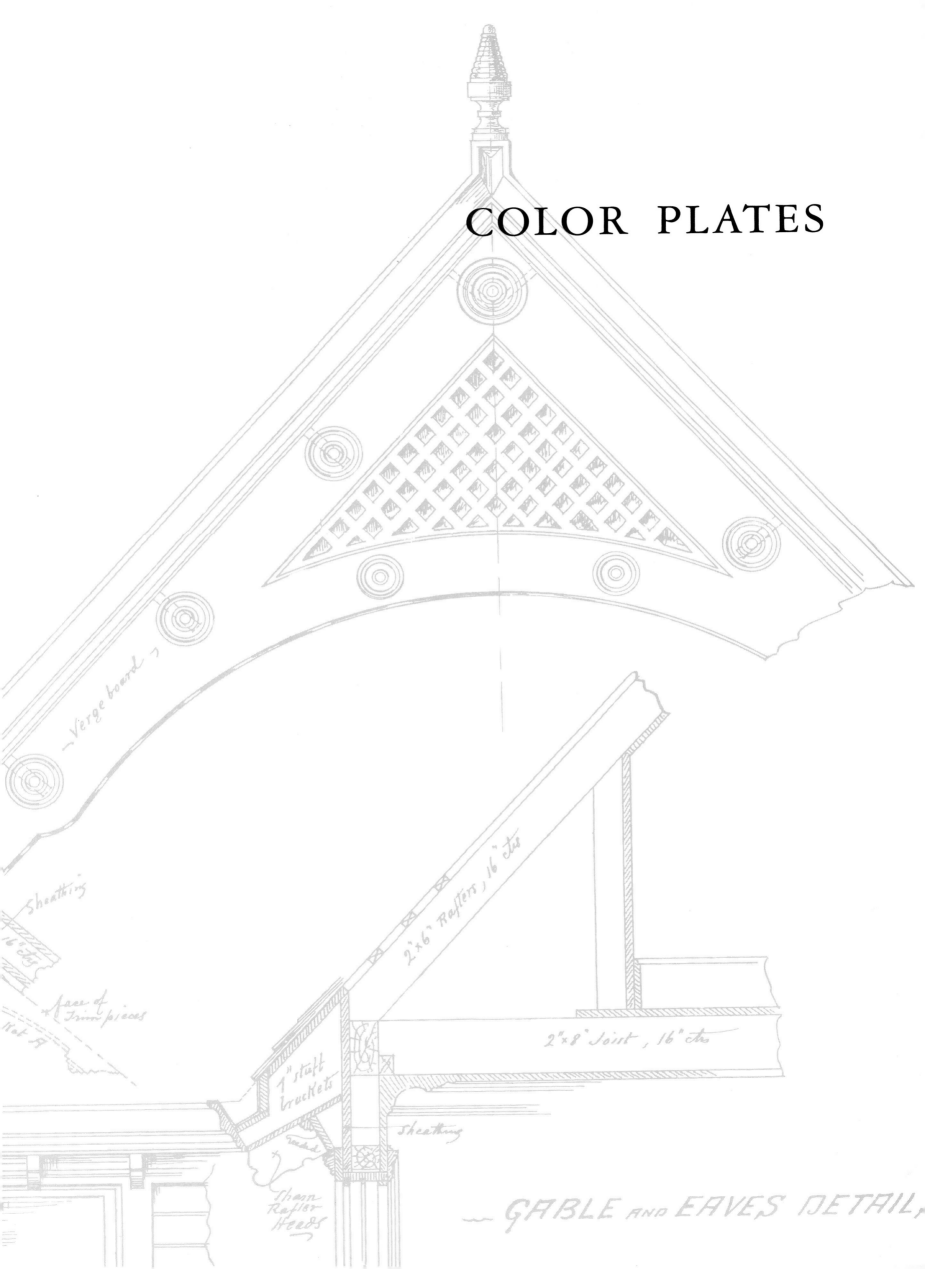

COLOR PLATES

PLATE 1

SUPPLEMENT TO THE SCIENTIFIC AMERICAN-ARCHITECTS AND BUILDERS EDITION-OCTOBER 1886.

·AN $1800 DWELLING· DESIGNED BY FRANK D. NICHOLS, BRIDGEPORT, CONN.

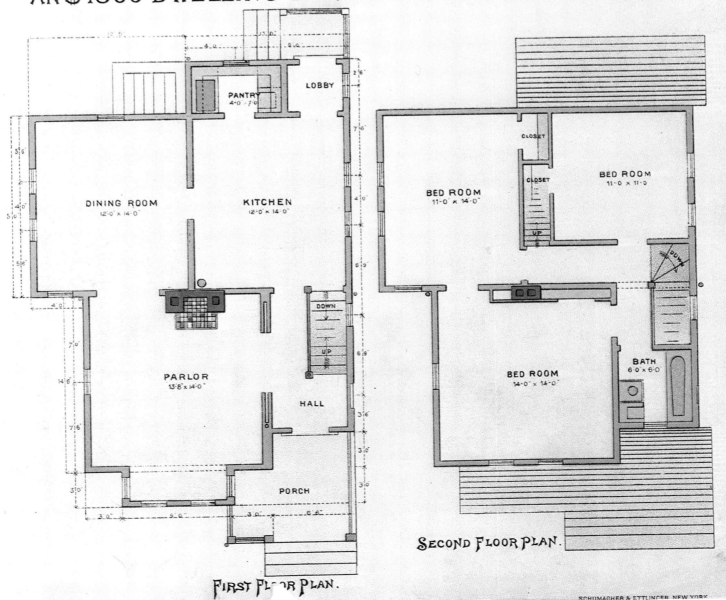

FIRST FLOOR PLAN.

SECOND FLOOR PLAN.

PANTRY 4·0 x 7·0

LOBBY

DINING ROOM 12·0 x 14·0

KITCHEN 12·0 x 14·0

PARLOR 13·8 x 14·0

DOWN

UP

HALL

PORCH

CLOSET

CLOSET

BED ROOM 11·0 x 14·0

BED ROOM 11·0 x 11·0

UP

DOWN

BED ROOM 14·0 x 14·0

BATH 6·0 x 6·0

PLATE 2

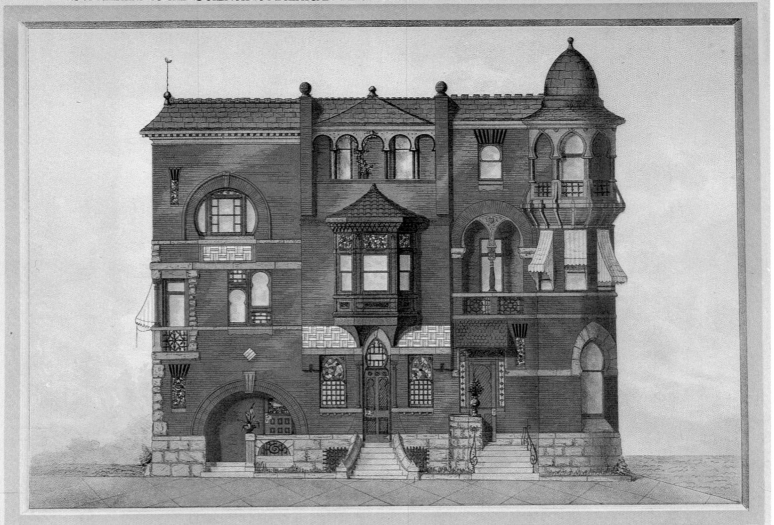

SUPPLEMENT TO THE SCIENTIFIC AMERICAN-ARCHITECTS AND BUILDERS EDITION-DECEMBER 1886

·A BLOCK OF BRICK DWELLINGS OF MODERATE COST·   W. CLAUDE FREDERIC, Architect, Baltimore, Md.

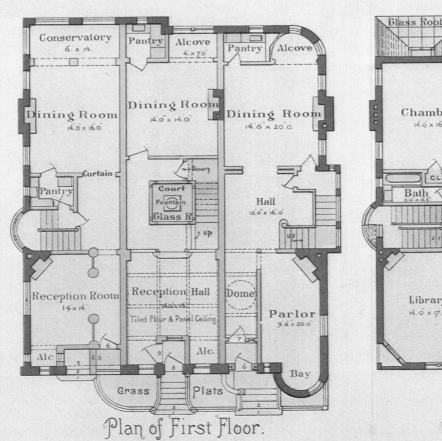

Plan of First Floor.

Plan of Second Floor.

PLATE 3

SUPPLEMENT TO THE SCIENTIFIC AMERICAN-ARCHITECTS AND BUILDERS EDITION-FEBRUARY 1887.

THE FARRAGUT CLUB HOUSE, CHICAGO. ROB. RAE, Jʀ Architect.

PLATE 4

A Two Thousand Six Hundred Dollar Cottage. GEORGE W. CADY, ARCHITECT.

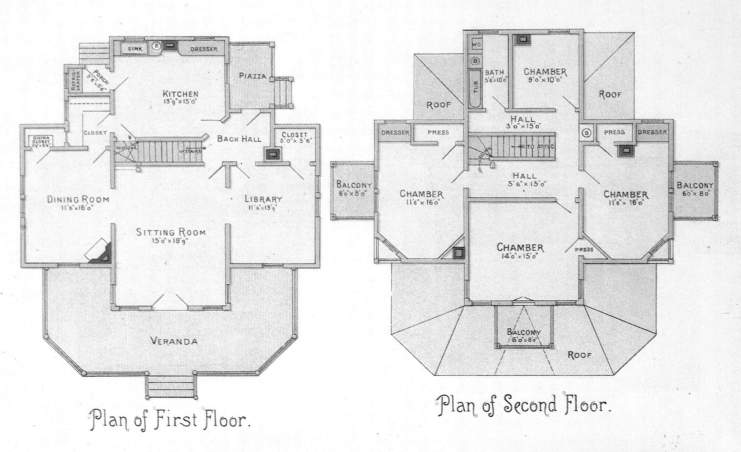

Plan of First Floor.

Plan of Second Floor.

PLATE 5

SUPPLEMENT TO THE SCIENTIFIC AMERICAN-ARCHITECTS AND BUILDERS EDITION- APRIL 1887.

RESIDENCE OF F.W. COOLBAUGH, ESQ. EAST ORANGE N.J.   GEORGE COOKE, ARCHITECT.

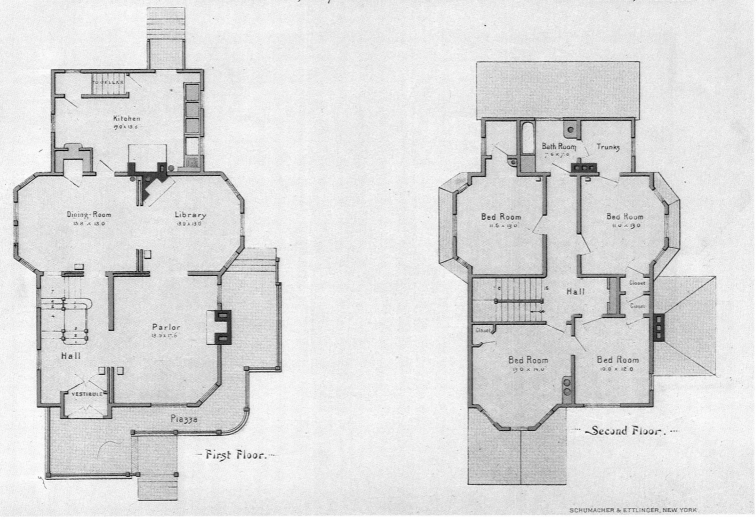

— First Floor. —

— Second Floor. —

PLATE 6

A Cottage Of Moderate Cost Intended For Future Enlargement.

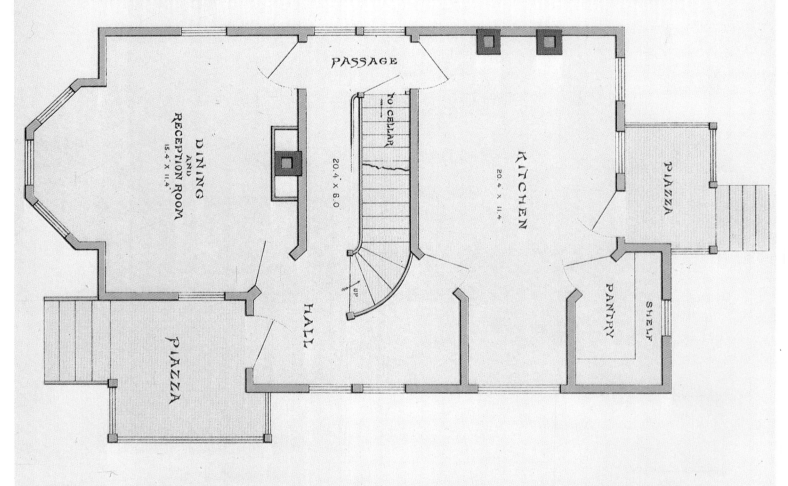

PLATE 7

⇒ THE COTTAGE (SHOWN IN APRIL NUMBER) AS ENLARGED ⇐

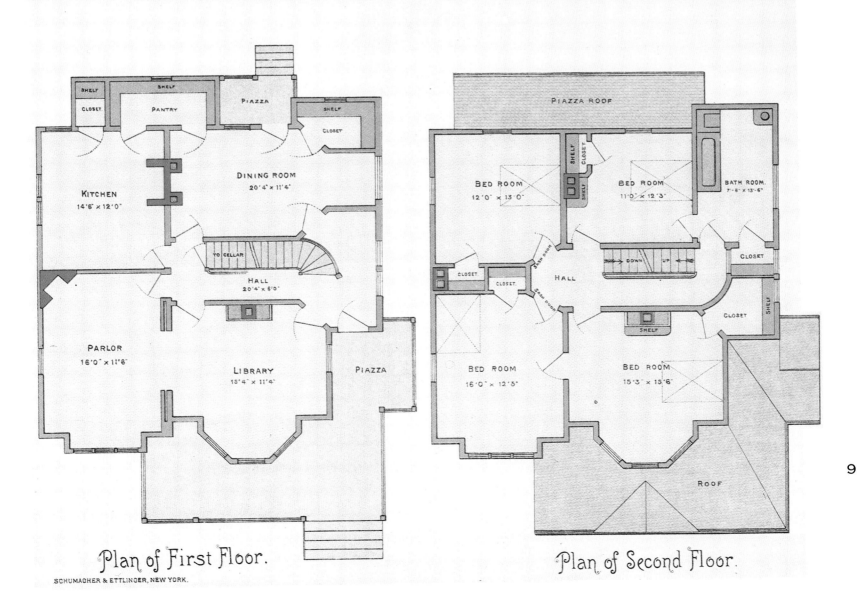

Plan of First Floor.

Plan of Second Floor.

SCHUMACHER & ETTLINGER, NEW YORK.

PLATE 7

SUPPLEMENT TO THE SCIENTIFIC AMERICAN-ARCHITECTS AND BUILDERS EDITION-MAY-1887.

⇒ THE COTTAGE (SHOWN IN APRIL NUMBER) AS ENLARGED. ⇐

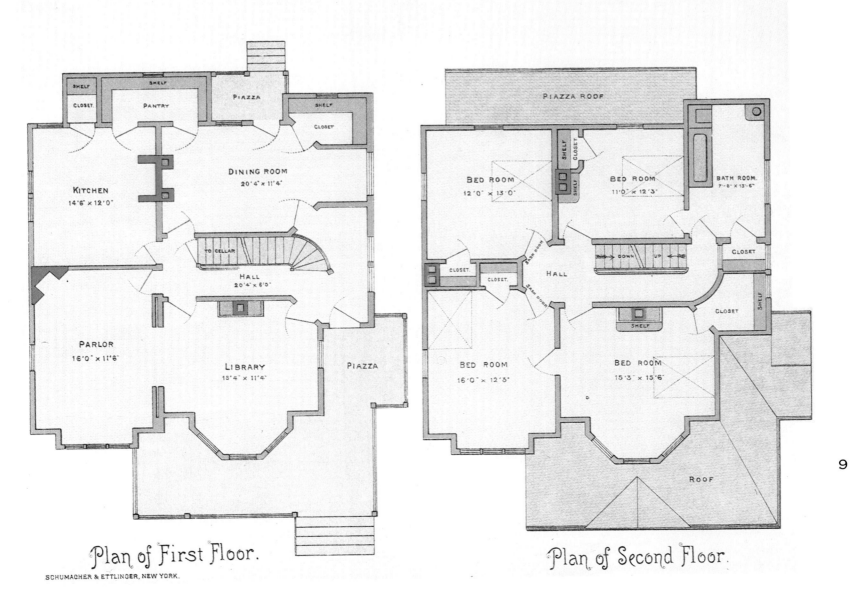

Plan of First Floor.

Plan of Second Floor.

SCHUMACHER & ETTLINGER, NEW YORK.

PLATE 8

A·Residence·Costing·Five·Thousand·Dollars·

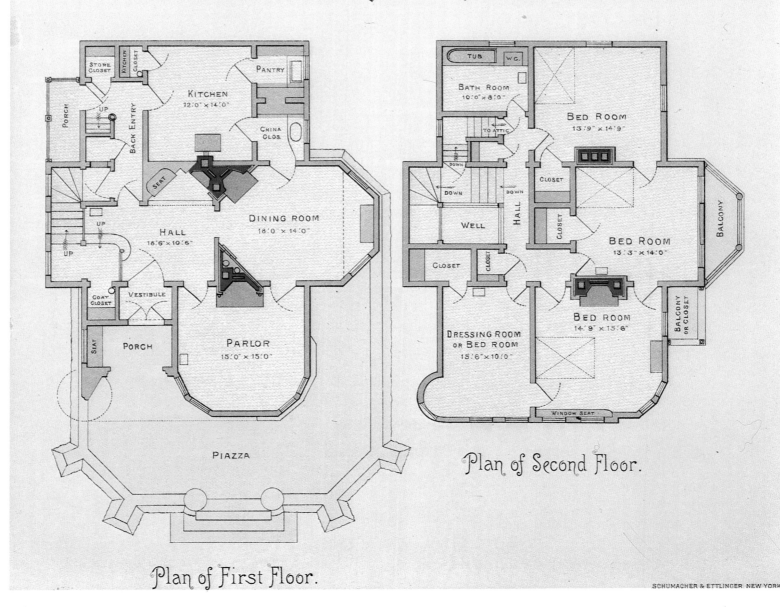

Plan of First Floor.

Plan of Second Floor.

SCHUMACHER & ETTLINGER NEW YORK.

PLATE 9

SUPPLEMENT TO THE SCIENTIFIC AMERICAN-ARCHITECTS AND BUILDERS EDITION-JULY 1887.

A·Residence·in·Kansas·City;·Mo.

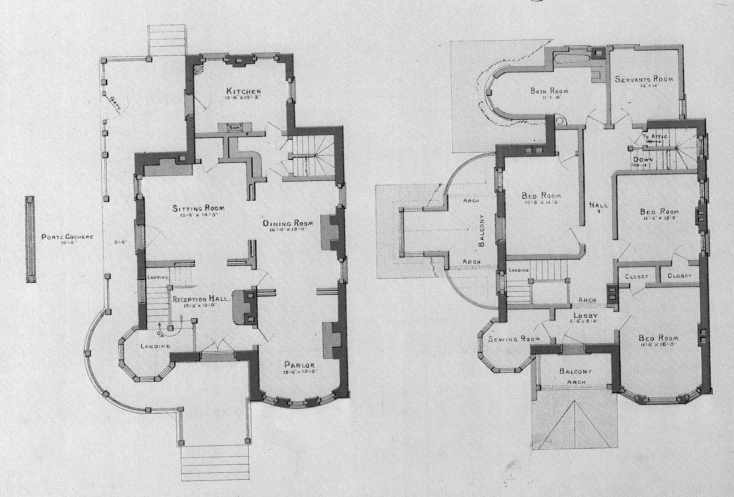

Plan of First Floor.

Plan of Second Floor.

SCHUMACHER & ETTLINGER, NEW YORK

11

PLATE 10

SUPPLEMENT TO THE SCIENTIFIC AMERICAN-ARCHITECTS AND BUILDERS EDITION-AUGUST 1887.

A Four Thousand Dollar Cottage.

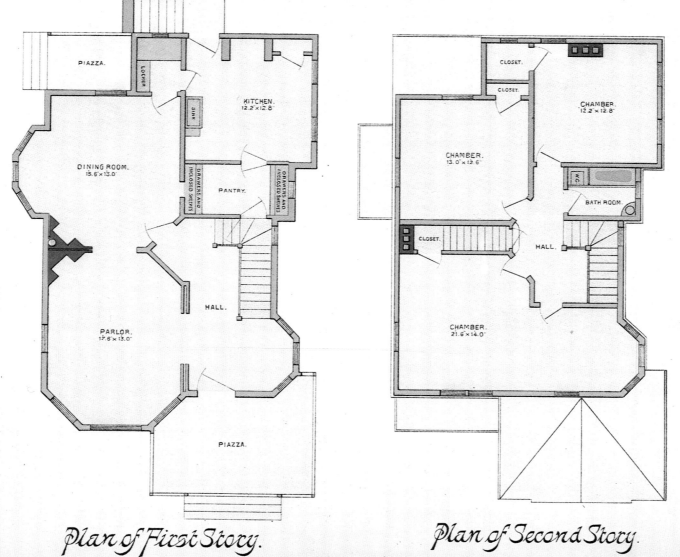

Plan of First Story.

Plan of Second Story.

PLATE 11

SUPPLEMENT TO THE SCIENTIFIC AMERICAN-ARCHITECTS AND BUILDERS EDITION-OCTOBER-1887.

❧ A COUNTRY STORE AND FLAT. ❧

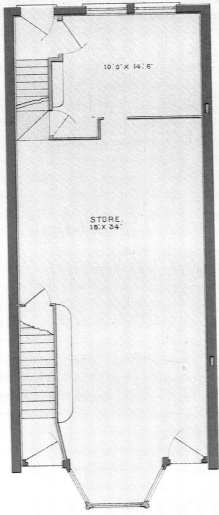

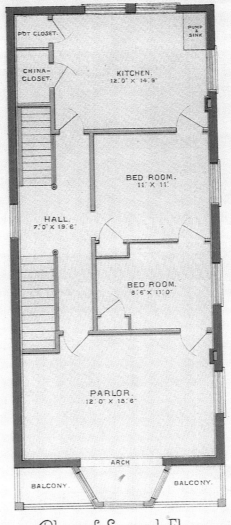

Plan of First Floor.

Plan of Second Floor.

PLATE 12

City Frame Houses of Moderate Cost.

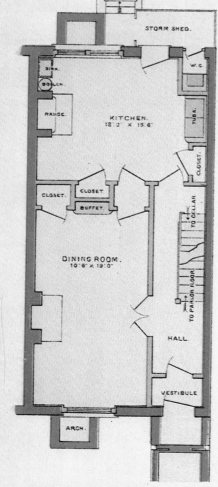

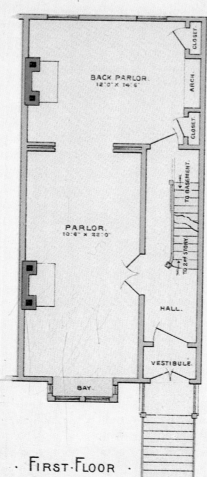

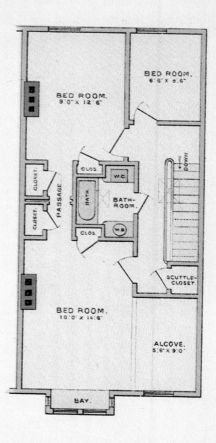

· BASEMENT ·   · FIRST·FLOOR ·   · SECOND·FLOOR ·

PLATE 13

SUPPLEMENT TO THE SCIENTIFIC AMERICAN-ARCHITECTS AND BUILDERS EDITION-MARCH 1888.

A Suburban Residence.

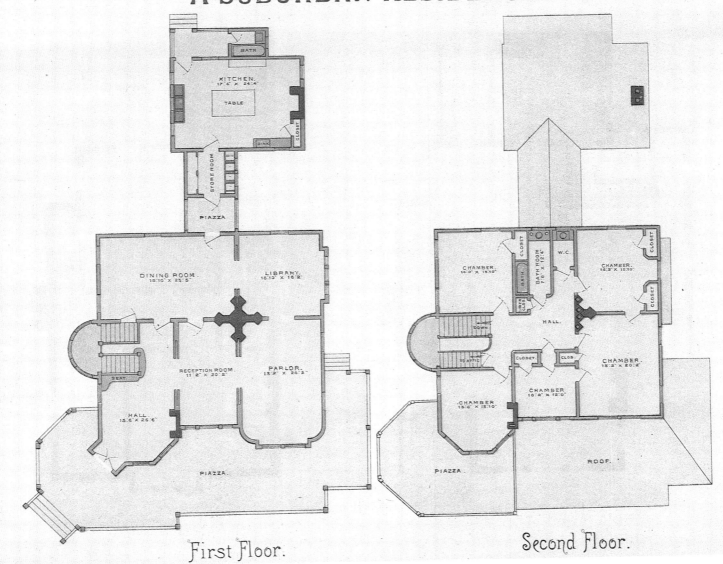

First Floor.

Second Floor.

PLATE 15

SUPPLEMENT TO THE SCIENTIFIC AMERICAN-ARCHITECTS AND BUILDERS EDITION-OCTOBER 1890.

· A LONG ISLAND RESIDENCE ·

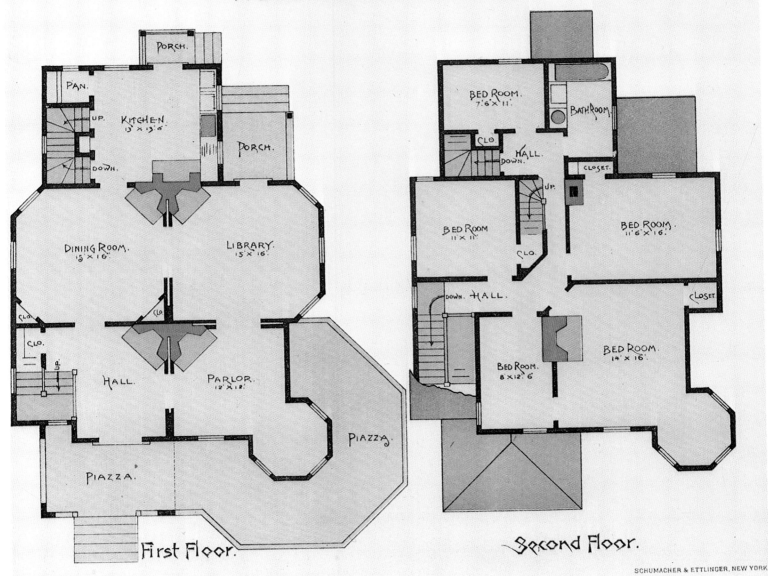

First Floor.

Second Floor.

SCHUMACHER & ETTLINGER, NEW YORK.

PLATE 16

A COTTAGE AT GRAND POINTE, MICH.

FIRST FLOOR.

SECOND FLOOR.

PLATE 17

A RESIDENCE AT BRIDGEPORT, CONN.

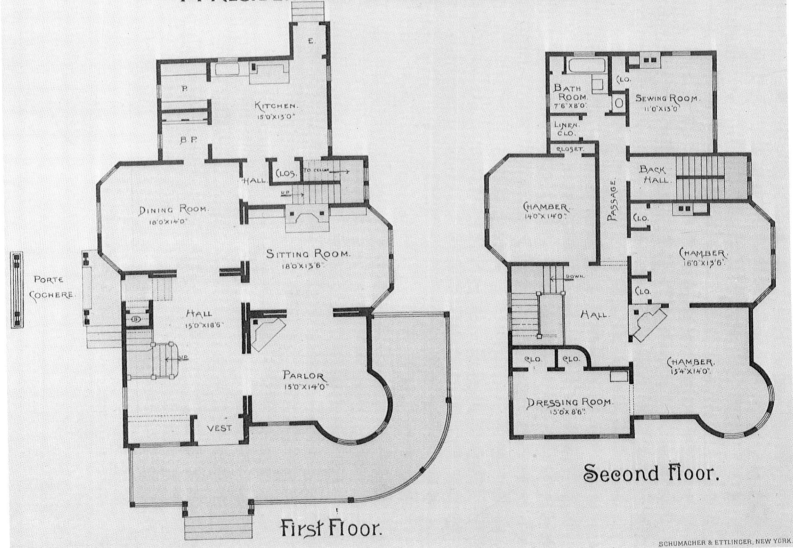

First Floor.

Second Floor.

PORTE COCHERE.

DINING ROOM.
18'0"x14'0"

KITCHEN.
15'0"x13'0"

HALL.   CLOS.   TO CELLAR
UP

SITTING ROOM.
18'0"x13'6"

HALL
15'0"x18'6"

PARLOR
15'0"x14'0"

VEST.

BATH ROOM.
7'6"x8'0"

SEWING ROOM.
11'0"x13'0"

LINEN CLO.

CLOSET.

PASSAGE.

BACK HALL.

CHAMBER.
14'0"x14'0"

CLO.

CHAMBER.
16'0"x13'6"

CLO.

DOWN.

HALL.

CLO.   CLO.

CHAMBER.
15'4"x14'0"

DRESSING ROOM.
15'0"x8'6"

19

PLATE 18

PHILADELPHIA HOUSES of MODERATE COST.

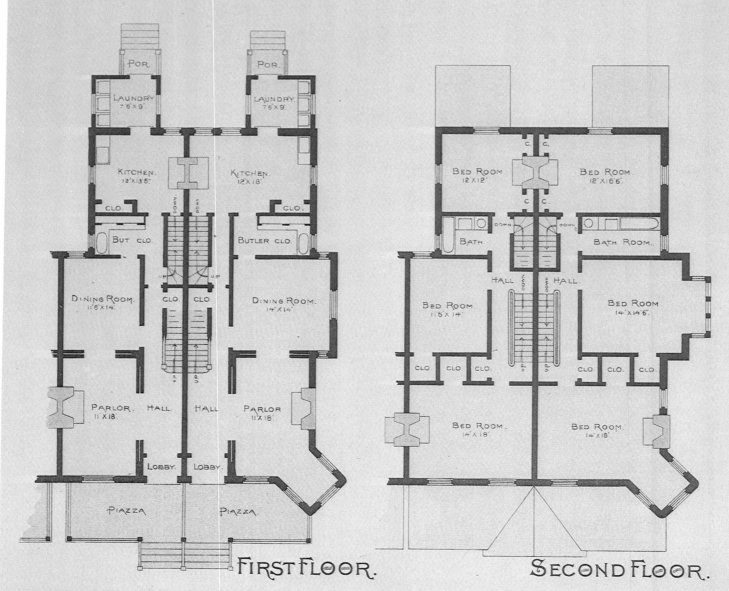

FIRST FLOOR.

SECOND FLOOR.

PLATE 19

SUPPLEMENT TO THE SCIENTIFIC AMERICAN-ARCHITECTS AND BUILDERS EDITION-NOVEMBER 1891.

A TWENTY FIVE HUNDRED DOLLAR HOUSE.

FIRST FLOOR.

SECOND FLOOR.

SCHUMACHER & ETTLINGER, NEW YORK.

PLATE 19

SUPPLEMENT TO THE SCIENTIFIC AMERICAN-ARCHITECTS AND BUILDERS EDITION-NOVEMBER 1891.

A TWENTY FIVE HUNDRED DOLLAR HOUSE.

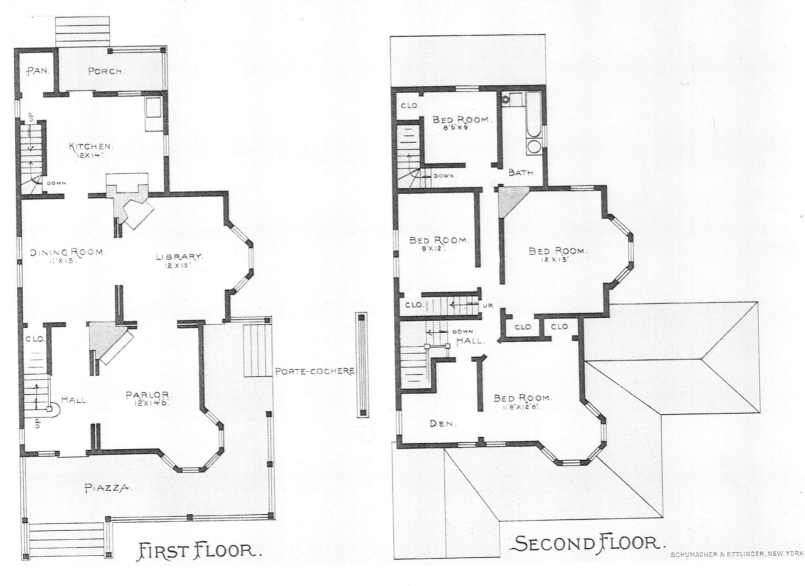

FIRST FLOOR.

SECOND FLOOR.

SCHUMACHER & ETTLINGER, NEW YORK.

PLATE 20

A RESIDENCE AT SPRINGFIELD, MASS.

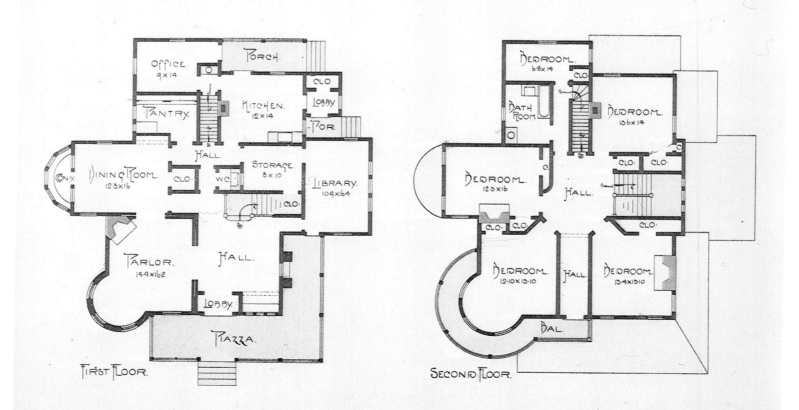

FIRST FLOOR.

SECOND FLOOR.

PLATE 21

A RESIDENCE AT PELHAM MANOR, N.Y.

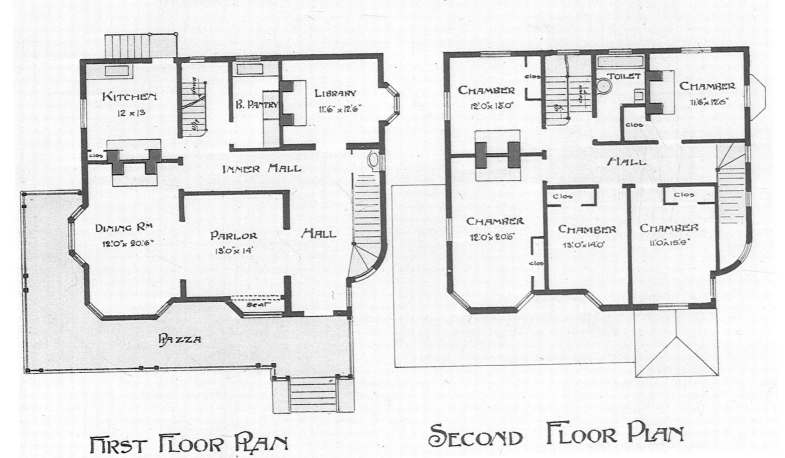

FIRST FLOOR PLAN

SECOND FLOOR PLAN

PLATE 22

A RESIDENCE AT EVANSTON, ILL.

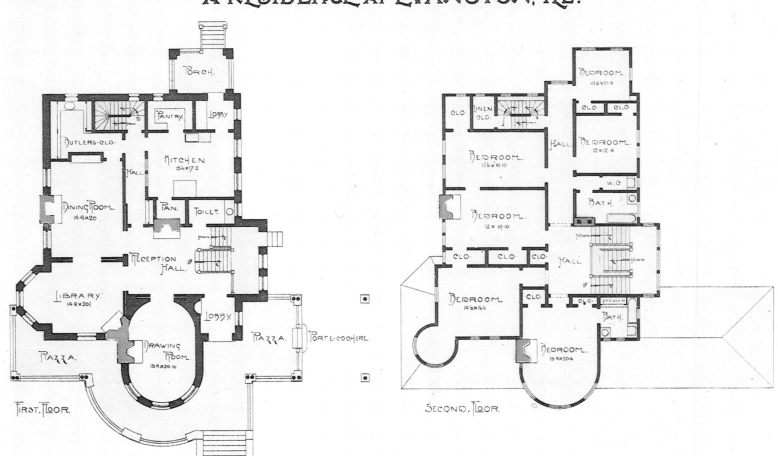

FIRST FLOOR.

SECOND FLOOR.

DESCRIPTIVE TEXT

*The text that accompanies the plates
is excerpted directly from the* Scientific American.

PLATE 1 October, 1886

"A Cottage at Bridgeport, Connecticut"
ARCHITECT: Frank D. Nichols
OWNER: Buckingham Marsh

One of our colored plates for this number illustrates an attractive dwelling of moderate cost, being $1800.

The whole treatment of the design is most satisfactory. A particularly attractive elevation, with a really well arranged plan, makes it one which could be utilized with advantage. It is a difficult matter to obtain a design with the cojoined advantages of a pleasing exterior and a good plan at low cost like $1800; and one only has to look around to notice the style of buildings of this class which are as a rule erected, to appreciate the advantages of Mr. Nichol's design.

The construction used in the execution of this design is of the usual kind, but thoroughly substantial. The foundations are of stone, with underpinnings of local brick. The body of the house is painted a light olive green in an attractive manner, with the trimmings of a darker tint of the same color picked out with English vermilion. The roof is of Bangor slates with terra cotta ridge and finials.

The casings and trim internally are all of yellow pine, finished to show plain wood. North Carolina pine is employed for wainscoting kitchen, pantry, lobby and bath room, relieved by black walnut mouldings. The parlor, dining room and a hall are connected by sliding and folding doors, and each ceiling is neatly paneled and corniced.

The kitchen has a rear entrance, which is fitted up with hat rack, the lobby serving as a protection against the weather on this elevation, which faces north. The pantry is fitted with shelves and cupboard, and with a sink supplied with hot and cold water.

On the upper floor are three good sized bedrooms, two of which are connected by a door, and each being accessible from the hall passage. The bath room is provided with a water closet, a wash bowl, and a bath tub supplied with hot and cold water. The usual objection to the use of the inside water closet is met by the location being on the outside, so that on opening a window, direct communication is made with the outer air, and by ventilators which are carried up above the roof.

In the roof is ample space for storage, and if it were wished, a large bed room could be fitted there without difficulty.

PLATE 2 December, 1886

"A Brick Row of Moderate Cost"
LOCATION: Baltimore, Maryland
ARCHITECT: W. Claude Frederic

One of our colored plates for the present month illustrates a design for a row of brick and stone dwellings, "Alhambra Terrace."

General Conditions: The contractor is to furnish all the materials of the best that can be procured, at the contract price. As the scheme for this row is an adaptation of the beautiful Moorish forms, the contractor must be careful to follow out, as far as possible, the idea intended, as in the selection of wall paper, gas fixtures, interior finish, etc. All workmanship must be thorough.

Terra cotta pillars, panels, tiles and ornaments from Boston Terra Cotta Company, all to be set in neat manner.

Stone for front coping and steps to be Hummelstown stone, rock faced. Carefully build all flues, fireplace arches, etc. Use Moorish terra cotta tiles for front of roofs, and line all the recessed work of the balconies, etc. with them. Set coal chutes in pavement for each house.

All stair work to be quartered oak, balusters to be spindle work. All to be smoothed, oiled and finished. Put shelves in all closets. Fit up pantries, dressers, etc. Build rough board fences in the usual manner. Furnish gates to alleys, and build servants' outhouses in each yard over the cesspools.

Good quality of hardware throughout must be used. All principal doors, casings, and window casings, mop boards, etc. must be ash, as also all woodwork in bath rooms, including a four-foot wainscoting. Set wood mantels as shown by detail in reception rooms, dining rooms, etc. Hang bells in kitchens to ring from front door, parlor, dining room and second story front, and speaking tubes from butler's pantry to kitchen. Plumber is to furnish each house with a double extra zinc bath tub, 2 ft. by 4 ft. 6 in., ornamental china wash bowl, all with nickel plated spigots, etc. and a good quality sanitary w.c.

Make necessary connection with city water supply. Lay all water and gas pipes through house where necessary, and test same to see if tight. Carry waste pipes from bath room, pantry, kitchen and laundry to gutter. Furnish selected, designed gas fixtures, and hang same.

Plaster all interior walls, ceiling, etc., with two coats in the usual manner, last to be skim finish, for papering, except in basement stairways, closets, kitchens, etc., which are to be white coated in best manner. Set plaster arches, panels, etc. in ceilings where indicated, and line the small domes with wire, lath and plaster. All corners must be true and square. Sod yards and front grass plots with good grass.

Furnace, etc.: Set a No. 2 Tubular furnace in the cellar of each house, to heat the front halls and rooms, and Baltimore Fireplace heater in dining rooms, to heat same and chambers over. Set a good single oven range in kitchen, with ventilator over.

Painting and glazing: Glaze all windows with good quality Baltimore glass. Bevel glass in panels of vestibule doors. Where colored glass is indicated, jewel glass in lead must be used. Firmly set all glass. Paint all exposed woodwork three

25

good coats of colors indicated. All interior work to be painted two coats light tints, to correspond with wall paper. Smooth and varnish all hard wood, and finish up everything in first class manner.

Paper hanger: Paper all rooms, halls, ceilings, etc. in the best manner. Arabesque design wall papers. Decorate all ceiling panels in best manner. Friezes to principal rooms to be Lincrusta Walton. See that all decoration is carefully carried out.

Finally, all the work hereinbefore specified or referred to is to be carried out to the true intent and meaning of the specifications and the accompanying drawing. Such a row can be built in Baltimore for about ten thousand dollars, all complete.

PLATE 3 *February, 1887*

"The Farragut Club House"
LOCATION: Chicago, Illinois
ARCHITECT: Robert Rae
OWNER: The Farragut Boat Club of Chicago

This club is, as its name indicates, an athletic organization, but, as may be presumed from the picture of its house, it is devoted in no small measure to the amenities of social life. A home so extensive, and even elaborate, would not be required solely for athletic purposes; and still, having gained great prestige and reputation upon the water, this club never loses sight of its "chief object in life," but simply adds to its attractions club features which interest the members during the season when out door sports are out of the question.

The intention was to provide a house which would combine all the essentials in the way of club rooms, and at the same time furnish an unusual area of balcony and observatory space for the use of members during the summer months, when aquatic sports are in progress on the lake. The site is so commanding that the entire harbor and lake front, and much of the city, can be viewed from the observatory or lantern of the club house.

The ground dimensions are 90 by 40 feet, and the building rises to the height of three full stories, and is surmounted by a gabled roof and tower. The material used is brownstone and pressed brick, while the balcony gables are finished in bronze and slate. The roof is covered with red slate, with coping of galvanized iron. The main entrance is through an archway and loggia paved with Minton tiles, and opens into an entrance hall from which springs a grand stairway in antique oak. An elaborate mantel of the same material occupies one side of this handsome hall, the decorations of which are in Turkey red and bronze. The other apartments on this floor are the grand parlor, library, directors' parlor, card room, billiard room and coat room, all handsomely frescoed, elegantly furnished. The ball room, with a twenty foot ceiling, a striking gallery and a thoroughly equipped stage for amateur theatrical purposes, is frescoed in soft buff tints and bronze. Large doors give egress to the main loggia, which in warm weather is thus made pleasantly tributary to the ball room. On the same floor are the ladies' parlor, gymnasium and superintendent's office. The spacious basement, eleven feet in the clear, is given up to bowling alleys, pool tables, dressing rooms, baths, steam heating apparatus and other conveniences.

The colored plate represents a cottage of pleasing appearance. The treatment of the roof and convenient arrangement of the rooms are both very satisfactory, and the whole design is one of considerable merit and usefulness.

SPECIFICATIONS

The house is to be built as per plans and figures on the same, substantially as shown, all dimensions to be verified on the works.

Walls: The cellar walls to be built up 18 in. thick, laid in cement mortar, underpinning faced both sides. Outside rubble work, natural face, the joints struck. Cellarway jambs the same. Chimney piers good common work.

Chimneys: To be built as per plans. Hearth places arched to trimmer. The several fireplaces to be laid up with Danvas pressed brick.

Lath and plastering: The first and second stories to be lathed on sides and plastered. One good coat of spruce lath, well nailed, and good, strong mortar. Slake and run lime through sieve. Mix with clean grit, sand and cattle hair in proper proportions. Put on and float. The three rooms and hall in the attic to have one good coat, sides and ceiling.

CARPENTERS WORK

Generally: The building to be well framed, with good mill sawed spruce timber, spiked and nailed securely together.

Roof: The main roof and piazza and porch roofs to be shingled with first quality of Eastern shaved shingles, laid out not over 5 in. to the weather and well nailed.

Floors: The attic floor to be ⅞ in. planed and matched spruce, well driven up and nailed. Other floors, except as hereafter designated, 1⅛ in. spruce, as above. Kitchen, closets, bath room and back hall floors 1⅛ in. Southern hard pine. Dining room floor, alternate strip of cherry and maple, 3 in. in width.

Doors: Front doors will be one pair 7 ft. 6 in. × 5 ft. 1¾ in. Vestibule doors the same size. Library and dining room doors the same as vestibule. Other doors, 2 ft. 10 in. × 6 ft. 10 in. × 1⅜ in., five raised panels and cope moulding, all alike. Second story doors the same, second quality. Attic doors 2 ft. 6 in. × 6 ft. 6 in., 1¼ in., four panels, third quality, all well fitted and hung.

Hardware: Knobs of kitchen, attic and all doors in rear of sitting room, etc. to be white porcelain, nickel rose and escutcheons, maple strikers behind all. Doors of library, dining room, sitting room, etc., to be pearl white, bright rose and escutcheon. Front door, bright bronze, bell pull the same.

Finish: Dining room to be finished in pine, sitting room to be finished in ash, and library to be finished in pine. Second story, front of back hall, in pine; rear room, bath, and hall, hard pine.

Mantels: There are to be six wooden mantels built with the finish of the rooms, all of hardwood, 4 in. pine and 2 in. ash, at an average cost of $10 apiece.

Painting: The outside finish to be painted two coats of Johns' asbestos prepared paint as follows: Gable shingles and that on the sides, red; the main finish light drab, the weather boarding dark drab, piazza floors oiled two coats. The inside hardwoods to be covered with shellac, two flowing coats; the pine work painted two coats, the floors to be oiled two coats where hard woods are used, all work to be well rubbed on first coat and puttied clean, and to match wood or paint.

PLATE 4 *March, 1887*

"A $2600 Cottage"
LOCATION: Providence, Rhode Island
ARCHITECT: George W. Cady
OWNER: W. P. Macomber

PLATE 5 *April, 1887*

"An East Orange Home"
LOCATION: East Orange, New Jersey
ARCHITECT: George Cooke
OWNER: F. W. Coolbaugh

Located in a slightly elevated position, at a well judged distance back from the road, the house at once gives the impression of being essentially a handsome one. The whole effect is well conceived, and exhibits evidence of much care and thought having been expended upon it, while many of the minor details are of a novel and interesting character.

Coming to the interior, one is immediately struck with the comfortable and homelike appearance and arrangement of the rooms, which open into one another, and are well calculated for the accommodation of guests. The kitchen leads off from the dining room, and a small serving lobby is placed between them.

The hall is very prettily arranged, the construction of the staircase being particularly novel and pleasing. This is executed in hard wood, and is formed with a quarter space, raised three steps up, and approached from two sides. On the second story four good sized bed rooms are provided, with bath rooms and ample space for closets and trunks. The top floor contains servants' and other rooms.

The decoration of the house is carried out in a very superior manner. In the vestibule, the walls are covered with stamped paper in imitation Lincrusta Walton; while the hall is provided with a dado and a filling of embossed paper. Most of the rooms are decorated in well chosen metal hangings, with deep friezes, and the ceilings are finished in light one-colored paper and borders. In several of the windows, stained lead lights are used, with charming effect. Some of this work is of a description not often seen, being partly composed of broken pieces of thick colored glass set in the lead work, and giving the appearance of crystals. Set in the wood work of the piazza are several rondels of colored glass, which aid in producing the good effect.

Among the special features in the house which greatly add to its comfort and completeness is a very nicely designed buffet, built in hardwood and fitted in the dining room, in the space underneath the stairs. Fitted wash basins, with marble tops, are provided in the dining and several of the other rooms, there being five in number altogether. A large heater, built in brick work, is provided in the cellar, with registers in the halls and all the principal rooms, and there are grate fires in the library and parlor in addition. The mantel pieces are of excellent design. Electric bells are fitted throughout in a most complete manner, the servants' call being so arranged that on pressing the button three bells in different parts of the house may be made to ring simultaneously. The drains are all ventilated with cool air spaces, and are built with special openings designed for the purpose of access in case of stoppage.

The cost of the house to duplicate would be about $5,000. Mr. Coolbaugh spent a total of some $6,000 in its erection, the extra sum being expended in decoration and plumbing, both of which are of a very superior kind. The original estimates did not exceed $5,000. The acting architect was Mr. George Cooke, of Orange, although to the talented wife of the owner, Mrs. F. W. Coolbaugh, is due the credit of arranging the general design and of planning the rooms. Indeed, to that lady is to be largely attributed the completeness and success of the whole structure.

PLATE 6
April, 1887

"A Cottage Adapted for Future Enlargement"
ARCHITECT: Christopher Myers

A problem of almost every day occurrence is the alteration and enlargement of existing buildings. A dwelling may be erected by a man for the accommodation of his small family, and a few rooms be quite sufficient for his wants. But, with increasing years, his family augments, and he finds it necessary to either build a new house or enlarge his old one. There are, generally, many reasons why he should do the latter. The individual and family associations connected with the old house render him anxious to preserve it in detail as far as possible. Then on the score of economy, he will wish that the old structure should be utilized.

To make extensive additions to a house under these circumstances is not, as a rule, easy; but that, with a little foresight, provision may be made for such a contingency, is shown by the design represented in this color plate.

Here we have a house complete in itself, and pleasing in appearance, which may be readily added to without in any way interfering with the existing building or necessitating the waste of material. This would be effected by building on the left hand wall. Exactly how it is proposed that it should be done will be shown in a future number. As it is now represented, the little house would be a convenient and attractive one.

Below is an estimate showing the cost of the house to be $1,819.37. These prices are based upon the high current value of labor and materials in New York and its vicinity. In many localities, the house might be erected for a good deal less.

ESTIMATE AND BILL OF MATERIALS

4,547 feet spruce, worked	$ 127.32
425 2″×4″×12″ studs, hemlock	81.60
800 feet hemlock boards for roof	16.00
800 slates	56.00
2,000 feet sheathing and paper, put up	44.00
1,500 feet siding	52.50
600 feet shingles on side	36.00
200 feet main cornice and gutter	60.00
100 feet band course	20.00
130 feet water table and piazza fascia	13.00
50 feet piazza columns	15.00
2 back piazza columns	3.00
1 short post on back piazza	2.00
10 feet rail and balusters back of piazza	2.00
13 feet filling in back piazza	3.90
2 turned columns front piazza	4.50
1 turned short column	2.00
13 feet rail, front piazza	3.90
6 brackets for same	1.50
100 feet piazza floor, ceiling, roof trimmed	25.00
Stoops, lattice, steps, etc. complete	18.00
7 cellar windows complete	12.25
13 windows on first story	104.00
11 windows on second story	77.00
4 third story windows	20.00
2 flights of stairs complete	75.00
Cellar stairs	4.00
300 feet of surbase	12.00
6 closets complete	18.00
Front door complete	10.00
7 doors, first story	38.50
6 doors, second story	30.00
4 doors, third story	18.00
Pump and sink	25.00
Incidental expenses	60.00
Mason's work	728.40
Total cost	$1,819.37

PLATE 7
May, 1887

"A Cottage After Enlargement"
ARCHITECT: Christopher Myers

By a careful examination of the plans and a comparison with those given in our last number (*American Victoriana* Plate #6) it will be seen that the object of providing a house which could be afterward enlarged without waste of material has been very successfully attained.

It will be observed that there is practically no waste of material. All that is done is slightly to alter one wall, remove certain windows and doors and place them in new positions. All the remainder of the work consists simply of the additions necessitated by the enlargement. The sheathing and all other material is utilized in the new building, so that it may be said that there is no waste whatever.

As altered and now represented, the house would form a very desirable and convenient residence, with well arranged rooms and a pleasing elevation. The design is one which is, at the same time, thoroughly economical.

Below is the bill of materials for the alteration. This, and our last number, taken collectively, therefore, provide for (1) the erection of the smaller house, (2) the alteration and arrangement of the same, and (3) the erection of the larger house.

Mason's work	$ 485.00
Carpenter's work	872.85
Painting all new work	50.00
Plumbing	325.00
Furnace, complete	170.00
Range	25.00
Total cost of alteration	$1,927.85

PLATE 8   *June, 1887*

"A Five Thousand Dollar Residence"
LOCATION: Pomfret, Connecticut
ARCHITECT: Howard Hoppin
OWNER: Mrs. W. B. Chapin

The treatment of the elevation is most pleasing, the arrangement of the roof lines producing a very graceful effect, while the dwarf stone wall surrounding the piazza gives the whole design a very substantial and superior appearance.

The cost of the house is estimated at $5,000, made up as follows:

MASON

Grading	$ 60.00
Excavation	70.00
Stonework	425.00
Brickwork and chimneys	225.00
Concrete, cementing, etc.	100.00
Lathing and plastering	385.00
Outside plaster	45.00

CARPENTER

Heavy timber	400.00
Joists and flooring	370.00
Studding and boarding	275.00
Shingling sides	75.00
Shingling roof	175.00
Outside finish	250.00
Outside mouldings	50.00
Sashes and frames	280.00
Doors, frames and trimmings	325.00
Staircases complete	175.00
Mantelpieces	100.00
Tinning, gutters, conductors, etc.	75.00
Plumbing	420.00
Painting, papering, etc.	300.00
Incidental items	170.00
Total	$5,000.00

PLATE 9   *July, 1887*

"A Kansas City Residence"
ARCHITECT: James W. Bryan
OWNER: Robert Beatty, Jr.

The building fronts east and south, the principal front facing the east. It sets back a sufficient distance from the road to allow of a fine lawn being formed in front, and presents with its well arranged sky lines and spacious covered balconies a very attractive and imposing structure.

The exterior walls are all constructed of pressed brick laid in red cement mortar; the roof is covered in with slates, and the woodwork is painted in pleasing colors.

The reception hall, sitting room and stairway are finished in red oak, the newel and the balusters of stairs are "spiral turned." The dining room is finished in white oak, the parlor in cherry, and the kitchen and second story all in natural woods, finished with three coats of oil and white shellac.

The mantels are of wood, correspond in general design with the trim, and have "over-mantels" and beveled plate glass mirrors. The house is furnished throughout with a complete system of speaking tubes, electric bells, annunciators, etc.

The system of heating is hot air, supplied by a McGee furnace, and distributed to all rooms except kitchen and servants' room. This, in conjunction with the fireplaces, proves most economical, and insures a more perfect ventilation, as in early spring and autumn fires may be lighted on the hearths without resorting to the furnace, and in colder weather both may be used.

The cost of the residence as represented was $7,500.

PLATE 10   *August, 1887*

"A $4,000 Residence at Flushing, N.Y."
SPECIFICATIONS:

Quality: All material used to be of good quality, free from defects impairing its strength or durability. All timber, except where otherwise specified, to be of good, well seasoned spruce.

Flooring: First and second story floors, except kitchen and bath room, to be laid with narrow pine flooring, well driven together and nailed to each and every beam. Attic to be pine, 9½" wide, well driven together, and nailed to every beam. Kitchen and bath room to be laid with white maple, 2" × 2½" × 2½"

Siding: Cover entire building, except where otherwise shown, with sound and clear No. 1 beveled clapboards, not less than 1" lap, nailed every 16", and set nails for putty.

Roof: The roof is to sheathed with rough hemlock boards; valley and gutters to be lined with the best I.C. charcoal tin; all joints to be carefully soldered. Do all necessary flashing around chimneys, dormers, bay windows, porches, etc., also counterflash all chimneys and junctions. Slate the entire roof with 16" × 8" royal black slate, not less than 3" lap.

Blinds: All windows, except cellar and attic, to have 1¼" outside blinds, made, hung and fastened in the best manner, painted at the factory three coats. The bay in reception hall, dining room bay, parlor bay and bay over hall to have Venetian blinds, with cornice made of stained wood, hung complete.

Exterior: The water table, corner boards, cornice, window frames, bay windows, porches and all other exterior ornamental work be made of the best quality of white pine.

Sashes: All sashes, except cellars, to be 1½" thick, to be glazed with second quality French double thick glass; cellar to be glazed with third quality. The double hung sash to have best Russian hemp cord, proper weights, and Berlin bronze sash fasts. Window on stair platforms to be stained cathedral glass, leaded in, designs selected by the owner, to cost $1.25 per square foot.

Doors: The front doors to be 2" thick, moulded as per plans, upper panels to be glazed with stained cathedral glass, to cost $1.25 per square foot, selected by the owner, hung with 4½" lacquered loose butts, fastened with 4½" mortise lock; night latch attachments, brass face, wooden furniture, and escutcheons, brass flush boltstop and bottom. Sliding doors to roll on Hatfield's patent 4" anti-friction sheaves, astragal face mortise locks, flush trimmings, bronze or brass.

Stairs: Build the stairs as shown, from the first to second story with 1¼" treads, ⅞" risers, and 1¼" strings, to be put up in the best manner; the steps to be wedged with glue and supported on strong carriage timbers. Newels, balusters, and hand rails to be made of cherry, all the treads and risers to be tongued and plowed together.

Trimmings: The architraves for all doors and windows throughout the house to be made 5" wide moulded on face. First and second stories to have turned corner blocks, the bases to be 7½" wide, moulded on top. All to be of seasoned and clear white pine.

Pantries: Kitchen pantry to be fitted up with wide shelves on two sides. China pantries also to be fitted up with shelves, doors and drawers complete. Bed room closets to have one shelf with strip fitted with japanned hooks for coats and hats.

Bath Room: Bath tub to have ash top; skirt the front of the bath tub with narrow beaded ceiling. Wainscot bath room 2' above the fittings all around, nosing and cove finish, ceil in front of wash bowl, and hang door complete, with catch. Put up water closet, with seat riser and lid hung with brass butts.

Mantels: The dining room, parlor and one bed room on second floor to be furnished with mantels and grates, of the prime cost in all, including setting, of $175, to be selected by the owner.

Picture Mouldings: Put up picture mouldings in principal rooms, first and second stories and halls, wood to match that of rooms, 1½" wide.

Coal Bins: Put up coal bins where shown, of planed hemlock boards and 3" × 4" stanchions, one bin for furnace coal and one for range, each to have one small door for access.

Air Box: Build cold air box as directed by the furnace man, of wide pine ceiling boards, with wire over entrance space through wall.

Painting: All the exterior woodwork usually painted to be painted two good coats of white lead and linseed oil paint, all knots and sap to be well shellacked before priming; all cracks, joints and nail holes and over nail heads to be well puttied after priming is done. All tin work to have two coats of Prince's metallic paint; also paint the chimney two coats. All the colors to be selected by the owner.

The interior will be wood filled with Wheeler wood filler, then two good coats of hard oil finish. The first story and main stairs and balusters and rails will be rubbed down to a smooth surface. All the doors, saddles, hearth borders and hard floors will be oiled; all sash and outside doors must be painted on top and bottom. The painters must follow immediately after the carpenters.

BILL OF ESTIMATE:

Materials	$1,607.19
Labor, putting up work	600.00
Painting	160.00
Mason	750.00
Plumbing and gas	320.00
Heating	195.00
Total	$3,632.19

PLATE 11 *October, 1887*

"A Country Store"

Our colored plate represents a country store and family flat

lately erected in an adjoining town, at a cost of thirty-eight hundred dollars. The costs are:

Mason work, complete	$1,900.00
Carpenter work, painting, tinning, etc.	1,900.00
Total	$3,800.00

The whole exterior of wood and tin work to be painted two good coats of English white lead and linseed oil, of such colors as may be selected. The priming to be done immediately after the work is put up. Putty up all nail holes after priming is done. Shellac all sap, knots, etc. before priming. All tin work painted two coats of Prince's metallic paint, including leaders. The cresting and finials to be painted two coats of such colors as may be selected, with gilded tips and points.

The store part to be finished in two coats of white shellac. The closet under stairs to have one coat of raw linseed oil. All door saddles oiled. The bottoms and tops of outside doors and all sash to be painted. The second story, including stairs, hallways, stair rails, first story hall and closets, to have Wheeler's wood filler, and well picked out. Then finish with two coats of hard oil finish. The stair rails will be rubbed down, including balusters and newels. All cracks and nail holes to be well puttied up. Putty to match color of wood. Also paint privy and shutters on the first story same as other woodwork.

PLATE 12 *November, 1887*

"City Frame Houses of Moderate Cost"
LOCATION: Brooklyn, New York
ARCHITECT: Charles E. Hebberd

Our colored plate is a view of three frame dwellings situated on the south side of Jefferson Avenue, near Ralph Avenue, Brooklyn. The lot is 50 ft. front, and the dimensions of each house 16'8" by 36' deep. Cellar of stone, basement of brick; 12" walls front and rear, and 8" party walls; two stories above, of frame, filled in with brick.

The design of the front is a decided innovation over the customary stereotyped city house, and meets a want that we feel our readers will appreciate. Our experience is that the general public are becoming tired of the monotonous row after row of exactly the same design of city houses, and there is a demand for houses of this description, while the ordinary front remains unsold and unoccupied.

The general ground plan is about the same as the average city house, with flat tin roofs and party walls. In fact, this arrangement has been thoroughly worked over and experimented on, and yet still retained as near perfect as can be devised for one family houses with the narrow city lot.

The exterior will bear a few explanations. The bay window on both parlor and second story and the large one-light window in the basement make all the front rooms decidedly inviting. The judicious use of sawed shingles along the front and at the base of the bay serves to relieve the monotony at small cost, and the ornamentation in gables and in panels under the bay window gives a decidedly bright, artistic effect.

This ornamentation is all worked from the solid, rather than planted on. The frame is sheathed on all sides, filled in with brick laid on edge, covered with building paper, and then clapboarded. Plastering throughout is three coats work. Slate mantels in parlors and dining room, and fireplace heater in basement. The net cost complete, including plumbing, was $2500 each.

PLATE 13 *March, 1888*

"A Suburban Residence"

Our color plate this month illustrates a pleasing residence,

of the following dimensions: Front, not including piazza, 48';
side, not including piazza and kitchen, 43'6"; store room and
back porch, 10' × 16'; kitchen, 18' × 25'; lavatory back,
5'6" × 7'6". Height of stories: Cellar, 7'6"; first story, 12';
second story, 11'; height of ceiling in attic, 8'.

The estimated cost without mantels and furnace is $12,500.
There are open fireplaces in the dining room, library, parlor,
reception room, hall and three chambers on second floor. The
four fireplaces on first story are in one chimney.

The kitchen is set apart from the main house, with porch
between. The attic is unfinished; there could be four nice
rooms therein.

The specifications are intended to embrace all of the labor
and materials necessary in the erection and completion of the
building in all its parts; the whole to be comprised within any
contracts that may be made for the same. The entire work is to
be constructed and finished in every part in a good, substantial, and workmanlike manner, according to the specifications,
to the full extent and meaning of the same, and to the entire
satisfaction, approval, and acceptance of the owner.

There is furnished a complete set of detail or working drawings for exterior and interior work, which, used in connection
with the above, show all dimensions in relation to the work
which is represented by the detail drawings. Where figures are
not given, all drawings must be accurately followed and measured according to their scale. All writing and figures are to be
considered a portion of these specifications and must be followed and considered. In every case where figures are given,
they must be used in preference to measurement.

It is also understood that the owner of the building shall
have the right to make any alterations, additions or omissions
of work or materials herein specified or shown on the drawings, during the progress of the building, that he may find
necessary, and the same shall be acceded to by the contractor
and carried into effect without in any way violating or vitiat-
ing the contract.

Particular care must be taken by the contractor of all the
finished work as the building progresses, which work must be
covered up and thoroughly protected from injury or deface-
ment during the erection and completion of the building.

The owner shall have full power, at any time during the
progress of the work, to reject any materials that he may deem
unsuitable for the purpose for which they are intended, or
which are not in strict conformity with the spirit of these
specifications. He shall also have the power to cause any unsafe
or inferior work to be taken down.

PLATE 14   *July, 1890*

"Residence of Henry Towne, Esq., Stamford, Connecticut"
ARCHITECT: H. Hudson Holly

Our colored plate illustrates the residence erected for
Mr. Henry R. Towne, at Stamford, Connecticut. First story,
partly of brick, pointed in black mortar, with trimmings of
stone and buff brick; the rest of the building is of wood
covered with clapboarding and shingles, painted light olive
green, with bottle green trimmings. Roof, slated.

The main entrance is at side, with stone steps and tiled
platforms; the walls to this entrance are laid up with tiles and
buff brick. Hall, trimmed with oak, contains a grand staircase, with carved newel and candelabra; the windows on landing glazed with stained glass. This hall, also, has a panel
wainscoting and ceiling beams. The floors throughout are of
ash and cherry, laid in narrow widths, etc.

The drawing room is trimmed with mahogany, the library
and den with cherry, and the dining room with ash. The open
fireplaces are furnished with tiled and marbled hearths, and

hardwood mantels elegantly carved. Butler's pantry, rear hall,
and kitchen, and other apartments are trimmed with hard
Southern pine, finished natural. Cellar contains the kitchen,
laundry, furnace room, and other apartments, all fitted up
complete. Lift runs to attic.

Second floor contains six bed rooms, with ample closets and
two bath rooms. These rooms, as well as the third floor, are
trimmed with whitewood finished natural. There are five bed
rooms, billiard room, and trunk room in attic or third floor.
This house is wired for electric illumination, and is also
provided with electric bells and speaking tubes, etc. Cost
$20,000.

PLATE 15   *October, 1890*

"A Long Island Residence"
LOCATION: Hollis, Long Island
ARCHITECTS: Schwietzer and Deimar
OWNER: E. J. Johnson

Dimensions: Front 34 ft., side, 47 feet, not including piazza.
First story clapboarded; the balustrade and columns to piazza,
second and third stories and roof are shingled with slate quarried at Bangor, Pa. The trim throughout is of whitewood; hall
stained and finished in oak; parlor and library in cherry,
dining room and rest of trim finished natural. Floors of yellow
pine, laid in narrow widths. Hall contains an ornamental staircase, and an open fireplace faced with tiles and capped with a
slate shelf; hearth of tiles. Parlor, library and dining room each
have fireplaces with tiled hearths and facings, and elegant slate
mantels with plate glass mirrors, etc. Kitchen and pantries are
wainscoted, and provided with wash trays, sinks, etc. complete. There are five bedrooms and bathroom on the second
floor. The third floor or attic is not partitioned off, but several
rooms could be finished if desired. There is a cemented cellar
under whole of house containing furnace. Cost, $5,500
complete.

PLATE 16   *December, 1890*

"A Summer Cottage at Grand Point, Michigan"
ARCHITECTS: Munn and Company (Scientific American)
OWNER: Mrs. M. Hutchinson

The house was built complete at a cost of twelve hundred
dollars, and was erected and occupied within six weeks after
the delivery of the plans to the builder. The house is plastered
throughout with adamant. This design has met with very
general favor, and has been extensively copied. We have heretofore published modified examples of the same. The present
illustration shows improvements which render the plans still
more desirable. The liberal piazza on three sides of the house is
a particularly desirable feature.

PLATE 17   *May, 1891*

"A Residence at Bridgeport, Connecticut"
ARCHITECT: Joseph W. Northrop
OWNER: George Comstock

The residence is a frame house constructed in a most thorough manner, and of best materials throughout. The lower
part is clapboarded, the upper covered with cut shingles, the
gables being paneled. The roof is of black slate, the windows
are glazed with plate glass, with bent glass in windows of
round tower.

The plan is roomy and conveniently arranged. Entrance is
had through the tile vestibule into the large and fine reception
hall, which is finished in quartered oak, and has a handsome

paneled and carved staircase winding up on one side, finely lighted by large stained glass windows. In the front part of the hall is a screened alcove, with very wide window and stained glass transoms over. The hall is also entered on the side back of staircase, from the side entrance and porte cochere.

The hall connects with parlor, library, and dining room through side sliding doors. The parlor has round corner bay window in tower, and the ends of library and dining room also finish in octagonal bay windows. These rooms are all handsomely finished in natural woods, and have fine carved mantels. The hall and dining room are in quartered oak, parlor in mahogany, library in cherry.

The rear part of the house is entered from dining room through butler's pantry, and from sitting room through lobby containing rear stairs. Ample kitchen and pantry containing accommodations in the rear part. The second story contains large square hall and passages to rear; four large chambers, three with bay windows, large dressing room, bath room and closets. In the third story are finished two chambers and stair hall.

The cost of this house, as built, is about $10,000.

PLATE 18 *July, 1891*

"Philadelphia Houses of Moderate Cost"
ARCHITECTS: G. U. & U. D. Hewitt
OWNER: W. S. Kimball

Our colored plate this month shows a row of dwellings, with ornamental fronts. *Dimensions*: The extreme width of each house, between walls, is 18 feet and the depth 62 feet, exclusive of the 9 ft. piazza. Height of ceilings: Cellar, 7 ft., first story, 10 ft.; second, 9 ft.; third, 8 ft. 6 in. The design is excellent, and it combines both elegance and convenience. The exterior walls are built of Philadelphia pressed brick, with trimmings of dark red sandstone. Roof covered with Bangor slates. Halls are trimmed with ash, and each is provided with an ornamental staircase, turned out of similar wood. Parlors and dining rooms are trimmed with cherry, and are connected by double sliding doors. Fireplaces, where shown, have tiled hearths and hardwood mantels, provided with beveled plate mirrors, etc. Kitchens, laundries and pantries are trimmed and wainscoted with Southern pine, finished natural with hard oil. These apartments are fitted up in the best possible manner. Second floor contains three bedrooms and bath room, all trimmed with ash, and the latter wainscoted and provided with tub, bowl, and closet, complete. Third floor contains three bed rooms and storage. Cemented cellar contains furnace. The cost of corner house was $7,500, and the inner houses $5,800 each.

PLATE 19 *November, 1891*

"A $2500 House"
LOCATION: Asbury Park, New Jersey
OWNER: C. L. Urlick

We publish as the subject of our colored plate a very attractive cottage. Among the principal features are the tower, bay window, and porte-cochere. Underpinnings are of brick and the exterior above this is of wood, covered with clapboarding and painted light olive green, with trimmings of a darker shade. Roof slated. *Dimensions*: Front, 25 ft.; side, 44 ft., not including front piazza and rear porch. Height of ceilings: Cellar, 7 ft.; first story, 9 ft.; second, 8 ft. 6 in. The plan is excellent, rooms of good size. The interior throughout is trimmed with yellow pine, finished natural with hard oil. Hall contains an ornamental staircase turned out of ash. Parlor has a chimney breast with mantel. Library has a bay window

and fireplace built of brick and furnished in the usual manner. Kitchen and pantries are replete in all their appointments. Second floor contains four bedrooms, den and bathroom. Three bedrooms can be finished off in open attic if desired. Cemented cellar under whole of house. Heated by a furnace. Cost $2,500.

PLATE 20 *July, 1893*

"A Residence at Springfield, Mass."
OWNER: S. E. Walton

The design is pleasing, and it has many bits of detail of interest. The underpinning and stonework around tower at first story is built of Longmeadow stone, with faces left rough as they came from the quarry. This stonework is neatly pointed in red mortar. The remaining part of the building is of wood. The exterior framework is sheathed, covered with clapboards, laid in narrow widths, and painted white. Blinds bottle green. Roof shingled and painted red. Lobby has a tiled floor. The hall, spacious, is trimmed with quartered oak. It contains a nook with a paneled seat, and an elegant staircase with carved newels. Parlor is trimmed with cherry, and it contains a fireplace built of brick and furnished with a tiled hearth and facings, and a hardwood mantel of excellent design. Dining room and conservatory are trimmed with cherry and bird's eye maple, library and office with ash, and store room and rear hall with cypress. Dining room has a paneled wainscoting and a buffet built in with drawers and shelves, enclosed with beveled plate glass doors. The floors in hall, library and dining room are laid in oak, maple and mahogany, laid in mosaic. Kitchen and pantries are wainscoted and trimmed with white pine. The second floor is trimmed with cypress, finished natural, and it contains five bedrooms, large closets and bathroom, the latter wainscoted with cherry and fitted up replete. The third floor contains one bedroom, besides ample storage. The cemented cellar is divided into three apartments—main cellar, laundry and vegetable cellar. The house throughout is plastered with adamant, and it is provided with water, gas, electric bells, speaking tubes and all the modern conveniences. Heated by the Gurney hot water system. Cost $10,000, including furnace, wall decoration and everything complete.

PLATE 21 *February, 1894*

"A Residence at Pelham Manor, New York"
ARCHITECT: F. Charles Merry

Our plan this month shows an elegant residence. It has a masonry basement, above which is a frame structure, covered with shingles, three stories high, the upper one being built in the roof. To the front it presents a large gable with a semicircular window. An open piazza extends across the entire front, and is returned around one end, a special feature being made of that part devoted to the entrance. The piazza roof is supported by square columns, between which are semicircular wooden arches, the spandrels being filled in with vertical bars. A gable faces the side, and the whole roof forms a fine combination of form. In its interior arrangements it shows a large main hall, containing a fine staircase, amply lighted by side lights. From this open direct a parlor and library, by sliding doors. A passage communicates with dining room and a service hall, in the latter of which is placed the service staircase. On the second floor there are provided five bedrooms and a main hall. A rear hall is also provided, and a bathroom, containing wash basin and water closet, opens directly from this. The service stairs run to the third story, where are placed the servants' rooms and store chambers. The estimated cost is $7,000.

PLATE 22 *June, 1894*

"A Residence at Evanston, Illinois"
ARCHITECTS: Raeder, Coffin and Crocker
OWNER: H. D. Cable

Our plate this month shows a handsome residence. The building has many interesting features, and is built of the best materials in a thorough workmanlike manner. The underpinning, first story, and chimneys are built of natural-faced stone, laid up in red mortar. The second story is of wood, and the exterior walls are covered with shingles and stained a mottled brown, with olive green trimmings. The circular wall at front bedroom is beamed, forming panels which are filled in with stuccowork. Roof shingled and painted red. The main hall is trimmed with oak. It contains a grand staircase, with carved newels and candelabrum, and is lighted by a cluster of leaded windows glazed with delicate-tinted glass. The fireplace is built upon rock-faced stone, with mantel shelf of oak. The walls are paneled and the ceiling heavily beamed. The floors are of hardwood. The drawing room is trimmed with sycamore. It has an open fireplace, with facings of Mexican onyx, hearth of tiles and a mantel of similar wood, elegantly carved and provided with a mirror. Library is trimmed with cherry and it has a paneled wainscoting, bookcases, bay window and an open fireplace. Dining room is trimmed with oak, and it has a paneled wainscoting, ceiling beams and buffet built in and carved in an exquisite manner. Kitchen and pantry and rear hall are trimmed and wainscoted with Georgia pine, finished natural. These apartments are furnished with the usual fixtures complete. The second and third floors are trimmed with similar wood. There are six bedrooms, ten closets and two bathrooms on second floor, and four bedrooms on third floor. Servants' hall and stairway are private from cellar to third floor. Bathrooms are wainscoted and furnished replete. Cemented cellar contains laundry, furnace and other apartments.

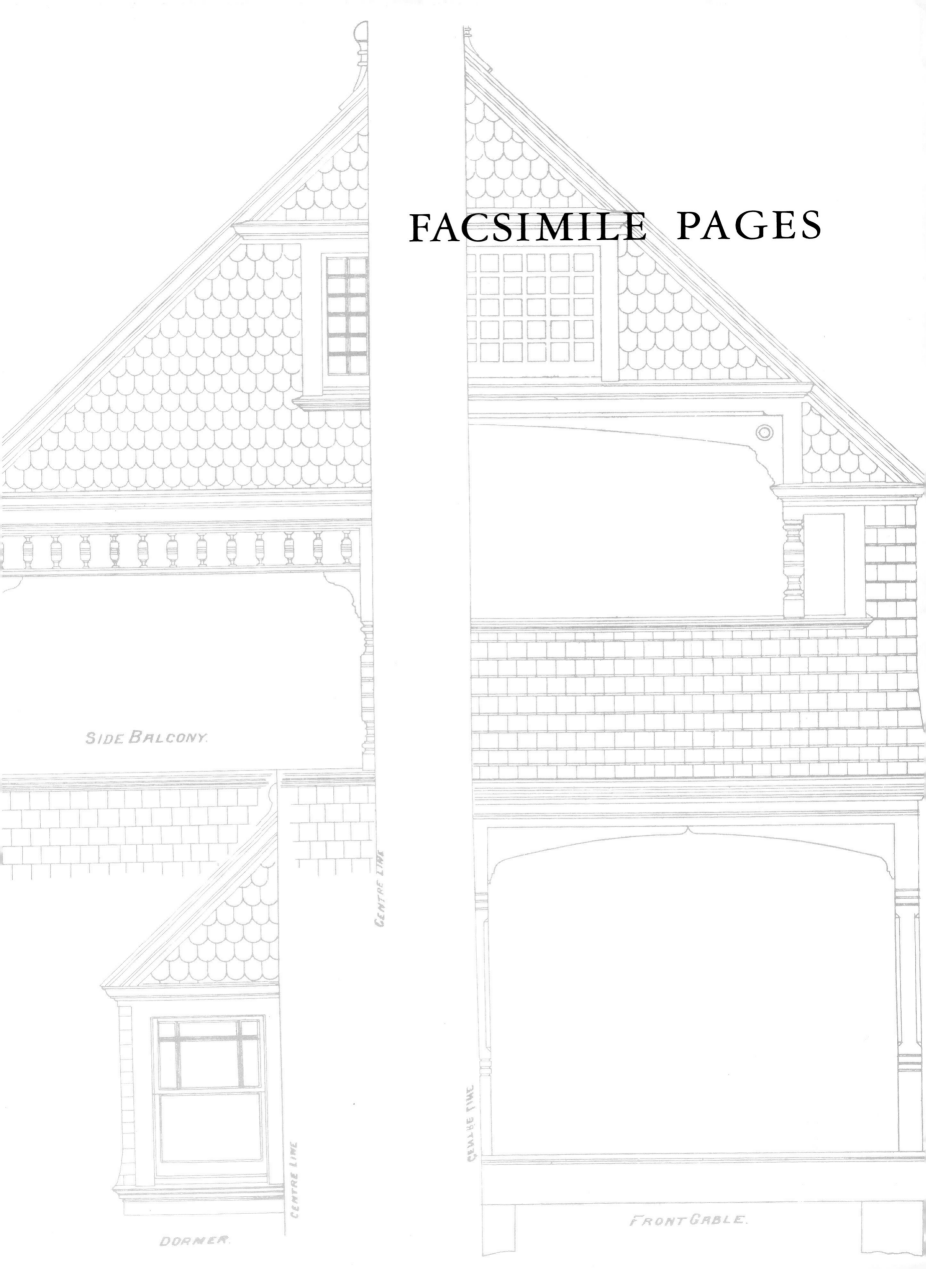

FACSIMILE PAGES

SIDE BALCONY.

DORMER.

CENTRE LINE

CENTRE LINE

CENTRE LINE

FRONT GABLE.

SCIENTIFIC AMERICAN

[Entered at the Post Office of New York, N. Y., as Second Class Matter.]

A WEEKLY JOURNAL OF PRACTICAL INFORMATION, ART, SCIENCE, MECHANICS, CHEMISTRY AND MANUFACTURES.

Vol. XLIII.—No. 4.
[NEW SERIES.]

NEW YORK, JULY 24, 1880.

[$3.20 per Annum.
[POSTAGE PREPAID.]

MANUFACTURE OF WALL PAPER.—WORKS OF CHRISTY SHEPHERD & GARRETT, NEW YORK.

34

THE WALL PAPER MANUFACTURE.

Among the many ways in which modern household decoration has been developed, perhaps no one occupies a more prominent position than the use of ready-made paper, instead of paint or tapestry, to cover the walls. And this method has become popular because of the degree of excellence which has been attained by manufacturers of wall paper within the memory of the present generation, the work now done being such as is sought after in the adornment of the most luxurious mansions in the world, while there is a great deal, also, the cost of which is so low that the lowest paid mechanic can afford to frequently brighten and freshen the walls of his living apartment therewith. A considerable manufacturing industry has, consequently, been developed for furnishing this one product, which affords no inconsiderable market for the paper manufacturer, and the dealers in colors, gums, and varnishes, besides giving employment to a large number of operatives. The illustrations on our first page this week give views of some of the leading operations in the conduct of this department of manufacture, as carried on by one of the leading houses in that line, Messrs. Christy, Shepherd & Garrett, at their large factory in West Twenty-third street, New York city.

Those who are in any way familiar with the art of printing will probably suppose that there is, from the start, some similarity between the processes of making letter-press work and the methods employed in producing the many-figured patterns which we find in wall paper. One does suggest the other throughout, but the means used and the mechanical part of the work are as different as the products. Wall papers are printed in water colors almost exclusively; very heavy pigments are used and stout bodies made, which require a great deal of time to dry, and these conditions also modify the character and substance of the type or blocks from which impressions are to be taken as well as the manner of taking them.

The "color mixing," an illustration of the department for which may be seen to the left hand at the bottom of the page, is one of the most important, as well as one of the most difficult branches of the business, where an extensive variety of fine wall paper is to be made. Besides the large room here shown for this purpose the firm have a special chemical department in an adjoining building at the rear, where they manufacture some of their own colors. In the mixing room, however, there may be found nearly every variety of earthy coloring matters, such as raw and burnt umber, sienna, etc., besides a good collection of mineral and vegetable colors, with an extensive assortment of gums and varnishes and the different kinds of clay which form the staple for making the body and carrying the color in every description of wall paper printing. The clay used comes principally from South Carolina and New Jersey. Both kinds are very nearly white, and readily divide into a fine powder, but the New Jersey clay has sufficient alum to render it best fitted for the second grounding in preparing the paper for "satining" or glossing. A large building in the rear is used for storing the clay, and a railway runs thence under the floor of the mixing room, 500 tons a year being about the amount of clay used here. The mixing of the colors is effected in large circular vats, in which arms operated from a shaft overhead are kept constantly revolving. From these vats the color is drawn off as wanted and transferred by a railway which runs through the room to an elevator leading to the various printing departments on the floors above.

On the basement floor, where the color mixing is carried on, is also the room for the reception of printing paper, which comes in rolls weighing about one hundred pounds each, and of just the regular width for wall paper, except such as is required for window shades, which is as much wider as may be desired.

The first part of the printing process, represented in one of the views at the top of the page, is the "grounding," or the covering of the whole white surface of one side of the paper with the ground color, on which the future patterns are to be printed. In this operation the color is put on the paper by brushes. Two wooden cylinders are arranged a short distance apart, carrying a wide belt of thick woolen cloth, the lower cylinder turning slowly in a trough containing the color, while a brush, operating against the cloth on the upper cylinder, transfers the color therefrom to the paper. The lower cylinder has a knife or rule pressing against the cloth as it comes out of the color, so that the quantity taken up may be regulated as desired. The brush which puts the color on has a slight, quick motion across the paper running through. The paper afterwards goes under brushes running lengthwise of the paper, and then again crosswise. This operation distributes the color evenly and leaves a good finish, varying slightly according to the work being done.

For all satin finished or glossed papers a second grounding is necessary. The first grounding, to adhere properly to the paper, requires an amount of glue which would render it too brittle to take a good polish, so a second coat is given, which carries a good deal more fine clay in a solution especially prepared to give a high polish. This operation is effected in a department not shown in our illustrations. It is done entirely on brushing machines, which work very rapidly, a cylinder about two feet in diameter revolving against smaller cylinders on its circumference, and the paper passing over one and under another until each portion of its surface has been vigorously brushed under six or eight cylinders.

All of the above work is preliminary to the printing proper, which is shown in the large view in the center of the page. For this purpose there are several large and small machines, the largest standing about fourteen feet high, and fitted to print twelve colors, but all working on the same principle. Each of these machines has a large drum in the middle, around which passes the paper, and, set at exactly the proper distances around its under side, are small rollers on which are the designs to be printed, each different color or shade being represented by a separate roller. It would hardly be proper to call these rollers or drums impression cylinders, in the sense in which printers use that term, for they bear very gently on the paper. The large drum is covered with a thick band of rubber, and is so light that it can easily be lifted away from the rollers carrying the design, as is always done in getting the press ready for work. It is, of course, absolutely necessary that the different colors should each come in their proper place, and so the small design rollers are all run by one large cog wheel, into which they are all geared. The color is taken up on cloth, in the same way as for the grounding, from little troughs or fountains near each of the design rollers, but it is pressed directly against the latter from the cloth itself as the rollers revolve, and each separate color is printed in succession as the large drum moves around.

Perhaps one of the most interesting details connected with the printing is the method of drying. Considerable time is required to thoroughly dry these heavy bodied pure water colors, and to do this work quickly and effectually the end of the paper first coming from the press is taken up and carried along by an endless belt, at nearly the height of the ceiling, and for a distance of some fifteen feet; the middle portion will then sag down, when a wooden slat is dropped on buttons on this belt, and taking the paper as it is coming from the press, carries it along and upward from that point, making a loop, for each fourteen or fifteen feet of the roll as it comes out. These slats carrying the loops of freshly printed paper are being constantly pushed forward on overhead railways which extend the whole length of the room, and underneath these railways are lines of steam pipe, each floor having special ventilators to carry off the moisture. At the end of the room there is an ingenious automatic arrangement by which the overhead railway carries the paper around a turn and back over a line parallel to that on which it came from the press, and so it continues to travel back and forth until thoroughly dry.

In making the bronzed papers, or those which have more or less of their patterns in silver and gold, the drying of the other colors must be effected before the bronzing. The size which is to carry the bronze is made especially for this purpose, and, when the colors which have been printed are entirely dry, the size, printed also at the same operation, is just in the proper condition to take and firmly hold the bronze. This is put on in a box-like machine with many brushes, into which the paper passes continuously from the press, after it has gone through its journey over the steam pipes on the overhead railroad.

Where embossed papers are wanted, in any style, the otherwise finished paper is simply run under a steel roller, of the desired surface, whereby it is pressed against a hard packing to give the required effect.

From the bronzing press, as from all the others, the paper proceeds, in the same manner as before, to the small machines for rolling, operated by girls, the work of which is shown in one of our pictures. Attached to each printing press is a gauge which indicates how many rolls are run, and makes a slight cut on the paper at the exact length required for each roll. The end of the paper being fed to the roller, it quickly turns until stopped by the operator at each of these cuts or marks, when a knife cuts it off, the roll is removed, and another roll started. This is the final operation of the manufacture. As the loops of paper are pulled out in the rolling, the slats which have suspended them drop at a certain point, to be gathered up and taken back to the presses.

One of the most important departments of the work, however, and the one which comes first in all the higher grades of goods, is the making of the designs for new patterns and styles. Old patterns are, nowadays, entirely unsalable, and the rule is that each year's patterns must be entirely new and distinct from those of the preceding season. So much so is this the case that the blocks are not saved, on the supposition that some old pattern might again become fashionable. It will be readily seen that this condition imposes upon manufacturers who have to constantly supply large lines of new and attractive patterns a task of no small magnitude. Messrs. Christy, Shepherd & Garrett have always stood in the front rank in their trade in this respect. They have artists regularly in their employment the year round, and also receive many patterns for competition from Europe as well as at home, and from the large number thus collected make selections of those they deem most meritorious. The artist makes the pattern and colors it as he deems most appropriate; but of any pattern they decide to use they make a great many different styles, by using different grounds with different combinations of colors, bronzes, etc., so that from one pattern sometimes as many as forty different styles are made.

From the designer's hands the pattern, after it has been accepted by the firm, goes to the block-cutting department shown in one of our engravings. Here it is drawn in outline on cylinders of wood carefully prepared to be of the exact size, and as many drawings made on different cylinders as there are to be colors in the pattern. The workman takes one of these cylinders and drives, in the line of the outline, little strips or pieces of brass, or it may be bits of brass wire, if a row of dots is wanted, or brass otherwise shaped to make a variety of small figures. A wire-drawing machine, with an assortment of dies, is kept to make many of the shapes wanted. When a large place is to be filled in to be printed in one color of which this brass work may form the outline, as a leaf, the center of a flower, etc., this space is filled with felt, firmly packed in. This brass and felt work, giving a perfect engraving on the circumference of the cylinder of all there is of one color to be worked in a pattern, stands up nearly a quarter of an inch from the wood; but that its surface may be entirely even and true, the face of the brass work is turned down under a file, and the whole is finally finished under an emery wheel.

Notwithstanding that, in nearly all of the operations of this establishment, the machinery works almost automatically, the firm employ during the busy months about 200 hands. The premises they occupy include a building 350 by 100 feet, and five stories high, besides several detached buildings in the rear. Their goods are exported to some extent to Europe, Australia, and South America, and have a large sale in every part of the United States; so that, although their facilities would seem to be so ample, they are frequently troubled to get the goods ready as fast as they are ordered. The total production last year amounted to about 6,000,000 rolls. The firm is one of the oldest, if not the oldest, in the country, having been established in 1836 by the late Thomas Christy, who died in 1874.

THE DEMAND FOR HEAVY HORSES.

The Factory and Farm states a fact which we have observed to exist in this city for some time past, i. e., an increase in the number of large horses used on trucks and heavy business wagons. During the past fifteen years, the writer remarks, there has been a great change in the demand for horses in this country. Formerly nearly every one bred in relation to speed and endurance. Now a large proportion of farmers breed with a view to increasing size and strength. This change is not the result of caprice. There has been a steady, increasing demand for heavy horses, and a corresponding falling off in the demand for light ones. Fashion has had little to do in the matter. Heavy horses are wanted because they supply an existing want. From present appearances it will be many years before the supply of heavy horses will equal the demand. The country is now well supplied with horses. At no time in its history, perhaps, were there as many horses to a given number of inhabitants as at present. Small work horses are low, but heavy draught horses continue to be high.

The importation of Clydesdale and Percheron-Norman horses increases every year. The first that were brought over were regarded as very uncertain ventures. At present they are of no doubtful value. The importers of horses from France and Scotland have suffered none of the reverses of the importers of short-horn cattle. With rare exceptions they have become rich. From present appearances we shall soon be sending Clydesdales to Scotland and England, and Normans to France and Belgium. The value of heavy draught horses was recognized in the Old World before it was in the New. Now that their worth is appreciated here, all persons having teaming to do seem anxious to procure them.

Large horses are less liable to injuries from the swinging of the poles of wagons than small ones. Their bones are firmer, and they are commonly more hardy. Large horses are more economical as respects harness, stall room, feed, and work required to take care of them. In all the countries of eastern Europe heavy horses have taken the place of light ones in general farming operations. That American farmers will soon generally employ heavy horses in field work seems certain.

Dangers of Elevator Cables.

To the Editor of the Scientific American:

I am informed that the superintendent of a well known hotel and apartment house, near Union square, this city, in order to learn what effect the continued bending and unbending of the wire elevator cable causes by passing over the pulleys and around the drum, detached the cable and, to his astonishment, found it actually rotten. In bending it twice across his knee it broke. This cable had been in use only two years. If this constant bending and unbending the cable causes such a disintegration, should it not be more widely known, that examinations may be made and possible disasters prevented ? 　　　SAMUEL SWAN, M.D.

13 West 38th St., New York.

SCIENTIFIC AMERICAN

[Entered at the Post Office of New York. N. Y., as Second Class Matter.]

A WEEKLY JOURNAL OF PRACTICAL INFORMATION. ART. SCIENCE. MECHANICS. CHEMISTRY AND MANUFACTURES.

Vol. XLIII.—No. 15.
[NEW SERIES.]

NEW YORK, OCTOBER 9, 1880.

[$3.20 per Annum.
[POSTAGE PREPAID.]

THE MANUFACTURE OF PARLOR FURNITURE.—FACTORY OF M. & H. SCHRENKEISEN, NEW YORK CITY

THE MANUFACTURE OF PARLOR FURNITURE.

It is said that when Jenny Lind first visited America, and after she had been some time in New York City, she inquired where our "poor people" lived. She saw so many signs of thrift, comfort, and prosperity everywhere, so many evidences of culture in every class of people with whom she came in contact, the residences so commodious, and the people so well clad, in comparison with what she had seen in the Old World, that it appeared to her, even after she had been for some time in New York, that she had only become partially acquainted with real life here. In the prosecution of no other one line of business, perhaps, is this distinction so clearly brought out as in the industry which we this week make the subject of our first page illustrations. In no other country in the world has such an industry heretofore been possible, carried on in the manner and according to the scale on which it is here conducted, for, although it is true that equally beautiful and far more elaborate specimens of household furniture and decoration are to be met with in the mansions and palaces of the older countries of the world, such work there is almost always made to order, and obtainable only by the few, at a cost far exceeding the price of quite as serviceable and very similar goods here.

There has been a rapid development of this branch of business within the past twenty years, and with its growth has come a natural division according to which the different specialties are made exclusively by particular manufacturers. The manufacture of dining-room and chamber furniture each constitutes separate lines of business, while parlor furniture is a specialty of itself, and the leading details of this department of the trade are shown by our artist, as the industry is conducted by Messrs. M. & H. Schrenkeisen, of New York City.

The first operation in the manufacture is represented by the view at top of first page, where the log, as it comes to the factory, is taken by a large band saw and cut into the thicknesses and lengths required. This saw runs on a wheel about five feet in diameter. An adjoining view shows a smaller band saw, used to cut up plank and boards and further divide the lumber into the different sizes to fit it for the several pieces to be made. There are seven of these band saws and nine jig or scroll saws in constant operation. The wood having been cut to the required size, the first detail of the manufacture consists in the marking of the patterns thereon. This was formerly done with a pencil, but now stencil patterns are made in zinc, by which the pattern is so plainly shown on the wood that there is much less liability to error in cutting than was formerly the case.

Previous to the work on the jig saws, nearly all the pieces have to go to the boring machine, where holes of different sizes are put through such parts of the pattern as required to enable the workman to pass through the end of the saw in cutting out the design. These holes are usually bored in places where the curves are so small that it would be difficult to work them out with the saw, although some of the jig saws are less than an eighth of an inch wide. The workmen in this department, however, from long practice, are able to follow the intricate patterns with such firmness and facility that the most complicated designs are worked out with great rapidity, and apparently without the least pause or hesitation.

The friezer, or machine carver, shown in one of the views at the top of the page, takes up but little room, but the variety of work it will do is almost unlimited. There are several modifications of this machine, for different classes of work, but the essential principle in them is the revolution, on a small axis, of different shaped knives, according to the design of the work, the wood being pressed against the knives in the line of guides and gauges adjusted to the particular pattern. In this way the machine may be adjusted to do almost any kind of carving desired, but it is found more economical in practice to do a large proportion of the carving by hand, rather than fit up the knives and patterns for the machine for all the new and elaborate designs in carving which are always being introduced.

The variety moulder, shown in one of the illustrations, represents only one of several machines in operation for this department of the work, but it is one which will cut almost everything known to the trade in the way of mouldings. The planing and turning machines, which are also the subjects of separate views, are of several sizes, and of patterns entirely familiar to all wood-workers, but the "jointer" is a machine less commonly known. It is to put a smooth edge or corner on pieces to be joined together, and it makes the edges and angles, either flat or any desired bevel, so smooth and even that when two pieces of wood of the same grain are placed together it is difficult to see where they join. The sand-papering machine shown at the bottom simply represents arms covered with sand paper, which are made to rotate very rapidly while the workman passes the rough surfaces over them to smooth off the unevenness made by the saw or planer.

The carving by hand, of which a view is given in one of our illustrations, forms a very important part of the work done at this establishment, at which from thirty to forty expert hands are kept regularly employed. This work is all done by the piece, from original designs gotten up by the house, the firm being constantly engaged in contriving something new which is likely to please the artistic taste of the community. In this way they will get up a suit of parlor furniture, subject it to criticism, make possibly considerable alterations in it, decide on the different ways in which it will be upholstered, and then have from one to two hundred sets made of this particular style. No one outside of their own immediate business is allowed to know what their new designs are until these sets of furniture are finished and ready to put on the market. In short the firm take the log as it comes from the woods, and do every part of the work necessary to make therefrom the completed furniture as it appears in the parlor, and all from new and original designs of their own.

One of the most important details of the work, without the most sedulous care in regard to which it would be impossible to make durable work, is the proper seasoning of the lumber. Only the best seasoned wood is used to start with, but it is almost impossible to thoroughly season a thick plank all through. After the work is cut out in the rough, therefore, the pieces all go to the drying room, a large apartment with slatted floors, under which run steam pipes, by which the temperature can be kept up to and above 100° Fahrenheit constantly. In this way the moisture is thoroughly evaporated, and all after danger of cracking from exposure to unusual warmth is avoided, as the finely finished work, in which the pores of the wood are all closed, and its surface has a glass-like polish, will not allow of its afterward absorbing moisture from the air. The cracking which sometimes happens in very old furniture does not arise from this latter cause so much as from the improper gluing of panels, etc., a detail which here receives careful attention.

The upholstering and finishing of the work is all done at the warerooms, on Elizabeth street, near Canal street, where the firm occupy a six story building, L-shaped, but covering a space equal to 50 by 150 feet. This building, as also the factory on Monroe street, 100 by 100 feet, and six stories high, are shown in the view in the center of the page. A 100-horse power engine furnishes the power required at the factory, and this is run almost entirely by the shavings and turnings made in the work.

Most of the goods now made are of cherry, "ebonized," as it is called, and black walnut. The ebonizing is done by dipping the furniture in an acid coloring bath, which turns it black and eats its way into the wood so as to give more than a surface coloring, and a scratch or light cut shows black underneath. In this style of furniture a large portion is finished with lines, bands, and beading in gold leaf, though some of it is also made in plain black, either brightly polished or what is called a dull finish. In the upholstering department the final work of finishing is never put on the goods until just before shipment, as finished furniture of the finest quality requires great care. In sofas, easy chairs, rockers, etc., steel springs, hair, and moss, are used, as may be required for different kinds of goods, but only the best qualities of any kind of stock are employed, and, although a fine finish is always obtained, the work is throughout of the most solid and substantial character.

The firm are the owners of several patents connected with the furniture manufacture, among the most successful of which have been their patents on spring rockers, for which they had a great run for several years after they were introduced, and which still form a leading article in the trade. They have also obtained a number of patents on band embroidery trimmings and coverings. The most of the goods used for coverings are imported, orders being given on samples sent here by European manufacturers, with the agreement that the firm shall have the exclusive control of these styles for a definite period, or until they shall have had time to put their goods on the market. The variety of these coverings is very extensive, embracing almost everything in the way of raw and finished silk, figured stuffs in satin, tapestries, reps, serge, damask, plush, etc., the patterns of only a small portion of which can be found in the large and handsome illustrated catalogue issued by the firm. In order, however, to keep their customers and agents fully informed in regard to the new styles they are constantly getting out, they have a photograph establishment fitted up in one portion of their warerooms, where they make prints of each new set of furniture when it is ready to put upon the market, and from which they receive orders from agents and dealers.

The firm have already done some business in the way of exporting furniture, but the foreign demand for ready-made upholstered parlor furniture, which is the particular specialty of this house, is relatively far less than is the call for these goods in our own country, where almost every well-to-do mechanic has his parlor, or "best room," furnished in a way which is almost unknown among the same classes in other parts of the world.

DECISIONS RELATING TO PATENTS.

By the Acting Secretary of the Interior.

EX PARTE GREAVES.—CONDENSING CYLINDER FOR CARDING MACHINES.

Bell, Acting Secretary.

1. The Commissioner of Patents may issue a patent for one or more of the divisions of a reissue application, and subsequently issue a patent to the applicant for the remaining divisions, if it be held that otherwise he is entitled to them.

2. Until an application for reissue is ended in all its divisions the vitality of the original patent continues so far as required to support that portion of the application which remains undecided.

By the Commissioner of Patents.

EX PARTE LEE.—COUPON RAILWAY TICKET.—APPEAL FROM THE EXAMINERS-IN-CHIEF.

Marble, Commissioner:

1. The patentable features of a railway or other ticket, like those of any other substantive thing, must depend upon peculiarities of mechanical construction.

2. The printed matter upon a ticket is nothing more than an arbitrary direction as to how such ticket is to be used, and can have no bearing upon the patentability of the ticket itself.

3. A railway ticket anticipated by an internal revenue stamp where the system and the manner in which it is carried out is substantially the same.

4. Duplication of checks or coupons as a matter of expediency, obviously suggested by the necessity of the case, does not require invention.

THE FRANKLIN SEARCH EXPEDITION.

The members of the Franklin search party under the command of Lieutenant Frederick Schwatka, U. S. A., were picked up, August 1, by a New Bedford bark, at Depot Island, Hudson's Bay, where they had been since March 4. The party had been for two years exploring the regions north and northwest of Hudson's Bay in search of relics of Sir John Franklin's expedition. Reports of the first year's work were received and published about a year ago. Having come to the conclusion that the records of the Franklin expedition might be preserved in cairns in King William's Land, Lieutenant Schwatka set out on the first of April, 1879, to look for them. During the succeeding eleven months he accomplished the longest sledge journey ever made in an unexplored Arctic country, traveling in all 3,251 statute miles. It was the first sledge journey ever made that covered an entire Arctic winter; and the temperatures experienced exceeded in frigidity anything ever before encountered by white men in the field.

On January 3, 1880, the thermometer sank to 71 degrees below zero, Fahrenheit, or 103 degrees below freezing point, and during the entire day it did not rise above —69 degrees. During sixteen days the average temperature was 100 degrees below the freezing point, and during twenty-seven days it was below —60 degrees. All this time the party traveled, in fact they never halted a single day on account of the cold.

During the summer and fall of 1879 they made a complete search of King William's Land and the adjacent mainland, traveling over the route pursued by the crews of the Erebus and Terror upon their retreat toward Back's River, and while so engaged the party buried the bones of all those unfortunates remaining above ground and erected monuments to the memory of the fallen heroes. Their research established the mournful fact that the records of Franklin's expedition are lost beyond recovery.

A large quantity of relics were gathered by the party to illustrate the last chapter of the history of Sir John Franklin's expedition. From each spot where the graves were found a few tokens were selected that may serve to identify those who perished there. A piece of each of the boats which had been found and destroyed by the natives was brought away, together with interesting though mournful relics in the shape of the prow of one of their boats, the sledge upon which it was transported, and part of the drag rope upon which these poor fellows tugged until they fell down and died in their tracks. In addition to these the party secured a board which may serve to identify the ship which completed the northwest passage.

They also brought the remains of Lieutenant John Irving, third officer of the Terror, which were identified by a prize medal found in his opened grave. The party endured many hardships and were threatened with starvation after their return to Depot Island, where they failed to find the supplies which were to have been left there for them by the schooner Eothen. The party suffered no serious sickness while in the field.

A Remarkable Group of Solar Spots.

To the Editor of the Scientific American:

One of the very finest groups of sun spots it has ever been my pleasure to witness was observed by me through the five-inch Newtonian telescope yesterday morning, September 12, 1880. It was situated then about midway from the center of the sun's disk and the western limb south of the equator. Its length was enormous, occupying a space equal to one-quarter of the sun's diameter, and therefore over 200,000 miles in length. I present herewith a sketch made of the group at the eyepiece of the telescope, and which conveys but a faint idea of its grandeur. At A and B were quite large spots surrounded by a very delicate penumbra, while at C was a most beautiful cluster of small spots. The whole group was remarkable for its brilliance and distinctness. In addition to this large group there was a fair-sized single spot near the center of the disk, with a faint penumbra and dark markings in its vicinity; also a faint double spot below this one.

WILLIAM R. BROOKS.

Red House Observatory, Phelps, N. Y., September 14, 1880.

SCIENTIFIC AMERICAN

[Entered at the Post Office of New York, N. Y., as Second Class Matter.]

PRACTICAL INFORMATION, ART, SCIENCE, MECHANICS, CHEMISTRY

NEW YORK, MAY 17, 1884.

THE PAINT AND VARNISH MANUFACTURE AS CONDUCTED BY F. W. DEVOE & CO.

38

Scientific American. [MAY 17, 1884.

THE MANUFACTURE OF PAINTS, VARNISHES, BRUSHES, AND ARTISTS' MATERIALS.

Only those directly connected with the business can fully realize how enormous has been the increase of American production in this line during the present generation. The growth has been far more than proportionate to the increase of the population, for two reasons—first, the manufacture here has been so improved that we now import very little except raw materials; and second, the condition of the great body of the people has been steadily improving, so that we have more comfortably and tastily fitted up homes, workshops, and business houses, to say nothing of the great demands which modern railway and steamboat traffic have given rise to. And all these causes contribute to making the business in paints and varnishes of much more importance, proportionately, in our industries, than it was a generation ago.

In our first page illustrations we give representations of some of the most important details of the manufacture, as conducted at the extensive paint works of Messrs. F. W. Devoe & Co., in New York city, and at their varnish factory in Newark, N. J. Their manufacture includes colors of all kinds, either dry, ground in oil or water, or in pulp, ready-mixed paints, colors in japan for coach and carriage and railway car painting, and fine varnishes and japans, with every variety of brushes, artists' materials generally, and mathematical and surveyors' instruments.

Although in many pigments the manufacture has been greatly changed within a recent period—more especially since the introduction of the aniline colors—the making of dry white lead and of zinc white, which constitute a large portion of all the paint used, and form the basis of many of the colors, has remained substantially unchanged through a long period. Formerly white lead was largely imported, but there are now some forty corroding establishments in the United States, and imported white lead is almost unknown. In zinc white, however, we still import our best qualities, Messrs. Devoe & Co. using the Vieille Montagne product, made in the largest establishments of the kind in the world, at Paris and Liege. This is a purer article than that made here, from the fact that the American zinc white is made direct from the ore, while that which they import is made from the metal, and, although the house makes all grades of colors which have a popular demand, they sell none carrying the label of their own name and trademark which is not strictly what it is stated to be. White lead and zinc white are much adulterated, for the cheaper paints, with chalk, barytes, and other adulterants.

In making and preparing for use the various pigments which go to make up the great variety of colored paints, an extended knowledge of chemistry is indispensable. Chemically manufactured colors, such as chrome yellow and green, Prussian blue, and vermilion, are not durable when in exposed conditions, but either of these may be mixed with vehicles which will add greatly to their permanence. Ultramarine blue, as now made—for that made from lapis lazuli has been entirely superseded by the cheaper artificial blue—is a durable color, but care is required in mixing it with white lead to be sure that the lead is pure, for that adulterated with barytes is very injurious, causing the blue to fade quickly. Carmine, also, if mixed with varnish instead of oil, is a durable color, although much of the durability of any color is largely dependent upon the ground on which it is spread and the exposure it receives, as well as the vehicles used in mixing. There has long been a good deal of difference of opinion among painters as to the use of white lead and zinc—some strongly advocating one and some another—but these differences are now resolving themselves into pretty general unanimity of opinion that zinc white has many advantages for interior work, and that for exposed situations the most durable white is a mixture of white lead and zinc white in nearly equal parts. But however the painters or the public may differ in opinion on this point, the doctors all strenuously oppose the use of white lead as eminently injurious to those who make it and the painters who use it.

In the manufacture of all their goods the firm start with the raw material, and carry it forward through all the successive stages. Mr. Isaac Wyman Drummond, E.M., Ph.D., has direct charge of the chemical examinations and experiments necessary, and the importance of the most careful attention in this department for the making of durable colors cannot be overestimated. The permanence of colors in secondary or mixed paints depends primarily on the chemical relations of the colors and pigments employed. These secondary colors are produced by various combinations, and the rule is to use the least number of colors possible to secure the desired tint. It is thus that, with the best of skill in the chemical manipulations, and experts to attend to the mixing and all the details of the manufacture, a variety of colors and an excellence in quality is attained which it would be impossible for any single workman to hope to reach.

In our illustrations are given thirteen views of as many different departments of the business, besides one showing the interior of the large and handsome store at the corner of Fulton and William Streets, New York.

In the left hand corner at the top of the page is shown the mixing and grinding of the pigments for standard colors, while adjoining it in the center is a view of the process of making the finer artists' colors furnished in tubes. The engravings are necessarily small, from the desire of the artist to bring into the group as many departments as possible. There is nothing, perhaps, that would be entirely new to the well informed mechanic in the manner of mixing and grinding the colors, but the advantages possessed by a large establishment for doing this work, with ample power and the most perfect mills, make it an easy matter to secure great fineness and uniformity in the product. The constituents required for the different colors and shades are accurately weighed and measured out before they are put into the mills, and the work is afterward done with mechanical precision. The grinding of the artists' tube colors is done on a circular glass table on which, in a regularly changing ellipsis, revolves a heavy granite block.

On sanitary grounds alone, the extent to which ready ground and mixed paints have come into use within the last few years is a matter of public good fortune. The grinding and mixing of paints were among the most unhealthful parts of the business, when done in the old way, as the dry powder was to some extent absorbed by the skin or taken in by breathing, while its being directly taken in through a scratch in the skin was not uncommon, and all tended to give a high death rate among painters before the attainment of middle life.

The pulverizing of dry colors, shown at the left, about the middle of the page, is done with powerful mills, the pigments, when large enough to require it, being first passed through a breaker and then ground between heavy stones, and bolted to secure uniform fineness, much in the same way that flour is ground.

The white lead and zinc grinding, shown immediately below, forms a most important part of the business. The lead or zinc, with its requisite quantity of oil, is placed in a mixer, which has a trough or gutter in a circle, on a bed about six feet in diameter, in which rolls around a stone also about six feet in diameter, and eight inches face, until the oil has been thoroughly incorporated to make a paste or pulp. Thence this is drawn by pipes into mills on the floor below, where it passes between powerful grinding stones, and comes out slowly in a thick paste of great fineness and entire uniformity.

In the grinding of colors for house painting, or what should be more properly styled the making of the ready mixed paints for use without change, the firm do an extensive business. A large portion of their goods are simply ground in oil to a paste consistency, leaving the painter to thin and put in such drier as deemed best; but in those goods sold in cans, pails, etc., ready for use, the requisite driers and all necessary ingredients are incorporated, and the buyer only has to select the color or shade required from the sample on the label or specimen sheet.

The making of vermilion, shown in one of the views, requires a large department. This is principally made from carbonate of lead and bichromate of potash, with water, the resulting liquid being left to settle in large tanks, the sediment being laid out in batches to dry, the final moisture being absorbed by chalk blocks on which the rough cakes are placed. This vermilion has been in practical use for several years; it does not turn brown or blacken, but retains its brilliancy under exposure to sun or weather.

In all the varieties of umber and sienna made, of which the manufacture includes everything known to the trade, the raw umber and sienna are imported by the hundred tons, and burnt, ground, and passed through all the requisite processes on the premises, as is also the case with the various grades of Vandyke brown. For their ivory black the firm buy ivory chips from the manufacturers of billiard balls and ivory goods, and burn it themselves, to be entirely sure of having a perfectly pure article, which they sell in the powder or in the form of drop black.

As a substitute for the chrome or Paris green, the firm have for several years been making a very popular shade of green, known as the "Park Lawn Green," which is much used for window blinds, agricultural implements, ornamental iron work, and machinery, and they also make another shade, known as "Clover Leaf Green," which is strong and brilliant, and with great covering properties.

Of coach and car colors, ground in japan, the firm make a specialty, and furnish all the supplies required by several prominent railway lines. It is absolutely necessary that the identical shade adopted shall be preserved in all subsequent orders, and that the materials shall be the same, so that the wear will be uniform, and on this account they usually make up large lots at one time, so as always to have a supply on hand. For these colors the firm received a gold medal at the National Exposition of Railway Appliances in Chicago last year.

Not the least among the departments of the business is the large tinshop, where the pails, cans, and painters' tinware are made. Everything of that kind required is made on the premises, the most improved machinery being employed, and every piece being made by a pattern that cannot fail to secure absolute uniformity.

The brush making department of the business covers the manufacture of every kind and grade of brushes known to the trade, from the fine sable to those made of bristle—brushes for the japanner or varnisher, the painter, or the artist—and for all classes of work. The deftness with which the hands put together this work, the facility with which they even up the tufts of almost silky fineness, or separate bristles which have split points, or which have been laid with the roots where the points should be, is something quite wonderful to one who has never seen the work in progress. Everything in this room is made according to sample, and specimens to work by are hung up near every work table.

The making of artists' canvas boards requires a large department. Only the best English linen is used, made especially for the purpose; this is first stretched tightly on the frames, and workmen go over each inch of the surface to remove all pin heads or imperfections of the flax—then come successive coats of specially prepared lead and filling, to make a smooth, firm surface, such as best adapted to make an even and permanent surface for the artist's work.

The manufacture of surveying and mathematical instruments, to be used in railroad construction and for engineers, architects, and draughtsmen, as well as for technical schools, has naturally grown out of the gradual expansion of the business into the filling of all the wants of artists, and everything required by contractors who use their paints. A view of this department has been necessarily omitted from our illustrations, but here are made squares, triangles, compasses, pantographs, and a large variety of other instruments, while the transits, theodolites, and levels furnished by the firm have been approved by and are in the use of the United States Coast Survey.

For the making of varnish and japan the works are at Newark, N. J., and representations of some of the leading details in this branch of the business are shown in the views on the right of the page. The first operation in order is the chipping, which is in reality little more than the removal of the outside crust or coating, and the separation of any impurities. There are in all some thirty different resins or gums of which varnish is made, included in which are principally amber, copal, gum cowrie, animé, and common resin. There are natural lacquers from India and China, and drying oils which resinify by oxidation in the air, but oil varnishes proper are composed of an intimate combination of a drying oil with a fused resin, which hardens by the oxidation of the air. Besides these there are varnishes which have a volatile liquid holding in solution resins or gums which, on the evaporation of the solvent, leave behind a vitreous coating on the surface varnished.

The oil used is principally linseed, which from its high drying property and its general constancy in quality is the great favorite in nearly all varnishes. It is obtained as new, sweet, and free from rancidity as possible, and then clarified and allowed to settle for weeks, after which it is drawn off for use. By boiling, the fatty constituents of the oil—glycerine, palmitine, etc.—are volatilized. The various methods of mixing the oils and gums or resins, and the manner and extent to which they are heated together or separately, necessarily vary with the particular kind of varnish or japan being made. It is a branch of the business which calls for the greatest knowledge, experience, and care, together with a skill which can only be acquired by long practice and observation. The resin must be so prepared as to be readily soluble in oil, and then so incorporated as to form a compound which shall be perfectly soluble in turpentine, and so that, on the evaporation of the latter, a hard surface will form before dust, under ordinary circumstances, will attach to the varnished surface. The high success of the firm in this branch of their manufacture, through many years of steadily increasing business, affords the best criterion of the quality of their goods.

The works of the firm in New York city have a frontage of 200 feet on Horatio Street and 175 feet on Jane Street, with a floor space of about four acres. This part of the business is under the especial superintendence of Mr. James F. Drummond, a member of the firm who has attended entirely to the manufacturing since 1856. A view of the main salesroom, at the corner of Fulton and William Streets, forms one of our illustrations, the business department being under the direct personal supervision of the two other members of the firm, Messrs. Frederick W. Devoe and J. Seaver Page. The first floor above, of the full size of the store, is devoted to artists' supplies and painters' sundries, including an assortment of almost everything even remotely connected with painting and decorating. The firm have a branch house in Chicago under the style of Coffin, Devoe & Co.

𝔖𝔠𝔦𝔢𝔫𝔱𝔦𝔣𝔦𝔠 𝔄𝔪𝔢𝔯𝔦𝔠𝔞𝔫.

ESTABLISHED 1845.

MUNN & CO., Editors and Proprietors,

No. 361 BROADWAY, NEW YORK.

O. D. MUNN.　　　　　A. E. BEACH.

NEW YORK, JANUARY, 1886.

THE

𝔖𝔠𝔦𝔢𝔫𝔱𝔦𝔣𝔦𝔠 𝔄𝔪𝔢𝔯𝔦𝔠𝔞𝔫,

ARCHITECTS AND BUILDERS EDITION.

This is a Special Trade Edition of THE SCIENTIFIC AMERICAN, issued Monthly,—on the first Saturday of the month.

It goes directly *into the hands of those who have the ordering of the great bulk of Building Materials and Appliances*, namely, the Architects, Builders, Constructing Engineers, and Contractors.

It has the largest circulation of any Architectural or Building paper in the world.

An Increase of Trade will necessarily accrue to all Manufacturers and Dealers whose establishments are conspicuously represented in this important edition of THE SCIENTIFIC AMERICAN.

TERMS OF SUBSCRIPTION:

For Architects and Builders Edition of SCIENTIFIC AMERICAN, $1.50 a year. In Clubs, four copies for $5.00. Single Copies, 15 cents each. Sold by all Newsdealers.

MUNN & CO., Publishers,
361 BROADWAY, NEW YORK.

CONTENTS

Of the January number of the ARCHITECTS AND BUILDERS EDITION of SCIENTIFIC AMERICAN.

(Illustrated articles are marked with an asterisk.)

OTHER PUBLICATIONS.

THE SCIENTIFIC AMERICAN

Weekly, $3.20 a Year; $1.60 Six Months.

Sixteen large pages elegantly illustrated.

THE SCIENTIFIC AMERICAN SUPPLEMENT

Is a distinct paper from the SCIENTIFIC AMERICAN. THE SUPPLEMENT is issued weekly. Every number contains 16 octavo pages, uniform in size with the SCIENTIFIC AMERICAN. **$5.00 a Year.**

Combined Rates.—The SCIENTIFIC AMERICAN and Supplement, one year, **$7.00.**

The SCIENTIFIC AMERICAN (weekly) and ARCHITECTS AND BUILDERS EDITION (monthly), $4 a year.

SCIENTIFIC AMERICAN (weekly), SUPPLEMENT (weekly), and ARCHITECTS AND BUILDERS EDITION (monthly), $8 a year.

The safest way to remit is by draft, postal order, or registered letter. Address

MUNN & CO., 361 Broadway, corner of Franklin Street, New York.

Table of Contents of

THE SCIENTIFIC AMERICAN SUPPLEMENT No. 522,

For the Week Ending January 2, 1886.

Price 10 cents.　For sale at this Office and by all Newsdealers.

ABOUT TERRA COTTA.

Terra cotta must now be regarded as a staple building material. The stage of experimenting is past, and the manufacturer is sure of his work and of the market. The architects and builders of our large cities are well acquainted with terra cotta, but to many others a concise account of this material and of the point to be observed in its use may not be unwelcome.

Terra cotta, like brick, is burnt clay. There is no patent composition about it, as many might suppose from its name. It was known to the ancients, as many discovered fragments from old ruins, and numerous literary references, testify. To make good terra cotta, the clay must be rich in natural silica and free from carbonaceous and sulphurous material and from grit. Soft, loamy clays, which require the addition of sand to make them fit for burning, are more suitable for common bricks and for stoneware pottery. A fine, even, plastic texture is necessary for terra cotta. Hard clays require to be crushed and pulverized, and all are greatly benefited by exposure to the oxidizing action of the air. The leading makers now employ expensive and special machinery, suitable to the particular clay at their command, so as to secure a perfect paste. Clays fit for terra cotta appear to be found in abundance in every country, at varying depth below the ground. The coloring matter is oxide of iron, and the color varies according to the quantity of this chemical, the degree of burning, the fuel, and the construction of the kiln. It ranges from a warm buff through every shade of red to a rich brown, and can be regulated at will.

The most ordinary way to shape terra cotta is to press the prepared clay into moulds from wood or plaster models or patterns. This is an important part of the business, similar in most respects to the pattern making in iron foundries. Allowance must be made for the shrinkage of the clay in drying and burning. It is best for architects to allow the manufacturer to arrange for this himself.

All terra cotta blocks above the smallest dimensions are modeled hollow, with suitable solid sides or ends, and sometimes partitions to give the necessary strength. By this method a nearly even thickness of clay is attained, varying from one to three inches, seldom more. Solid lumps of material are thus avoided, the baking takes place evenly and simultaneously all around and all through the clay, and cracking and warping are considerably reduced. This tendency of the clay to warp, twist, and crack under fire is the greatest difficulty the manufacturer has to contend with.

Not only must each maker suit the manner of burning to the nature of the clay he uses, but the same material seems to behave in an erratic manner under apparently identical conditions. Different patterns of kilns are used—square and round, down-draught and up-draught, muffled kilns, where the flame does not come in direct contact with the clay, and open ones, in which it does.

A perfect kiln is the great desideratum of terra cotta manufacture, and experience alone must guide each maker toward this desirable achievement. The preparation of the paste has almost reached perfection; the kiln and also the fuel must be suited to this to insure the best possible work. Vigilance and judgment on the part of the workmen intrusted with the burning process are of the utmost importance. For the foregoing reasons, architects should joint their lateral terra cotta work, such as belt courses, cornices, window sills, etc., in pieces not exceeding two feet in length, especially when they are of a flat section.

Before being dried, the moulded clay is thoroughly dried in rooms kept at a moderate temperature. The amount of exposure in the kiln varies from an ordinary red heat to a white heat sufficient to melt iron, all according to the nature of the clay, the depth of color desired, and the durability to be attained. All terra cotta should be well burned to be thoroughly hard and chemically and physically homogeneous; beyond this point further burning is of no advantage, as it only tends to make a brittle fabric, and increases the chances of warping.

Terra cotta is now used for every kind of architectural work, from the simple moulded brick to the most elaborate cornices. Entire fronts have been carried out in this material, and important constructive functions have been assigned to it. It is, however, an open question whether terra cotta should be used in this sense. Some recent failures seem to indicate the contrary. Although strong, it is not well to expose it to great weights and strains. Nor can it be said that elaborate continuous features, like, for instance, a modillion entablature or a fluted pilaster shaft, are of a thoroughly satisfactory appearance when viewed closely. From reasons already explained, the separate moulded pieces are too unequal to make perfect buttjoints and true continuous lines. Some cornices in New York city buildings have a distinct wavy outline, and much imperfect work seems to indicate that there is a tendency to strain this material to uses which are beyond its capabilities. The proper sphere of terra cotta is that of an auxiliary decorative and constructive material in connection with brickwork or stone masonry. Under such conditions its very imperfections are converted into points of merit. Terra cotta is used to best advantage in moulded bricks for the edges of door and window openings, in plinth and belt courses and cornices of modest projection, in moulded architrave blocks, keystones, tiles, panels, etc., for separate features or continuous friezes, in pilaster capitals, figured and ornamental subject panels, balusters, cappings, copings, chimney pots, in roof tiles and ridges, and other isolated ornamental features, also for fireplace mantels. A plain brick building may, with the means above indicated, be invested with artistic interest at a comparatively small cost, and elaborate and high art effects may be obtained with terra cotta at a cost much below that of convex masonry.

The bedding of the separate blocks is made to work in with ordinary brick bond; is either 2¼ inches, 4 inches, or 8 inches, and so on, according to the size of the block and the projection. They are built in with cement mortar like stonework, and are inclosed secure or held by superincumbent weights in the same manner as stonework of great projection is. The buttjointing of terra cotta work is peculiar. For balustrade cappings and similar top courses of light section, where neither weight nor anchors can hold the work, it is well to dowel joint the pieces. For window sills, top courses of cornices, wall copings, etc., it is best to lap-joint the blocks, to protect the joint against wet and frost. This practice gives a very good effect when the joints occur regularly.

About cost it is difficult to give data of any value, unless accompanied by a precise description of the work understood. The illustrated catalogues of the leading manufacturers give full information.

A most important point is to order terra cotta early enough in advance of the general estimate for a building. This will save much delay and annoyance. It is also well to order a reasonable surplus of bricks or tiles, to make up for any accidental breakage in transit or on the building. Every architect and builder should seek the opportunity of visiting the establishment of a terra cotta maker, to see for himself the various manipulations and the variety of the articles made and their diversified application. There is no other building industry that has made equally phenomenal strides in an equally short space of time.

Cast Iron Columns.

The design and execution of the columns of the Royal Bank, Dublin, was matter of the most anxious attention, on account of their unusual length, the great loads they were intended to carry, and the architectural necessity of diminishing their diameters to the utmost extent consistent with safety. The dimensions finally adopted were: Length, 26 feet; diameter of base, 14 inches; diameter of head, 12 inches; thickness of metal, 1¼ inches. The ultimate strength of this pillar, according to Hodgkinson's practical adaptation of Euler's formula, was 770 tons, and the safe load may be estimated at one-sixth of that amount.

Having decided the proportions of the column, it was of the utmost importance to secure good, sound casting, straightness, concentricity of bore to the external surface, and perfect bearing with flat ends on a good foundation. Soundness of casting and straightness were alone to be obtained by careful moulding and ventilation, but the certainty of obtaining uniformity of thickness required special precautions. It is well known that in moulding columns the hollow part is formed by means of a " core," composed of a perforated metal pipe, wrapped with hay and plastered with loam till it assumes the proper shape and size. This core is placed horizontally in the external mould, and held securely in the sand at both ends, " chaplets," or supports of tinned iron, being placed in addition at intervals throughout its length. These chaplets answer very well for small castings, as the sand of the external mould into which they are stuck has sufficient power to resist the distorting action of the molten metal; but in columns of such length as those here described, they would not be sufficiently secure to be trusted. It was necessary, therefore, to make a metallic connection between the top and the bottom boxes of the mould and the metal core barrel.

The strength of a column is very much influenced by the perfection of its bearing and fixity of its ends, and to insure these the ends of the columns were turned truly in the lathe; and the base, which was 2 feet square 3 inches thick, was turned on the upper and planed on the lower face. The foundation stone having been set perfectly level and chiseled to fit the plate exactly, the latter was laid truly in its place, and se cured by means of iron dowels run with lead. The up per face of the plate being level, the column when reared on it was, of course, quite vertical, and in absolute contact with the plate all around. The cap, which is also turned on its under side, was slipped in between the beam and the column, and the space between it and the beam filled with bars of flat iron, and cast iron cement tightly driven in. Both the cap and base had projections a quarter inch high entering the column to prevent any lateral displacement.—*William Anderson, in the Architect.*

PASSAIC CITY, NEW JERSEY.

The open country adjacent to the city of New York is in many respects most beautiful and attractive. This is especially the case in respect to the region situated westerly from the metropolis. Crossing the broad Hudson River on commodious boats, the passenger takes seat in the steam cars, in a few minutes traverses the Jersey meadows, and at once enters among the rolling hills and valleys pertaining to the flanks of the Shawangunk Mountains.

The scenery in all directions is interesting, and here are scattered hundreds of hamlets, villages, and rural cities, where thousands of people, doing business in the great city, have built their dwellings.

We have thought our readers might be interested in knowing something concerning the houses and their surroundings; for this purpose we have selected, as a type, the suburban town of Passaic City, N. J. The enterprise and courteousness of the Citizens' Improvement Association of Passaic City, of which Mr. A. Swan Brown is the president, has resulted in placing at our disposal, ready made, much interesting material.

The Association, with a view to make more widely known the merits and attractions of this beautiful city, have issued an elegant little book of fifty pages, containing much reliable information, with engravings. To its pages we are chiefly indebted for our illustrations and the facts we now present.

Passaic is situated at the head of tide water and navigation on the Passaic River, eleven miles northwest from New York city; is reached by the New York, Susquehanna & Western Railroad in less than forty minutes from New York city. The growth of the place has been healthy and natural; from a mere hamlet in 1867, it has grown to a municipality with a population numbering at the present time nearly

land. In the southern and western portion of the city the greatest altitude is attained, affording charming views of the surrounding country, from the Palisades of the Hudson on the east to the Orange and Garret Mountains on the west, while far to the north, beyond the beautiful valleys of the Passaic and of the Saddle

Rivers, may be discerned the peaks of the rugged Ramapo and Haverstraw Mountains, and to the south Staten Island and the Bay of New York are in sight.

It contains the homes of many New York business men, and is not a place of summer homes, but of "all year" residents, who appreciate its advantages in all seasons of the year.

The air is pure, dry, and invigorating as compared with places nearer the coast. Reference may be had in this connection to many citizens, former residents of Brooklyn, who have experienced great relief and marked benefit from the change.

Another characteristic of the situation is the prevalence of the cool southern breeze on summer evenings, making rest and comfort possible even in the warmest weather.

The drives and walks in the neighborhood are numerous and beautiful, the surrounding country being one of great natural beauty, and the views from the high lands are unsurpassed in the neighborhood of New York city. To the east lie Rutherford, Hackensack, Englewood, and the Palisades; to the south, Belleville and Newark; to the west, Bloomfield, the Orange Mountains, Montclair, Little Falls, and the great Notch; while to the north are Clifton, Dundee Lake, Paterson, the Passaic Falls, the Passaic Valley, the famed Paramus region, and the Saddle River Valley, all within a radius of nine miles from the center of Passaic, and objective points of charming rides. The roads are generally good.

The beauty of the Passaic River is well known; among the illustrations will be found some views, which convey, however, from their want of color, a very inadequate conception of its natural beauty and attractiveness. A few miles above Passaic City are the "Great Falls," where the river cleaves through the mountains, with a descent of nearly ninety feet, and nearer by is the beautiful Dundee Lake, and "Slauter Dam," with a fall of some eighteen feet. The river forms the eastern boundary of the city, and the lovers of rowing or sailing find ample facilities for the enjoyment of either pastime. During the season, a steamer plies between Passaic and Newark, making several trips daily, and affording opportunities for delightful excursions.

In the winter season, each snowfall affords opportunity for the enjoyment of sleighing, coasting, or tobogganing, for which latter pleasures the hillsides of the neighborhood are especially fitted.

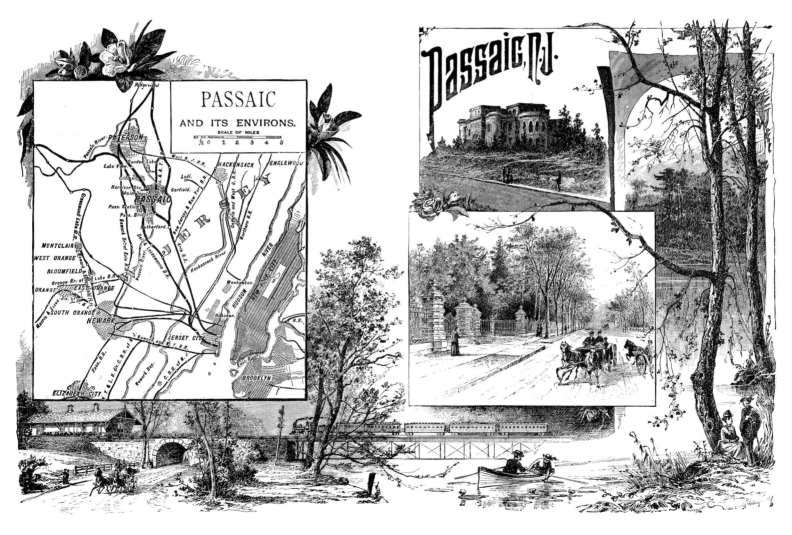

10,000. All of the conveniences of the great city are obtainable, with the comforts and attractions of the country. Good stores and markets abound, and the educational facilities and church privileges are unsurpassed.

The greater portion of the city is located upon table

Inasmuch as the natural drainage is perfect, the neighborhood is free from all zymotic, malarial, or miasmatic influences, making Passaic a very healthy city. The extreme cleanliness of the town in all its parts is a distinctive feature which invariably elicits favorable comment on the part of visitors.

The soil of the city and vicinage is a very fertile loam, suitable for gardening purposes and the making of lawns. It is very adaptable for flowers, fruits, and vegetables of all kinds, shrubs, deciduous and evergreen trees. It is especially favorable to the latter variety, which make rapid growth in it

Land is held at very reasonable rates, and persons wishing to purchase will find desirable property in either section of the city. To persons of small means, desirous of escaping the rents of the larger cities and of owning their own homes, special facilities are offered by several citizens who build to suit the views of the applicant, and arrange for payment in installments.

The city has an abundant provision of water for all purposes, the supply being taken from Dundee Lake, a beautiful sheet of water, only two miles distant from the city, and one of the attractions of the neighborhood. The mains of the Acquackanonk Water Company are laid in nearly all the streets, and running water may be had even in the highest portions of the city.

In addition to four ward public school buildings, accommodating 800 pupils, a central school building, capable of accommodating 600 pupils, is in progress.

All necessary books and appliances are furnished at the public cost. Hence the trouble and expense incident to change of place is avoided.

In addition to the public schools, there are several private and parochial schools, all of the best character.

Passaic City, especially that part situated on and adjacent to the canal of the Dundee Water Power and Land Company and the Passaic River, is especially attractive for manufacturers.

Its contiguity to New York city, Newark, and Paterson, and the low rates of railroad fare, make it a part of the great labor market formed by the three cities named, in which a surplus exists at all times.

Within three-quarters of an hour from New York, and with telephonic communication, its location is an exceedingly happy one for the shipment and distribution of goods. A great proportion of manufactured

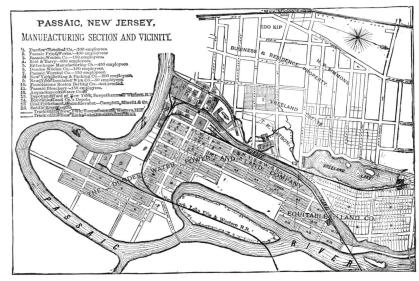

PASSAIC, NEW JERSEY,
MANUFACTURING SECTION AND VICINITY.

shipped from Passaic by the Erie and Delaware, Lackawanna & Western railroads direct, and by the Pennsylvania and West Shore *via* the New York, Susquehanna & Western Railroad, at the through rates prevailing in New York city in all cases. This is an especial advantage, as the large Western houses enjoy rebates

and extra low rates on New York shipments, due to the competition of the many roads that center in the metropolis. Passaic is only a few miles above Newark, on the Passaic River, and accessible by steamboats and sailing vessels. In fact, lumber, bricks, cement, coal, machinery, crude chemicals, and other bulky materials are now received by the river.

An important requisite is the permanent supply of a pure and soft water. The water furnished by the Dundee Water Power and Land Company, which they obtain by damming the Passaic River, of which stream

cotton printing business, for the manufacture of rubber, compounding of chemicals, the manufacture and dyeing of woolen cloth, and last, but not least, the bleaching of cotton fabrics of all kinds. The water is furnished to mills with a twenty-three foot head and fall, at a cost of $700 per annum for 3,000,000 gallons per day, or for smaller quantities in proportion ; this price also includes the mill site. The water, when used for motor power, costs $35 per annum per horse-power.

When steam is used, the cost of course depends on the price of coal, and there is no place outside the coal regions where coal can be purchased as cheaply. It can be bought, delivered at the mills, at the regular prices charged at the dumps at Jersey City. The difference in price in Passaic and New York city and the Eastern States during the past season has been from fifty cents to two dollars per ton in favor of Passaic.

One of our illustrations is a view of the "Van Wagoner homestead," the oldest house in Passaic or neighborhood, the erection of which was commenced before the Revolutionary War, but not completed until A.D. 1778. The old house is in an excellent state of preservation, and stands as built, without any architectural alteration, and in repainting the woodwork the present owner has retained the original colors. It was the homestead of Harmonus Van Wagoner, whose name will be found in all the title searches relating to property in the hill section of Passaic, which is built on a portion of the Van Wagoner farm, a princely estate in the "Olden Time," extending, as it did, from the banks of the Passaic River to the Garret Mountain, and covering many hundreds of acres.

The rising ground to the rear of the old homestead is known as "Toney's Nose," deriving its name from

RESIDENCE OF EDO KIP ESQ., ON DUNDEE DRIVE.

PASSAIC AVENUE, LOOKING SOUTH.

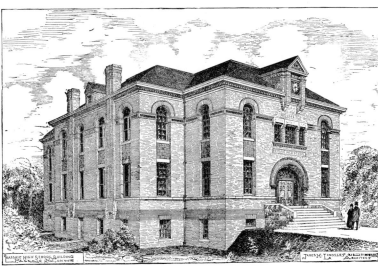

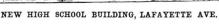

NEW HIGH SCHOOL BUILDING, LAFAYETTE AVE.

RESIDENCE OF JOHN J. BOWES, ESQ., PENNINGTON AND GREGORY AVES.

goods, except for large Western houses, goes to New York ; and in Passaic every advantage to be derived from an immediate delivery of goods is obtainable without expensive storage in the city. New York is also a great center for raw material, and proximity to it is an advantage also in that respect. Goods for the West are

the minimum flow is not less than 200,000,000 gallons per diem, is both permanent and soft, coming from a red sandstone formation. It is used in Paterson for making paper, for dyeing silk in all its delicacy of shade and nicety of color, for the manufacture of chemicals ; and in Passaic for all the purposes of a

Sir Anthony Howe, who was in command of a detachment of the British army which encamped upon the heights, acting as an "army of observation," with the view of intercepting the Continental army under Washington in its retreat from the Hudson River to the neighborhood of Morristown. History records,

RESIDENCE OF B. F. POPPLE, ESQ., PARK PLACE AND PROSPECT ST.

GROVE TERRACE, BETWEEN PASSAIC AND BLOOMFIELD AVES.

RESIDENCE OF DR. E. W. VONDERSMITH, RIVER ROAD.

A "QUIET HOME" ON PAULISON AVE.

RESIDENCE OF E. N. FRISBIE, ESQ., PASSAIC AVE.

RESIDENCE OF A. SWAN BROWN, ESQ, PENNINGTON AND PAULISON AVES.

RESIDENCE OF M. E. WORTHEN, ESQ., PASSAIC AVE.

THE "VAN WAGONER MANSION," A.D. 1778.

43

however, that Washington's forces crossed the river further to the north, and thus avoided meeting Sir Anthony and his troops at Acquackanonk, by which name Passaic was then known. The neighborhood is rich in historical reminiscences. The neighborhood of the old "Van Wagoner Mansion" in the beginning of the present century was a bustling and thriving place, the landing opposite it being the headquarters of a great trade with the West Indies in hoops, staves, shooks, lumber, and other products of the neighboring country. A large fleet of vessels was engaged in the traffic, the river affording at that date the only means of transportation to New York. Going back to an earlier date, it is worthy of note that this point was the rendezvous of all the neighboring tribes of Indians on their expeditions down the river. The old Indian trail on the west side of the river, leading from the landing, followed the present line of Prospect Street and the Dundee Drive, Passaic, and thence northward along the line of the present Weasel Road.

Frozen Lumber Will Shrink.

There has been going the rounds of the newspapers a statement that lumber worked when frozen would not shrink. A lumberman, in the language peculiar to his trade, communicated to the *Northwestern Lumberman* his experience in testing the frozen lumber theory.

"I was once running a little mill, and along about the middle of winter we got short of flooring, when an able-bodied liar came along and give it to me. He not only asserted that frozen lumber would not shrink in a floor, but he got on to his hind legs and swore to it. He had known it tried in many cases, and it was always successful and made a better floor than the best seasoned flooring. I was caught. I swallowed it whole. I took green

strips, frozen, and dressed them frozen, put them down frozen so hard that you could hardly get a nail through them, and they shrank almost out of the matching.

A GLIMPSE OF THE PASSAIC RIVER, FROM THE ERIE R.R. BRIDGE.

LOOKING DOWN PAULISON AVE. THE "SHEOWEN HANK" HILLS IN THE DISTANCE.

I simply kicked myself for being such an idiot as to believe the story, which is certainly at variance with all natural laws, and have been looking for that ablebodied liar ever since."

Phosphatic Slag as a Fertilizer.

As the new basic plant for the dephosphorization of steel at Pottstown, Pa., is expected to be in full blast before the end of the month, the utilization of the slag for agriculture may in time assume importance. As yet it is the only basic plant in America. The *Newcastle Chronicle* thus speaks of its use in England:

The following are additional particulars as to the new idea of utilizing slag for manure: The so-called "basic cinder" taken from the furnaces contains as much as from 14 to 20 per cent of phosphoric acid, associated with a number of other substances, chiefly lime, iron, and alumina; and various processes—more or less expensive—have been applied for the conversion of this phosphoric acid into forms suitable for agricultural use. It has now, however, been demonstrated that the slag or "cinder" itself merely ground into the form of meal has a very considerable manurial value, and when used in sufficient quantity can hold its own against superphosphate and other well-tried forms of phosphatic manure. The experiments of Messrs. Wrightson and Munro have so far only been carried out in two districts, but they are sufficiently striking to suggest a more extended trial of the material, the interest in which centers in the fact that it is a waste product and is cheap. We may add that the number of producers of basic slag in England is limited.

THE Boston and Albany Railroad has a circulating library of two thousand volumes free to its employes.

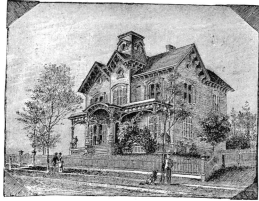

RESIDENCE OF RICHARD OUTWATER, ESQ., PENNINGTON AND PAULISON AVES.

RESIDENCE OF J. B. HOFFMAN ESQ. PASSAIC AVE.

RESIDENCE OF WM. C. McGIBBON, ESQ., PASSAIC AND PAULISON AVES

RESIDENCE OF J. T. GRANGER, ESQ., PARK PLACE.

A SADDLE RIVER "NOOK."—ROAD ALONG THE PASSAIC RIVER.

CONCRETE CONSTRUCTION.

Concrete may be described briefly as pieces and particles of rock or like material aggregated together with lime or cement. The origin of its manufacture is unknown. The massive ruins in Italy testify to its durability and of its extensive employment by the Romans. Since the introduction of Portland cement, the use of concrete has greatly extended. In England, where the first cement was manufactured, Drake states that thousands of concrete buildings have been erected of late years. The great desirability of concrete as a building material is well recognized, and rapid strides are being made in its application. Rapid as has been the increase of concrete building during the past few years, the progress would have been still greater had it not been hindered by the general lack of knowledge on the subject, the great cost of moulding or shaping the material, and the want of adequate appliances for mixing the concrete.

There are many localities where sand rock or gravel can be obtained at a nominal cost, in which concrete could be profitably introduced by any metallurgical man. And in these same districts are men plodding along in the grooves of better known trades who, by turning their attention to concrete construction, could establish themselves in a good business.

To accomplish the best results in this class of construction, it will be advisable to consult Mr. Ransome, who has had great experience in this class of work, and obtain the right of using his patented apparatus, with which buildings can be put up with unskilled laborers, provided the men are intelligently directed.

On this page we give an illustration of a building in process of erection on the system invented by Ernest L. Ransome, of this city. Mr. Ransome has received patents covering building construction, concrete mixer, and a concrete apparatus for moulding walls, houses, and other buildings.

The engraving gives an isometrical view of a building in course of erection, with part of the scaffolding removed. Ransome apparatus for moulding the walls consists of slotted standards, which being placed in pairs, one on either side of the site of the wall, and bolted together, hold in place the mouldboards, between which the concrete is placed. These standards are arranged to slide upward upon the outer face of the mouldboards as the wall progresses, and can be made to conform to any breaks or projections that may be required in the building.

The moulding boards may be of any size. If they are permanently required for the apparatus, they should be surfaced and squared, and about 1¼ inches thick, 6 to 12 inches wide, and as long as could be conveniently obtained or handled. If, on the other hand, they are only needed temporarily for this purpose, then their dimensions should be determined by their future use. For instance, if they are subsequently needed for flooring, then flooring could be used; if fencing is wanted, then use fence boards; if planks are required, then let planks be taken. In using them for the mould, the boards or planks are but little damaged; the bolt holes required in some of them are not large, and could easily be filled up.

Ordinary bolts may be used for connecting the standards together, but those having winged nuts will be found more convenient. The washers should be of good size.

The *modus operandi* is as follows: The foundations being prepared and the standards and lower moulding boards all in position, concrete is put into the mould continuously, layer after layer. Moulding boards are added from time to time, as needed, until the concrete is brought to about the top of the standards. The bolts are then slackened, a set at a time, and the standards pushed up a few inches, or a foot or two, dependent upon the character of the work.

As soon as the lower bolts are in the way of the upward movement of the standards, they are withdrawn and replaced at the top of the slot. The moulding boards, liberated by these movements, are reused above those already placed as often as needed.

This action is repeated as often as may be necessary to obtain the height desired. It forms a continuous operation, and offers no interruption to the filling in of the concrete. In building retaining walls, posts are inserted in the face of the bank and sunk below the foundation of the wall at intervals of from five to ten feet, and the slotted standards are attached to these by means of lag screws.

For a plain building, say 100 ft. long by 50 ft.

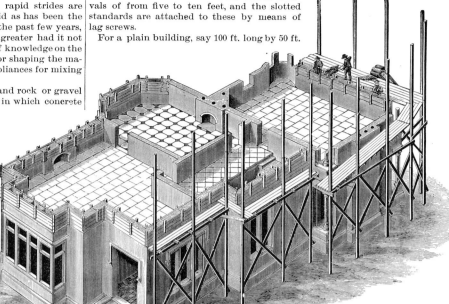

ISOMETRIC VIEW OF CONCRETE BUILDING IN COURSE OF CONSTRUCTION.

wide and 50 ft. high, the cost of the apparatus, irrespective of height, would not exceed $150, and the expense of working it would not be more than a cent per cubic foot of concrete. After building a wall, the apparatus is good for ten or twenty more. By this system the first cost is small and the expense of working slight. There is no difficulty in keeping the wall plumb, and there is no trouble in moulding projections if desired.

The large factory and warehouse recently built for the Arctic Oil Works, on the Potrero, were constructed after this manner by the patentee of the system. The fireproof roof of the warehouse was also built by him. Mr. Ransome has built many concrete foundations for buildings, machinery, etc., the largest being that of the Starr & Co. Mills, at Wheatport, Contra Costa County. The foundations of this mill were all built of concrete. In the piers, arches, and floor platforms there are 140,000 square feet of concrete. Mr. Ernest L. Ransome, whose office is at 402 Montgomery Street, San Francisco, California, is prepared to rent tools, sell licenses and territorial rights for his various inventions in connection with concrete construction, and give suitable instruction so that people can build for themselves.

SUGAR, glycerine, and gum arabic are the articles used to produce the glossy appearance of ink.

The Ordinary Vest a Poor Lung Protector.

Mr. James Hess makes a very sensible suggestion, it seems to us, in the *Herald of Health*, when he calls attention to the absurdity of our present curious habit of wearing cambric-back vests, while the fronts are of heavy material and sometimes wadded, and urges the propriety of protection for both sides of the lungs. The habit of course has grown from a belief that the outer coat is sufficient protection for the back, while the chest needs warmer covering on account of the coat being open. But it seems a disproval of the reasoning that the first unpleasant sensations of chilliness are the so-called "creepers" running down the spine. Even when the warmest woolen material is selected for a suiting, the tailor, unless otherwise ordered, will invariably make the back of the vest of some thin, flimsy material, like cambric or silk, though he may deem it advisable to pad the front with cotton wadding. There is no proper reason why the back of the vest should be made so insufficient. The front may be made uncomfortably thick and still fail to protect the lungs, unless the back is made equally thick and warm. In front they are protected about five times as much as in the back by clothing, ribs, flesh, muscle, and fat. In the back, the lungs almost come to the surface, and therefore need more protection. Mr. Hess asserts that it has been his custom for two years past, and that many gentlemen to whom he has mentioned the matter have had their vests made with good, warm backs, and after a winter's trial are quite enthusiastic over the change.

They have passed through the entire winter and spring without once taking cold, which is the best evidence in support of the thick vest-back proposition that could be adduced.

THE LAYING OUT OF GARDEN PATHS.

Where a garden is to be laid out in a perfectly flat situation, there is not, of course, the same scope for effective ornamentation as can be produced where there is a diversity of surface. One means, however, of dealing with level ground is to provide oval and circular and serpentine paths, with plainly marked borders, but so that, to the eye, the lines of the borders will be broken by trees and shrubbery, and the complete plan will not be suggested from what can be seen at any one point. Such walks should, wherever possible, lead to or by some bright little spots which one will come upon unexpectedly, and the surprise of which will heighten the pleasure obtainable from the beauty of the scene. An idea of thus laying out a circular walk may be obtained from the accompanying illustration, the planting of quick-growing shrubbery giving extension and outline to a general direction of paths, which would be governed by any growth, as of trees, that would require years to mature. When a general plan has once been adopted, however, it should be carefully kept in view in all future work in the garden, and the pruning and planting kept steadily in line with the plan laid out.

TOBACCO blindness is becoming a common affliction. At present there are several persons under treatment for it at one London hospital. It first takes the form of color blindness, the sufferers who have smoked themselves into this condition being quite unable to distinguish the color of a piece of red cloth held up before them. Sometimes the victim loses his sight altogether. Although smoking is to a large extent the cause of the malady, heavy drinking is also partly responsible.

ART IN THE GARDEN.—A CIRCULAR PATH.

Cheap Method of Heating Factories.

It frequently happens that chimneys are now built round, without corners to retard the draught. This is done by inserting in the chimney, as the building progresses, cores consisting of iron pipes cast in sections, or tile piping. Air spaces are thus left between the core of the chimney and the outer wall, and of course the air in this space becomes heated to a high temperature. It is quite practical to utilize this air for heating purposes, if this is found desirable. The air spaces being closed at the top, and openings being made to the open air at the base of the chimney, tin piping is connected with the spaces for conducting the heat to different parts of the factory. Of course, this method is not designed for heating the stories nearest the ground, as the current of air in ascending has not had sufficient exposure to become heated until it has reached the third or fourth story of the building.

LINCRUSTA-WALTON.

Several stores in New York, Boston, and St. Louis have been decorated with Lincrusta-Walton, and are marvels of beauty. One recently fitted by Mr. Conkling, at the corner of Broadway and 31st Street, may be inspected as showing what can be done with this material. Mr Conkling was his own architect and designer in this instance, and has finished the decoration in dull

smoke inside. As sanitary inspectors everywhere have especial reasons for being extremely vigilant during the coming year, this method of testing pipes and drains may prove valuable in many instances where it is not convenient to apply other tests.

On the Coagulation of Blood.*

Brucke's researches on the conditions of coagulation of blood have shown that, on the one hand, contact with foreign bodies makes blood coagulate, and, on the other, that contact on all sides with the fresh vascular wall obviates coagulation (Durante). Lacker has proved the influence of foreign bodies on blood coagulation by microscopic observation of coagulation in its first stages. In partial contradiction to these results was the observation of Grunhagen that blood, when received into glycerine, and so long as it did not mix, remained liquid. To determine the nature of these influences the following experiments were made. Blood was drawn under oil from the carotid artery of a dog, and let stand at ordinary indoor temperature; after twenty-four hours it was *not* coagulated. Then the blood was drawn into a vessel smeared inside with vaseline, and it too *did not coagulate.* When it was stirred with an oiled glass rod, no fibrine was separated; but when, even after several hours, part of this blood was poured into an ungreased vessel, it coagulated in a few minutes. Moreover, contact with an ungreased glass rod sufficed to make the blood in the greased vessel coagulate outward from the rod.

The membranes lay several hours in 0·6 per cent chloride of sodium solution ; the blood was drawn off through a vaseline-lined canula into the bladders and tubes, which were then so hung in a liter of the salt solution that the mass of blood was under the surface. In these experiments also the blood remained liquid, the surrounding salt solution having no cogulative effect, while some of the blood, poured after twenty-four hours into an ungreased porcelain vessel for comparison, soon coagulated. Like the blood vessels, which, unlike manufactured vessels, after being emptied of the blood, retain no coloring matter, the membranes, even after several days, showed neither imbibition with blood-coloring matter nor any trace of coagulated fibrine. Thus, by soaking in salt solution, a property of the blood vessels was imparted to the fish bladders and parchment tubes.

It can hardly be doubted, then, that while, on the one hand, lack of adhesion prevents blood from coagulating, so, on the other, the presence of adhesion gives the impulse to coagulation.—*Nature.*

The Mullein Plant.

A good deal has been written lately about the mullein plant, and its efficiency as a cure for consumption. In reference to the use of the above, Dr. Quinlan, of Dublin, writes to the *British Medical Journal* that 3 oz. of the green leaves should be boiled for ten minutes in a pint of new milk. The liquid is then strained, sweetened to taste, and drunk while warm. This dose can be repeated twice or three times a day. This high

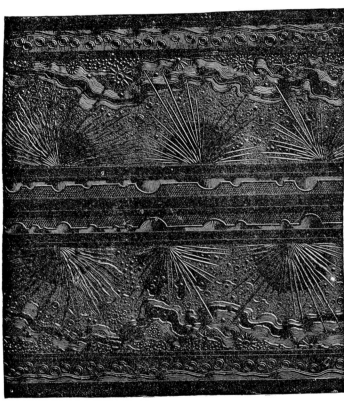

Fig. 1.—LINCRUSTA-WALTON—TWO-BAND BORDER. (Scale ¼ of original.)

Fig. 2.—LINCRUSTA-WALTON HANGING OR FILLING. (Scale ¼ of original.)

black, having the appearance of carved ebony. This, contrasting with the polished brass ornamentation, gives a delightful and really artistic effect. It is flattering to Mr. Conkling to find that he has been asked to advise in decorating many other stores with Lincrusta. In this instance about twenty patterns of Lincrusta-Walton were employed.

Figure 1 is a two-band border reduced to ¼ of the original size. It is a quaint design, and capable of very pretty ornamentation. Figure 2 represents a hanging or filling. If decorated in the color of mahogany, it cannot be distinguished from that material. The panels and rosettes in relief are sharp in their outlines, and have all the character of carved wood. Messrs. Fr. Beck & Co., the manufacturers of Lincrusta-Walton, are just publishing a supplementary book of designs.

Smoke Testing of Drains.

Cosmo Innes, the Secretary of the London Sanitary Protection Association, writes to the *Journal of the Society of Arts,* suggesting a smoke test, instead of that of some strong volatile liquid, for detecting defects in sewer pipes, as the smoke test will be apparent to the eye as well as the nose. That such testing may be done cheaply, he has devised a style of smoke rocket, charged so as to burn for ten minutes ; the fuse is to be lighted and the rocket inserted in the drain with a plug behind it, when the observer is to walk through the house to see if any smoke escapes, finishing on the roof, where the smoke will come in volumes from the ventilating pipe. If it is desired to increase the severity of the test, a wet blanket may be thrown over the top of the ventilating pipe, giving a slight pressure of

Further experiments showed that the drying of the upper layers of the blood, and the presence of small quantities of dust, caused coagulation even in the greased vessel ; if this was guarded against, the blood remained liquid for days, and the corpuscles sank to the bottom, the plasma remaining as a clear liquid above.

After pouring out the blood, the greased walls of the glass vessel showed neither blood coloring matters nor traces of a separated albuminous body. A repetition of these experiments at 37° C. gave the same result. In all the experiments blood was also, for comparison, drawn off into ungreased vessels, and in all these it coagulated, at the most, in a quarter of an hour.

In further experiments a small vaseline-lined glass tube was used as a canula; and the blood drawn through this into vaseline-lined vessels also remained uncoagulated.

When the outer orifice of a canula inserted in the carotid was closed, the blood column in it pulsated, without showing the least sign of coagulation even after two hours.

In all these experiments there was nowhere in the vessels with which the blood came into contact even a point for adhesion—such a point would have caused in shorter or longer time coagulation of the whole mass of blood. Thus the coagulative influence of foreign bodies appears to be due to their adhesion.

But to demonstrate that the anti-coagulative property of the vascular walls is due to the lack of adhesion, a further series of experiments was made with soaked fish bladders and parchment tubes.

* By Ernst Freund, in *Wiener Medicinische Jahrbucher,* 1886, Heft 1.

authority has no doubt of its efficacy as a curative in the earlier and a palliative in the later stages of pulmonary consumption. Care should be taken to use the leaves of the great mullein, known by its thick, mucilaginous, and woolly leaves.

Prize for the Best Method of Preventing Blasting Accidents in Coal Mines.

The mining owners of Ostraw Rarwin have decided to offer a prize of 1,000 ducats (about $2,500) for the best invention for preventing accidents in the shooting and ballasting connected with coal dust in mines, or rendering the operation harmless. The invention should answer to the following conditions, namely: 1st. Its use, effects, or explosion should not cause the coal dust to ignite. 2d. It should not produce after the explosion or use more injurious gas than through the methods heretofore employed. 3d. No specially difficult, dangerous, long preliminary arrangements or complicated apparatus should be required in using, setting up, loading, transporting, or lighting. 4th. Should not by its use and result be much more expensive than the former blasting methods. All applications should contain full particulars, and also of practical tests already made, stating name and address of applicant, and be sent on or before the end of 1886 to the K. K. Berghauptmannschaft, at Vienna. All projects, also the one which will be awarded the prize, will remain the property of the tender. From the Imperial Royal Ministry of Agriculture, Vienna.

A PATENT has been granted in Russia for a lucifer match that can be used an indefinite number of times.

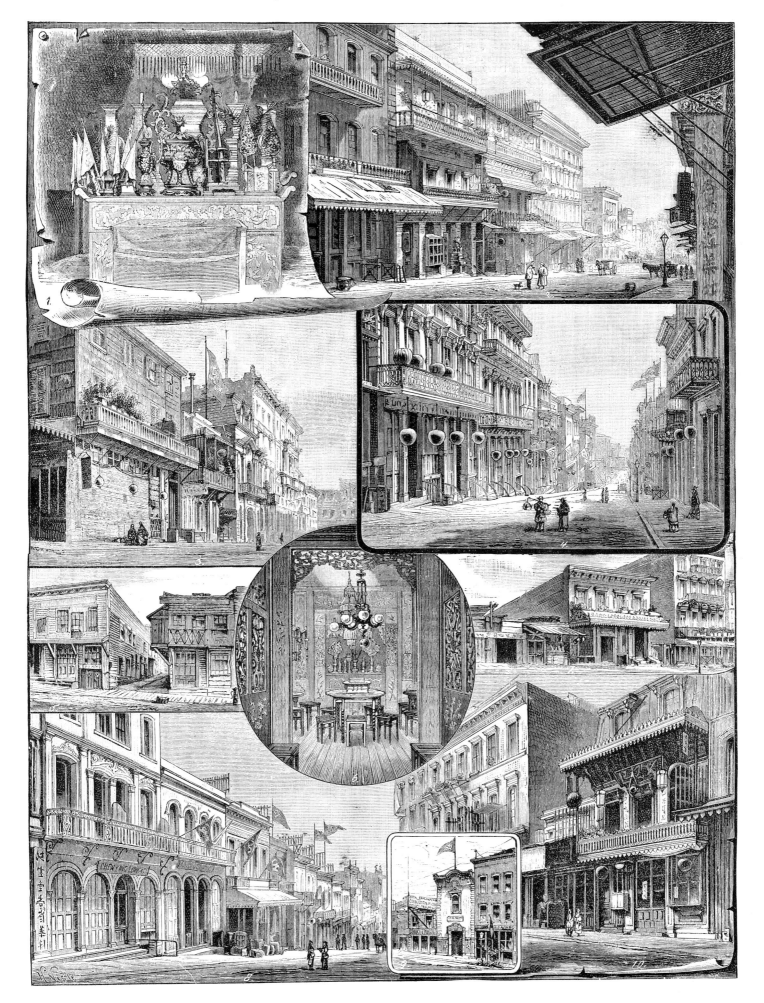

VIEWS IN THE CHINESE QUARTER, SAN FRANCISCO.

1. Altar in the Josh House.   2. Jackson St.—principal business street in Chinese district.   3. Chinese Block on the Plaza.   4. Sacramento St.   5. Dwellings of the Chinese poor.
6. Council Room of the Chinese Authorities.   7. Wholesale business houses.   8. Residences of Merchants.   9. Chinese Company Headquarters.   10. Restaurant on Dupont St.

Architects.

The complaints made by architects of the treatment they receive from clergymen and building committees indicate some very serious misapprehensions as to the money value of professional services. When an architect is asked to submit a plan, and the plan is used, it should be paid for. The stone mason and the carpenter have no stronger claim for remuneration than has the architect who conceived the design and rendered the execution possible by his drawings. If but a part of his design is used by being incorporated with some other design, he is entitled to some return for what is used.

These are very obvious principles, but we are told that sometimes every other claim is met before the architect receives anything, and in other cases the ideas which have been carefully elaborated are appropriated without any acknowledgment whatever. Instances are recited where preliminary sketches have been handed over to builders, and churches and chapels constructed from them without even asking the permission of the architects, to say nothing of making no return for what certainly has as definite a value as the services of a physician or the advice of a lawyer. This breach of good faith has become so serious and so annoying that many architects refuse to make even a preliminary study until some positive contract for remuneration has been made. It is a misfortune, to say the very least of it, that persons having in charge the construction of religious edifices should ever exhibit ignorance or carelessness of the principles of fair dealing.

The writer prefers to think that there is rarely any positive attempt to take advantage of an architect, and that the abuses referred to grow out of ignorance of the value of the architect's work, and also out of the dread of paying too dearly for services which seem to consist simply in putting a few lines on paper. It must be borne in mind that the calling of the architect has grown in importance year by year because of the demand for tasteful and convenient buildings, and because the calling itself has been dignified by the training given the men who fill it. Whereas once the village carpenter or the master builder who could do a little sketching were almost the only architects, now we have men in every city who have gone through a long course of training, and whose preliminary education has been gained at as heavy an expense as that incurred by men in fitting themselves for the bar or for the practice of medicine. Year by year reliable builders recognize more fully the need of well conceived plans and of carefully prepared drawings, and rely more and more upon the judgment and skill of the architect. It has grown to be a calling of great importance, and its successes are seen in the superior convenience and finish of our churches and other religious edifices.

When, therefore, a parish or a mission thinks of building, it is almost absurd in these days of improved taste to try to get along without an architect; and if one is employed, his labors should be rewarded. There are various ways of employing an architect. Sometimes a parish will want not only drawings, but personal superintendence. After he has prepared all the working details, the master builder and the building committee look after the work in progress. Sometimes only preliminary sketches are required, if the building is simple, or if it is a trifling enlargement or alteration of an old building. But for all of these three classes of an architect's work there is a recognized money value, and it should be considered part of the cost of the building.

The dread of meeting this expense is the secret of many of the blunders in construction and of the violations of good taste so often met with. There ought to be nothing so cheerfully paid as the small fee necessary to gain good advice in putting up a church. a chapel, rectory, or any other edifice belonging to the parish.

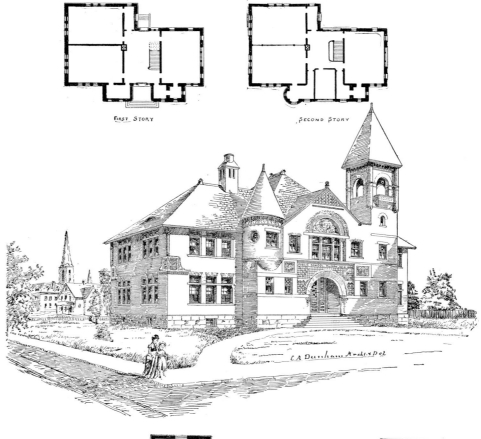

FIRST STORY   SECOND STORY

C. A. Dunham Archt. & Del.

No. 2

FIRST STORY   SECOND STORY

C. A. Dunham, Del.

MODERN SCHOOL HOUSE DESIGNS.—C. A. DUNHAM, ARCHITECT, BURLINGTON, IOWA.

Besides this, there is nothing so economical as starting right and continuing under good guidance. It would not be difficult to point out new buildings where from twenty-five to fifty per cent has been added to the cost of construction and alteration, simply because of the effort to save a few dollars by not employing an architect. But, however this may be, the purpose of this article is simply to call attention to the complaint so frequently heard, and to save any of our clergy and building committees the reproach of failing to treat fairly a very honorable calling when it does have dealings with its representatives.—*The Churchman*.

Buying Houses "on Easy Terms."

"If these easy terms houses were just what they look to be," said the retired builder, "the deal would be perfectly square. But that is the costly rub. For instance, you want to buy a house for $3,000, and you pay $500 down and move in. Then you begin to pay off the balance at the rate of $20 a month. That's easy, isn't it? Just take your pencil, and figure it up. Twenty dollars a month is $240 a year. Interest at 5 per cent is one hundred and twenty-five; taxes and water-rent, sixty more, and the total is four hundred and twenty." "Thirty-six dollars a month?" "Pretty nearly. But that isn't all. There's the repairs, my boy. You're lucky if you don't have to put on a new roof the second year; your pavement is sure to need repaving; the plumber will call on you about six times a year, and, in short, you will soon find another hundred a year tacked on to your easy terms. Now, what do you naturally do?" "I naturally kick," I replied with considerable energy. "It won't do you any good," said my friend. "You've signed an ironclad contract. You must pay or go." "Exactly," responded the ex-builder, with a genial grin, "that's just what 50 per cent. of the victims do. They do what they should have done first—figure it up; and it scares them. They look forward to 12 years of this sort of thing, and they see that they have the hot end of the poker; then they drop it." "Do you mean to say," I inquired severely, "that none of the money is returned?" "Well," said my friend, meditatively, "there was a rumor once that a contractor did return about a third of the purchase money to a certain man, but as I never could find either the man or the contractor, I guess it was a ghost story."—*Phila. Call.*

Marble.

The physical or external character of marbles constitutes the chief consideration with reference to their use for decoration or ornamental architecture, their color and internal structure being the most important. Their chemical character has reference more to the facility with which they may be converted into use, and their capability of receiving and retaining a certain polish. In their simplest and purest state, marbles chiefly consist of carbonate of lime, which is of a white color; the whitest kind, however, is frequently associated with quartz or silex, which more or less deteriorates it. This is more or less united both chemically and mechanically in various ways with nearly all the marbles. The variations in color arise chiefly from accidental causes, in the greater or less admixture of carbon, or the stains of various metallic oxides, or the sectional outlines of embedded fossils. Magnesia enters largely into the serpentine variety of marble. The more crystalline and least earthy marbles are the least durable, the compact or finely granular crystalline marbles being superior to those which are largely crystalline or of a slaty texture. Almost all the varieties burn into quicklime; several of them, however, exfoliate in the conversion before they become caustic, and fall into sand when exposed to the ordinary mode of separating the carbonic acid; such qualities are, therefore, very inferior for ordinary cement, as they make a costly and meager mortar.   G. WILKINSON.

Mistakes in Building.

Owners are often sadly disappointed and grieved at their mistakes in the means adopted by them to avoid the expense of an architect, and obtain plans for their buildings. Sometimes they know or become acquainted with some "honest mechanic," to whom they are induced to intrust the whole matter of plans specification, and instruction, only to repent when it is too late. The party to whom the proposition is made, elated with the splendid opportunity opened to him, and full of conceit in his own abilities, uses all possible means to secure and consummate the arrangement, and plans are made—*and such plans!* —and the work progresses. Once under way, there is no stopping it, and step by step the owner discovers and realizes, one after another, grievous errors which are difficult to remedy. And when the building is completed he simply feels disgusted. Imperfect arrangement, poor construction, homely design, and incurable defects crowd upon him as the reward of his folly; and regrets for his error haunt him day and night, but it is too late—the building is erected, and he must endure its defects.

But the first general dissatisfaction is primary and bearable compared with after experiences in their various details. The plumbing work has, perhaps, been done by some tenth-rate man—some spoiler of good materials, who calls himself a "practical plumber," but who has not the slightest idea of what constitutes a really good job, not to say first-class. Nor would the payment of ten times the value of the work done secure skillful workmanship at the hands of such men, for the simple reason that they do not possess, and, therefore, cannot practice, mechanical skill and abilities. And owners who employ this class of plumbers are unfortunate indeed, But to continue. defects show themselves in all connections. Pipes, under the old free and easy rule, were put in of insufficient capacity, wastes entirely too small, and sometimes so cramped in making bends as to diminish their practical size one-half. "Tinker" instead of "wiped" joints; leaks at various points and places; wetting and spoiling ceilings and walls, and frequently carpets have to be torn up to escape the deluge. All this is followed by a still more serious defect—one affecting the health and lives of the occupants, viz., imperfect or insufficient traps, pipe ventilation, bad sewerage, etc., resulting in the distribution of the vicious and poisonous sewer gases through the building, and, as a consequence, the ill health and sometimes premature death of loved ones. The intended pleasant home is thus transformed into a mere fume castle, a disease-breeding charnel house, not fit for human habitation.

All this is followed by continual repairing, tearing up floors, removing finishes to get at concealed places, etc.; and for all this the owner has been made to pay a good round price, amounting to more, as a rule, than it would have cost him to have secured a good building, erected under the superintendence of a trustworthy architect. But bad plumbing work is not the only serious defect which so often occurs in such cases. The foundation is often wholly insufficient, and set-

tling occurs, with any quantity of ugly cracks in the plastering. The structure is perhaps so poorly braced that the edifice trembles with every wind that blows. And when the rains fall, leaks are found at every exposed window and opening, and the roof itself yields its proportion of internal wettings. But we will not continue our enumeration of "bad things," as to do so would consume columns of space. Such cases are known to all architects, and many a "served him right" is indulged in, upon the principle that a competent physician laughs at the sufferings of a patient whose pains and agonies result from self-treatment or quack practice, and the educated lawyer smiles when his client gets himself into a *terrible fix* by intrusting his case to some pettifogger, or who tries to work out the intricacies and problems of law by his own self-conceived legal ingenuity.—*Trades Journal.*

The Latest and Greatest Gun.

The house of Krupp is stated to have completed a cannon 46 ft. 8 in. in length, weighing 125½ tons, and having a caliber of 16 in. The monster has been turned out to the order of the Italian Government.

Ornamentation of Rooms.

A soft and pretty tint for the two bed chambers on the north side of the house will be old pink of medium depth—a pinkish terra cotta shade, as it is now called; tint the ceilings in a fainter tone of old pink. A frieze of golden olive ground with a pretty wild rose design on it, with olive greens and yellow in the foliage and pinks in the flowers, will make the wall much more finished; it can be a paper frieze. The parlor and sitting room, supposing they are on the south and have peacock-blue and bronze and green shaded carpets, are susceptible of two treatments—namely, a light treatment and a dark one. For the former, a lemon-yellow tint for the walls and a paler shade for the ceilings; or an old gold for the walls and lighter shade of same for the ceiling. For a darker treatment, bronze green for the walls and pale yellow for the ceilings.

With either coloring, have a frieze of rich design in paper with a flock ground of bronze green to harmonize with the lemon-yellow, or deep lemon-yellow if you use a bronze green; if you use old gold coloring on the walls, let the frieze be dull peacock blue. This will not be very expensive, and will greatly improve the appearance of the wall. This frieze should have a picture rail of wooden mouldings painted and gilded. From these mouldings, with brass picture rod hooks, you can suspend all your pictures, and thus obviate driving nails in the walls. Paint woodwork a bronze green, and the two bed rooms in buff, which will harmonize with the old pink of the walls.

Sitting room and parlor furniture should have ebonized frames or mahogany-finished cherry frames, or be in pieces of both; black walnut will not look well. The ebonized pieces will look well upholstered in copper-colored reds. Rather light peacock-blue or blue-green felt will be handsome for the parlor windows. For the sitting room use double-face canton flannel of the same color or copper-red; copper-red would look well in the parlor also. Holland shades of deep ecru tint will suit in the rooms. Ash furniture will look bright and cheerful in the sitting room. Hang the parlor curtains by brass rods; of the sitting room, by ash rods and rings.—*Art Interchange.*

Fast Time.

The newspaper train on the New York Central on Sunday made a remarkable run, the time between Syracuse and Buffalo being claimed to be the fastest ever made in this country over the same distance. The train, which consisted of a coach and baggage car, is due to leave Syracuse at 9:25 A. M., but on Sunday it was 10 o'clock before the start. The train, which was drawn by engine No. 541, John Cool driver, was in charge of Peter Wagner as conductor. The train was put to its best speed, and the run of 149 miles to this city was made in 144 minutes, including a stop of 6 minutes at Rochester, leaving the actual running time but 138 minutes. The fastest run was from Syracuse to Fairport, 70¼ miles, in 61 minutes 20 seconds; from Syracuse to Rochester, 81 miles, being made in 72 minutes, and from Rochester to Buffalo, 68 miles, in 66 minutes. For a part of the time, mile after mile was traveled in less than 52 seconds.—*Buffalo Express.*

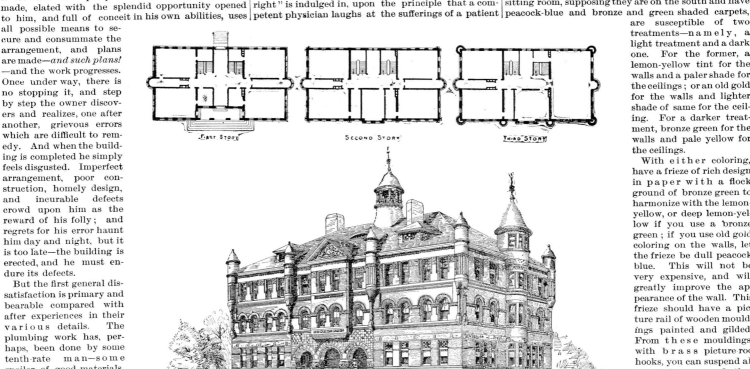

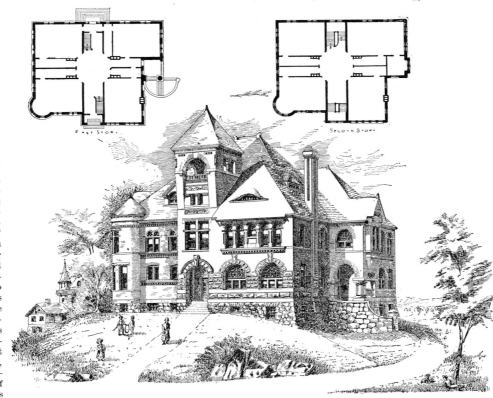

MODERN SCHOOL HOUSE DESIGNS.—C. A. DUNHAM, ARCHITECT, BURLINGTON, IOWA.

49

Scientific American.

ESTABLISHED 1845.

MUNN & CO., Editors and Proprietors,

No. 361 BROADWAY, NEW YORK.

O. D. MUNN. A. E. BEACH.

NEW YORK, SEPTEMBER, 1886.

THE

Scientific American,

ARCHITECTS AND BUILDERS EDITION.

This is a Special Trade Edition of THE SCIENTIFIC AMERICAN, issued Monthly—on the first Saturday of the month.

It goes directly *into the hands of those who have the ordering of the great bulk of Building Materials and Appliances*, namely, the Architects, Builders, Constructing Engineers, and Contractors.

It has the largest circulation of any Architectural or Building paper in the world.

An Increase of Trade will necessarily accrue to all Manufacturers and Dealers whose establishments are conspicuously represented in this important edition of THE SCIENTIFIC AMERICAN.

TERMS OF SUBSCRIPTION:

For Architects and Builders Edition of SCIENTIFIC AMERICAN, **$1.50** a year. **In Clubs**, four copies for **$5.00.** Single Copies, **15 cents** each. By mail to foreign countries, **$2** a year.

Sold by all Newsdealers.

MUNN & CO., Publishers,
361 BROADWAY, NEW YORK.

CONTENTS

Of the September number of the ARCHITECTS AND BUILDERS EDITION of SCIENTIFIC AMERICAN.

(Illustrated articles are marked with an asterisk.)

Architects.......... 46
Billiard balls, coloring.......... 48
Boat, torpedo, fast Chinese.......... 52
Boy with cat's eyes.......... 67
Bracket, scaffold, new*.......... 51
Bridge, pioneer, old*.......... 50
Building, mistakes in.......... 47
Buildings, slowly combustible.......... 54
Business and personal.......... vi
Buying houses "on easy terms.".......... 46
Cabinet, carved*.......... 68
Carriages, light American, criticism of.......... 52
Church, removal of a*.......... 51
Church, town, prize medal design for a*.......... 57
Combustion, slow.......... 53
Congress, American forestry.......... 67
Corundum and its uses.......... 63
Cottage at Block Island, R. I.*.......... 49
Cottage, design for a*.......... 54
Cottage, design for a*.......... 56
Decoration.......... 48
Designs, school house, modern*.......... 45, 46, 47
Doorways, early English.......... 55
Drawings and contributions.......... 48
Dust, emery wheel, curious accretion of*.......... 62
Embryo, influence of magnetism upon.......... 66
Exteriors of small dwellings*.......... 64
Fastener for window stop beads*.......... 51
Fire department, Parisian.......... 45
Fire extinguishing apparatus, improved.......... 60
Floors, concrete.......... 61
Floors, stable.......... 56
Forging, steel, a great.......... 62
Gas line, an old.......... 67
Gas, natural, in the blast furnace.......... 50
Germs in water.......... 56
Girders, cast iron.......... 45
Gun, latest and greatest.......... 47
Harrow, adjustable*.......... 66
Home costing about $1,200*.......... 53
Horse, a shying.......... 63
Houses, the airing and lighting of*.......... 58
Ink, marking.......... 51
Iron, protecting.......... 68
Jarrah wood.......... 59
Lavatories.......... 55
Library, Minneapolis*.......... 52
Lumber estimates.......... 50
Machine for cutting scrub, cane, etc.*.......... 66
Malta, the island of.......... 60
Marble.......... 46
Morningside Park*.......... 60, 61
Mortars and concretes.......... 68
Notes and queries.......... vi
Old Falcon Cocoa House, Chester*.......... 67
Orange flower, Mexican*.......... 54
Organ movement, new electric*.......... 62
Ornamentation of rooms.......... 47
Patents, decisions relating to.......... 60
People's Palace, London*.......... 64, 65
Photographic notes.......... 60
Press, illustrated paper, a fast.......... 66
Railway along Niagara Falls.......... 51
Raisins, medicated.......... 57
Reidence, country, and caariage house*.......... 55
Residence, design for a*.......... 64
Residence, a suburban*.......... 49
Roads, how to make pleasant.......... 53
Roofs, defective.......... 55
"Saltpetering" in stone.......... 52
Sash holder, convenient*.......... 51
Scarlet fever communicated by clothing.......... 54
Sheet metal construction.......... 51
Station, passenger, mammoth.......... 67
Statistics, professional.......... 64
Steel, casehardening.......... 66
Structures, rustic.......... 48
St. Sophia, Constantinople.......... 59
Tetanus treated by rest.......... 63
Time, fast.......... 47
Tree growth.......... 54
Volume, our first.......... 48
Weatherboarding and doors, fixing.......... 50
Weather strip, "Perfection"*.......... 51
Wedge cutter*.......... 66
Whistling nuisance, locomotive.......... 67
Wool, mineral.......... 66
Wrench, improved pipe*.......... 63
Yeast, preservation of.......... 67

OTHER PUBLICATIONS.

THE SCIENTIFIC AMERICAN

Weekly, $3.00 a Year; $1.50 Six Months.

Sixteen large pages elegantly illustrated.

THE SCIENTIFIC AMERICAN SUPPLEMENT

Is a distinct paper from the SCIENTIFIC AMERICAN. THE SUPPLEMENT is issued weekly. Every number contains 16 octavo pages, uniform in size with the SCIENTIFIC AMERICAN. **$5.00 a Year.**

Combined Rates.—The SCIENTIFIC AMERICAN and SUPPLEMENT, one year, **$7.00.**

The SCIENTIFIC AMERICAN (weekly) and ARCHITECTS AND BUILDERS EDITION (monthly), $4 a year.

SCIENTIFIC AMERICAN (weekly), SUPPLEMENT (weekly), and ARCHITECTS AND BUILDERS EDITION (monthly), $8 a year.

The safest way to remit is by draft, postal order, or registered letter.

Address

MUNN & CO., 361 Broadway, corner of Franklin Street, New York.

Back Numbers.

At present we are able to supply to new subscribers the back numbers of this journal from its beginning in November last. Each number is accompanied by a sheet of colored plates and a sheet of details.

PATENTS.

Messrs. Munn & Co., in connection with the publication of the **Scientific American,** continue to examine improvements and to act as Solicitors of Patents for Inventors.

In this line of business they have had *forty years' experience*, and now have *unequaled facilities* for the preparation of Patent Drawings, Specifications, and the prosecution of Applications for Patents in the United States, Canada, and Foreign Countries. **Messrs. Munn & Co.** also attend to the preparation of Caveats, Copyrights for Books, Labels, Reissues, Assignments, and Reports on Infringements of Patents. All business intrusted to them is done with special care and promptness, on very reasonable terms.

A pamphet sent free of charge, on application, containing full information about Patents and how to procure them; directions concerning Labels, Copyrights, Designs, Patents, Appeals, Reissues, Infringements, Assignments, Rejected Cases, Hints on the Sale of Patents, etc.

We also send, *free of charge*, a synopsis of Foreign Patent Laws, showing the cost and method of securing patents in all the principal countries of the world.

MUNN & CO., Solicitors of Patents, 361 Broadway, New York.
BRANCH OFFICE.—622 F Street, Washington, D. C.

DECORATION.

Rapid strides have been made both here and abroad during the past few years in the matter of the decoration of our houses, and although the improvement is marked and undoubted, it still leaves much to be desired. In houses of the smaller class especially, where the decoration is confined within moderate limits of cost, there is considerable room for improvement.

The decoration of rooms by the use of paper hangings is so inexpensive and convenient, and at the same time effective, that it is rapidly increasing in favor. Where they are used, it is the best plan to choose them as the first step in the decoration. Frequently the selection is made in the paper manufacturer's store, but the proper method is to choose each paper in the room in which it is to be used, for in this way one is enabled to observe it under the conditions of light and shade peculiar to the room itself, and can observe the effect of such conditions and the contrast between the colors of the furniture, paper hangings, floor cover, etc., and judge more accurately of the final effect when it is put upon the wall.

Paper hangings should never be chosen from a book of patterns, for it is almost impossible for any one who has not had considerable experience to judge of the effect from a small piece, such as will be found in a pattern book, and much disappointment has often arisen from this very cause. A paper in a small piece looks very different from its appearance when on a wall. The method of choosing papers which is recommended is to make a careful search through the pattern book, and to select two or three patterns for each of the principal rooms. The paperhanger should then bring one or two rolls of each of the papers chosen and pin them on the wall to the full height of the room, so that they may be viewed in the actual position they are to occupy. There is a further advantage in this method, which is that the eye does not get dazzled and the mind confused, as they are sure to do if a large number of patterns are examined in quick succession. Decorators all know how often people, choosing hangings and colors, will, from this cause, finally decide on what they at first rejected, and without having the smallest idea that it is so.

Having decided upon the papers, the colors for the woodwork will next be chosen to match. It is impossible to lay down any hard and fast rules as to the colors to be employed, so much depends upon the situation and aspect of the room, the kind and color of the furniture, and the individual taste of the owner. Do not, however, use graining. Happily, the system is rapidly dying out, although in the smaller and simpler class of houses it still retains its hold. Graining is objectionable from an artistic point of view, because it is a sham, but the effect of using plain colors is so very much more pleasant that it is difficult to understand how the more expensive and so much less artistic method could have remained popular for so long.

The woodwork, then, should be painted in plain colors, in two or more tints, the panels being always a lighter tint than the stiles and rails, with the mouldings picked in with a more decided tint or color. Drawing rooms, or parlors, should, as a rule, be finished in more delicate tints than dining or morning rooms. The decoration of a drawing room will be almost decided, or at least considerably modified, by the style and color of the upholstery. The writer has obtained excellent results from a variety of grays relieved with gold. In one case a paper was chosen of a decidedly light gray of a really beautiful design, but it had rather a cold appearance, as, indeed, that color always has in decoration, unless very carefully treated. The woodwork was painted in grays of three different tints, the stiles and rails being light gray, the panels lighter and the mouldings the darkest. The whole of the work was finished with a flatting coat of paint mixed without oil, to give a perfectly flat, dead surface, and a very small member of the moulding was run in with leaf gold. The decoration of the ceiling was carried out in three grays, to accord with the other portion of the decoration, the result being exceedingly satisfactory. The decoration of this room was quite inexpensive, and might be followed with advantage. The flatting has a very good appearance, and is, moreover, useful in hiding any irregularities in the woodwork.

The use of gold-leaf as an article of decoration must be very carefully limited. A free use of gold will make the best room look gaudy and glaring. Some decorators object to its use altogether; and although they undoubtedly err on the right side, its use need not be absolutely forbidden. It may be taken as a general rule that its use should be strictly limited to throwing into relief some feature of the decoration, but it must never be used in such a manner that the force of the decoration depends upon it. As illustrating the proper use of gold, a case may be referred to in which a room having a frieze and heavy cornice was decorated in good taste, but in somewhat insipid colors. The addition of a very thin line of the bright brick red sometimes called "Pompeiian red" on a member of the frieze immediately above the line of paper entirely altered the appearance of the room, and considerably improved the effect. The use of gold should be the same as the bright red in this case, used very sparingly and with the one and decided object of emphasizing the decoration.

The ceilings of the rooms of our ordinary houses are neglected in a conspicuous manner, generally being little more than a white blank expanse, with a cornice or perhaps frieze of more or less tasteful design. A ceiling lends itself very readily to the purposes of tasteful decoration, and should never be neglected. There are many methods of decorating it, among which that of picking out the cornice and stenciling on a border in one or more colors, to accord with the decoration of the remainder of the room, is one of the most simple and effective. In whitening ceilings the custom is, as a rule, to mix a small quantity of blue with the calcimine to increase the apparent whiteness. Where a color is used for the decoration throughout a room in varying tints, the color of the calcimine should be just broken by the addition of a small quantity of the same color, and the effect will be to bring the ceiling, as it were, within the system of decoration, and to considerably heighten the good appearance. H. S. J.

DRAWINGS AND CONTRIBUTIONS.

To those of our readers who have a mind to employ their leisure time in writing articles for this paper, we would say, the editor will be glad to receive their contributions, and will publish such as are approved.

Articles on practical subjects, aimed to interest and instruct every class of artificers connected with building, are especially desired; and for such articles special arrangements will be made.

Architects and builders who have desirable plans of buildings, which they wish to see illustrated in our columns, are invited to send them in. For colored plates, we need copy colored up as intended. For ordinary illustration, the drawings should be executed in black lines. We aim to give prominent credit to the authors of new designs. Those whose drawings have been issued have derived therefrom much benefit, owing to the very wide publicity thus given to their names and work specimens. It should not be forgotten our Building Edition now has, by far, the largest circulation of any architectural periodical in the world.

OUR FIRST VOLUME.

The first volume of our ARCHITECTS AND BUILDERS EDITION is now ready for delivery, bound in handsome paper covers. Price, $1.50. To be had at this office, and of book and news dealers throughout the country. Those who have not seen a half year's collection of our numbers bound together will be surprised at the wealth and variety of contents which the volume presents, as well as at the cheapness of the price.

The volume contains all the numbers of the work from its commencement up to and including June, 1886. It embraces sixteen splendid plates in colors, representing the perspective elevations and plans of various dwellings, all having attractive features; eight large double sheets of details of construction of the same structures; nearly one hundred additional engravings of architectural subjects, public works, buildings, dwelling houses, cottages, etc., with plans; and upward of three hundred other engravings, mostly of superior character, illustrative of works and subjects interesting to architects and builders. Including all the separate diagrams and engravings of construction details, the volume presents not far from one thousand illustrations. The reading matter covers a large variety of useful and excellent subjects, interesting to every one. No architect, builder, contractor, engineer, or householder can afford to be without this splendid work. It is beautifully printed, and is by far the cheapest architectural volume ever presented to the public.

Coloring Billiard Balls.

M. Guyot (*Repertoire de Pharm.*) says he was asked to redden a billiard ball, the color of which had been worn away in use. He had nothing but fuchsine at hand, and he tried to redden the ball by macerating it in an alcoholic solution of that coloring matter. This, however, did not answer at all; the color wiped off completely. After a few experiments, he found the following plan answer perfectly: To pass the ball rapidly through a bath of nitric acid, then wash it in plenty of water, and, finally, dip it into an alcoholic solution of fuchsine. The color is fixed instantaneously; the ball is washed, and polished with a piece of flannel.

Rustic Structures.

Ornamental summer houses, rustic fences, rustic bridges, settees, chairs, vases, etc., add an attractive feature to the landscape of a country place. Mr. John Wheeler, of Orange, N. J. (see advt. another page), has erected a large number of ornamental structures of a varied kind in Llewellyn Park and on the premises of other residents of Orange and vicinity. These varied rustic structures, scattered here and there through the park and on lawns, are the admiration of strangers, and they add more attraction to a country place than their cost to construct.

GOOD LIGHT WITHOUT VIEW.

LIGHT AND VIEW.

NEITHER LIGHT NOR VIEW.

HOW A ROOM SHOULD BE LIGHTED.

Jarrah Wood.

Jarrah wood (*Eucalyptus marginata*) is a product of Western Australia, where it is found in considerable abundance. Mr. Thomas Laslett, Timber Inspector to the Admiralty, in his valuable work, "Timber and Timber Trees, Native and Foreign," says of it: "It is of straight growth and very large dimensions, but, unfortunately, is liable to early decay in the center. The sound trees, however, yield solid and useful timber of from 20 feet to 40 feet in length, by 11 inches to 24 inches square, while those with faulty centers furnish only indifferent squares of smaller sizes or pieces unequally sided, called flitches. The wood is red in color, hard, heavy, close in texture, slightly wavy in grain, and with occasionally enough figure to give it value for ornamental purposes; it works up quite smoothly, and takes a good polish. Cabinet makers may, therefore, readily employ it for furniture; but for architectural and other works, where great strength is needed, it should be used with caution, as the experiments prove it to be somewhat brittle in character. Some few years since a small supply of this wood was sent to the Woolwich Dockyard, with the view to test its quality and fitness for employment in shipbuilding; but the sample did not turn out well, owing to the want of proper care in the selection of the wood in the colony."

The clerk of works at Freemantle, in reporting upon the opinions expressed by shipbuilders and others, says: "The sound timber resists the attack of the *Teredo navalis* and white ant. On analysis by Professor Abel, it was found to contain a pungent acid that was destructive to life. The principle, however, was not found to be present in the unsound portions. Great care is therefore necessary in preparing the

"Undoubted authority is unanimous in declaring that the timber of the jarrah, under certain conditions, is indestructible."

Professor Von Mueller, Government Botanical Director of Victoria, says: "Its wood is indestructible; is attacked neither by chelura, teredo, nor termites, and is therefore much sought after for jetties and other structures exposed to sea-water. Vessels built with this timber have been enabled to do away with all copper-

found the most enduring of all woods. On this condition it defies decay; time, weather, water, the white ant, and the sea worm have no effect upon it. Specimens have been exhibited of portions of wood which had been nearly thirty years partly under water and partly out. Others had been used as posts, and for the same period buried in sand, where the white ant destroys in a few weeks every other kind of wood. For this peculiar property the jarrah is now much sought after for railway sleepers and telegraph posts in India and the colonies. It is admirably adapted for dock gates, piles, and other purposes, and for keel pieces, keelsons, and other heavy timber in shipbuilding. Vessels of considerable burden are built entirely of this wood, the peculiar properties of which render copper-sheathing entirely unnecessary, although the sea worm is most abundant in these waters."

Though in the foregoing there are a diversity of opinions, yet the general tendency is to testify to the usefulness in an extraordinary degree, under stated conditions, of jarrah wood, and the practical mind will quickly see many opportunities for taking advantage of a wood possessing so many valuable qualities as this wood has been found to contain; and it is not saying too much to express a hope that the shipments now in the London docks will be but the prelude to many other, and more important, consignments to

GOOD LIGHT WITHOUT VIEW.

LIGHT AND VIEW.

NEITHER LIGHT NOR VIEW.

HOW A ROOM SHOULD NOT BE LIGHTED.

plating. It is very strong, of a close grain, slightly oily and resinous in its nature, works well, takes a fine finish, and is, by shipbuilders in Melbourne, considered superior to oak, teak, or any other wood for their purpose."

The committee of Lloyd's, after the representations of His Excellency Governor Weld, determined to rank this timber with those in line 3, Table A, of the Society's rules; thus ranking it with *Cuba sabicu*, pencil

this country, where intrinsic merit is the only passport necessary to gain public favor and support where commercial interests are concerned.—*Building News.*

St. Sophia, Constantinople.

St. Sophia at Constantinople, of which at last authentic particulars have been obtained in the work of Salzenburg of Berlin, who, taking advantage of the scaffoldings erected by Fossati for the repair of the building, measured carefully every part of it. From this it appears that the diameter of the drum of the dome is 100 Prussian feet, or 102 feet 11 inches English, but the dome itself is 4 feet more, or 107 feet in diameter. It is constructed of forty ribs, projecting each 2 feet, which die away toward the center, leaving about one-third of the dome perfectly plain. The form is segmental, 45 feet 6 inches in height, and described consequently from a point about 8 feet below the springing. Round the base are forty windows, which throw in a flood of light; and altogether its appearance internally is as beautiful as any I know of. Originally, it was even flatter than it now is; but being in that form beyond the constructive power of its architect, it fell in, and the present form was adopted; but even then the architect tried to keep it as low as possible, judging correctly that the flatter it was the greater would be its apparent size, and also that of the floor it covered, and all of the parts around it. To obtain these internal advantages, however, the architect sacrificed the exterior entirely, and it is on the outside perhaps the ugliest dome ever constructed. But the same remark applies to the whole church. No pains

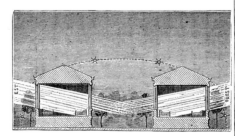
DIRECTION IN WHICH BUILDINGS SHOULD BE SET IN NORTHERN COUNTRIES.

wood for use by flitching the log so as to cut all the defective portions of the heart out, and using only the perfectly sound timber."

Very much has been said about jarrah being subject to split when exported to England in log. It must be borne in mind that its density renders seasoning very slow, and that the inner portions of the larger trees are often in a state of decay, even while the outer portions are in full vigor. A tree under these conditions, the inner portions comparatively dry, and the outer full of sap, shipped at once to such a variable climate as that of England, very naturally bursts from unequal shrinkage, being also exposed to very great changes of temperature. To obviate this peculiarity and apparent defect, let the jarrah be fallen when the sap is at the lowest ebb, and carefully flitched, as previously suggested.

The methods adopted in seasoning jarrah are as follows: The logs are thrown into the sea and left there for a few weeks; they are then drawn up through the sand, and after being covered with seaweed a few inches deep, are left to lie on the beach, care being taken to prevent the sun getting at their ends. The logs are then left many months to season. When taken up they are cut into boards seven inches wide, and stacked so as to admit of a free circulation of air round them for five or six months before using them.

In a communication forwarded to India by H. E. Victor, Esq., C.E., of Perth, in reply to inquiries made by some gentlemen engaged in the carrying out of several large contracts for public works in India, he says:

cedar, etc., for the construction and classification of ships. The purposes to which jarrah may be applied are innumerable; it fills the place where saul and teak could not be admitted, as well as where they are used; and as the material can be supplied at a price considerably less than the timbers named, in the log, and at half their price in scantling, it should be employed where hitherto timber has been considered undesirable—for instance, in sea-facing, dock-lining, landing-stages, breakwaters, and beacons; curbs, road paving, block-flooring, weather-boarding, and wainscot partitions, wallings, ceilings, and roof-coverings.

A Western Australian almanac says: "None of the neighboring colonies possess timber of a similar character to the jarrah, or endowed with equally valuable properties. If cut at the proper season, when the sap has expended itself and the tree is at rest, it will be

whatever seem to have been taken with the exterior, though every part of the interior is designed with the greatest care, and ornamented with the most profuse liberality.—*J. Fergusson.*

Swiss carved work in whitewood affords excellent opportunities for hand-painting, and many pretty articles for home decoration can be made from it.

DIRECTION IN WHICH BUILDINGS SHOULD BE SET IN SOUTHERN COUNTRIES.

GOOD LIGHT WITHOUT VIEW.

LIGHT AND VIEW.

NEITHER LIGHT NOR VIEW.

HOW A ROOM SHOULD BE LIGHTED.

Jarrah Wood.

Jarrah wood (*Eucalyptus marginata*) is a product of Western Australia, where it is found in considerable abundance. Mr. Thomas Laslett, Timber Inspector to the Admiralty, in his valuable work, "Timber and Timber Trees, Native and Foreign," says of it: "It is of straight growth and very large dimensions, but, unfortunately, is liable to early decay in the center. The sound trees, however, yield solid and useful timber of from 20 feet to 40 feet in length, by 11 inches to 24 inches square, while those with faulty centers furnish only indifferent squares of smaller sizes or pieces unequally sided, called flitches. The wood is red in color, hard, heavy, close in texture, slightly wavy in grain, and with occasionally enough figure to give it value for ornamental purposes; it works up quite smoothly, and takes a good polish. Cabinet makers may, therefore, readily employ it for furniture; but for architectural and other works, where great strength is needed, it should be used with caution, as the experiments prove it to be somewhat brittle in character. Some few years since a small supply of this wood was sent to the Woolwich Dockyard, with the view to test its quality and fitness for employment in shipbuilding; but the sample did not turn out well, owing to the want of proper care in the selection of the wood in the colony."

The clerk of works at Freemantle, in reporting upon the opinions expressed by shipbuilders and others, says: "The sound timber resists the attack of the *Teredo navalis* and white ant. On analysis by Professor Abel, it was found to contain a pungent acid that was destructive to life. The principle, however, was not found to be present in the unsound portions. Great care is therefore necessary in preparing the

"Undoubted authority is unanimous in declaring that the timber of the jarrah, under certain conditions, is indestructible."

Professor Von Mueller, Government Botanical Director of Victoria, says: "Its wood is indestructible; is attacked neither by chelura, teredo, nor termites, and is therefore much sought after for jetties and other structures exposed to sea-water. Vessels built with this timber have been enabled to do away with all copper-

found the most enduring of all woods. On this condition it defies decay; time, weather, water, the white ant, and the sea worm have no effect upon it. Specimens have been exhibited of portions of wood which had been nearly thirty years partly under water and partly out. Others had been used as posts, and for the same period buried in sand, where the white ant destroys in a few weeks every other kind of wood. For this peculiar property the jarrah is now much sought after for railway sleepers and telegraph posts in India and the colonies. It is admirably adapted for dock gates, piles, and other purposes, and for keel pieces, keelsons, and other heavy timber in shipbuilding. Vessels of considerable burden are built entirely of this wood, the peculiar properties of which render copper-sheathing entirely unnecessary, although the sea worm is most abundant in these waters."

Though in the foregoing there are a diversity of opinions, yet the general tendency is to testify to the usefulness in an extraordinary degree, under stated conditions, of jarrah wood, and the practical mind will quickly see many opportunities for taking advantage of a wood possessing so many valuable qualities as this wood has been found to contain; and it is not saying too much to express a hope that the shipments now in the London docks will be but the prelude to many other, and more important, consignments to

GOOD LIGHT WITHOUT VIEW.

LIGHT AND VIEW.

NEITHER LIGHT NOR VIEW.

HOW A ROOM SHOULD NOT BE LIGHTED.

plating. It is very strong, of a close grain, slightly oily and resinous in its nature, works well, takes a fine finish, and is, by shipbuilders in Melbourne, considered superior to oak, teak, or any other wood for their purpose."

The committee of Lloyd's, after the representations of His Excellency Governor Weld, determined to rank this timber with those in line 3, Table A, of the Society's rules; thus ranking it with *Cuba sabicu*, pencil

this country, where intrinsic merit is the only passport necessary to gain public favor and support where commercial interests are concerned.—*Building News.*

St. Sophia, Constantinople.

St. Sophia at Constantinople, of which at last authentic particulars have been obtained in the work of Salzenburg of Berlin, who, taking advantage of the scaffoldings erected by Fossati for the repair of the building, measured carefully every part of it. From this it appears that the diameter of the drum of the dome is 100 Prussian feet, or 102 feet 11 inches English, but the dome itself is 4 feet more, or 107 feet in diameter. It is constructed of forty ribs, projecting each 2 feet, which die away toward the center, leaving about one-third of the dome perfectly plain. The form is segmental, 45 feet 6 inches in height, and described consequently from a point about 8 feet below the springing. Round the base are forty windows, which throw in a flood of light; and altogether its appearance internally is as beautiful as any I know of. Originally, it was even flatter than it now is; but being in that form beyond the constructive power of its architect, it fell in, and the present form was adopted; but even then the architect tried to keep it as low as possible, judging correctly that the flatter it was the greater would be its apparent size, and also that of the floor it covered, and all of the parts around it. To obtain these internal advantages, however, the architect sacrificed the exterior entirely, and it is on the outside perhaps the ugliest dome ever constructed. But the same remark applies to the whole church. No pains

DIRECTION IN WHICH BUILDINGS SHOULD BE SET IN NORTHERN COUNTRIES.

wood for use by flitching the log so as to cut all the defective portions of the heart out, and using only the perfectly sound timber."

Very much has been said about jarrah being subject to split when exported to England in log. It must be borne in mind that its density renders seasoning very slow, and that the inner portions of the larger trees are often in a state of decay, even while the outer portions are in full vigor. A tree under these conditions, the inner portions comparatively dry, and the outer full of sap, shipped at once to such a variable climate as that of England, very naturally bursts from unequal shrinkage, being also exposed to very great changes of temperature. To obviate this peculiarity and apparent defect, let the jarrah be fallen when the sap is at the lowest ebb, and carefully flitched, as previously suggested.

The methods adopted in seasoning jarrah are as follows: The logs are thrown into the sea and left there for a few weeks; they are then drawn up through the sand, and after being covered with seaweed a few inches deep, are left to lie on the beach, care being taken to prevent the sun getting at their ends. The logs are then left many months to season. When taken up they are cut into boards seven inches wide, and stacked so as to admit of a free circulation of air round them for five or six months before using them.

In a communication forwarded to India by H. E. Victor, Esq., C.E., of Perth, in reply to inquiries made by some gentlemen engaged in the carrying out of several large contracts for public works in India, he says:

cedar, etc., for the construction and classification of ships. The purposes to which jarrah may be applied are innumerable; it fills the place where saul and teak could not be admitted, as well as where they are used; and as the material can be supplied at a price considerably less than the timbers named, in the log, and at half their price in scantling, it should be employed where hitherto timber has been considered undesirable—for instance, in sea-facing, dock-lining, landing-stages, breakwaters, and beacons; curbs, road paving, block-flooring, weather-boarding, and wainscot partitions, wallings, ceilings, and roof-coverings.

A Western Australian almanac says: "None of the neighboring colonies possess timber of a similar character to the jarrah, or endowed with equally valuable properties. If cut at the proper season, when the sap has expended itself and the tree is at rest, it will be

whatever seem to have been taken with the exterior, though every part of the interior is designed with the greatest care, and ornamented with the most profuse liberality.—*J. Fergusson.*

Swiss carved work in whitewood affords excellent opportunities for hand-painting, and many pretty articles for home decoration can be made from it,

DIRECTION IN WHICH BUILDINGS SHOULD BE SET IN SOUTHERN COUNTRIES.

51

Concrete Floors.

These are sometimes formed on a centering of pieces of fir of proper scantlings resting on a trestle or on the lower flanges of the girders. Across these, transverse pieces are laid, and boarded with boards of, say, 1 inch thick and close jointed. The concrete is laid in bays; each is finished in one operation, so as to form a slab. The ingredients may be as follows : 1 part cement to 4 parts of breeze or other porous substance, iron slag, hard bricks, well burnt clay, which have to pass through a ¾ in. mesh. If fine stuff is required, clean smith's ashes may be used, as being better than sand, the fine stuff not exceeding one-third of the whole. Portland cement, if fine ground, capable of passing through a sieve of 2,500 meshes per square inch, should be used, and the following test is given : When made up wet and filled into a glass bottle, and struck level with the top, it must not in setting crack the bottle or rise out of it, or become loose by shrinking. When filled into moulds, and after being seven days in water, it must have an ultimate strength under tensile stress, slowly applied, of 250 pounds per square inch of section. The mixing is to be performed by turning the ingredients over twice dry, then shoveled to a third heap, at the same time adding from the rose of a hose water enough to make the ingredients cling together. The broken material and breeze should be damped before mixing. The concrete, after being laid, is slightly rammed with wooden beaters, and the surface should be kept damp by water fourteen days after laying. The soffits should be well wetted, and a setting coat of fine stuff given. These are the instructions given in a specification for concrete floors, and may be usefully followed. Slabs of concrete 6 inches thick have been found to break at from 1 cwt. to 2½ cwt. per foot super., the size of the slab being about 14 feet by 13 feet in the former case and 14 feet by 7 feet in the last. Experiments have not been sufficiently numerous or conducted with enough exactness to insure any reliable rule, the slabs crack suddenly, and there is little warning after the ultimate resistance has been reached.—*Building News.*

ILLUSTRATIONS OF MORNINGSIDE PARK, NEW YORK CITY.

EXTERIORS OF SMALL DWELLINGS.

The owner of a small farm wishes to erect a cheap dwelling; and while he has not the means to use costly ornaments, he wishes to secure "a neat and symmetrical exterior," and desires suggestions from us. In compliance with his request, we give a few small views of houses of moderate or small cost, from

Fig. 1.

which he may make a selection, and we trust they will afford useful hints to others of our readers.

For a quite small house, Fig. 1 gives a view of one with both neatness and symmetry, the only part of which requiring a single dollar in expenditure for the sake of ornament is the curved top of the front entrance. The broad eaves and brackets are an essential protection of the walls from storms and rain, and their cost is small. A dwelling may be built after this style, with small dimensions, with two rooms below, besides the kitchen added, and with two sleeping apartments above stairs; or it may be made larger with double cost, and wider rooms with ample closets.

A handsomely built Gothic cottage is represented by Fig. 2. The steep roof of this style has the advantage

Fig. 2.

of less danger of leakage from rains, and is well fitted for a slate roof. The house is of larger size than the one last described, and rather more attention is given to ornament.

A cottage intended for nearly all the room which it gives to be on the common floor, to avoid frequent passing up and down stairs, is shown in Fig. 3. It makes no pretension to outside ornament, and yet such a dwelling neatly constructed, and surrounded with handsomely planted grounds, might constitute a rather pleasing as well as comfortable home.

For a neat farm house, with a slight air of elegance,

Fig. 4 is a good representation of the bracketed style. But little explanation is needed. Cheap and substantial side walls are made with boards or plank outside, with vertical battens both outside and within; and on the inner battens thick, tarred building paper, with battens again on this paper to receive the lathing and plastering. We have found dwellings constructed in this way to be quite as secure from cold winds as the best walls laid in with brick, where they possessed some additional advantages.—*Country Gentleman.*

THE PEOPLE'S PALACE, LONDON.

The foundation of a People's Palace at the East End, London, was lately laid by the Prince of Wales. The funds for this undertaking originated in a nucleus of £12,500, part of a larger sum left for the benefit of the East End by Mr. Barber Beaumont. About an acre and a half will be covered with buildings, leaving three and a half for recreation purposes, such as running, cycling, tennis, etc. The Drapers' Company have contributed £20,000 for the establishment of technical schools and ranges of workshops, where all the principal trades carried on at the East End will be taught by practical artisans, so that no lad in future need begin life without the knowledge of some trade. These buildings are designed for the accommodation of 20,000 students. Indeed, the trustees wish to see the whole institution so framed that, whether in science, art, or literature, any student may be able to follow up his education to the highest point; in fact, that the Palace may become the university for East London. At the same time, the Palace will afford ample means for recreation and social enjoyment. There will be a winter garden and concert hall, a library and reading-rooms, gymnasia, and a swimming bath (the last contributed by Lord Rosebury), and, as we have said, an extensive recreation ground, where on summer evenings efficient bands are to be provided, so that workmen, with their wives and children, may find a pleasant resort for social intercourse after the day's work is done. The main building, of which we give an illustration, is to be constructed from the plans of Mr. Robson. The architectural features are decidedly Oriental. The structure is to be of red brick and white stone, and facing the main thoroughfare will be a semicircular portico, supported upon columns, and surmounted by a large and handsome dome, right and left of which will tower a lofty ornamental minaret, capped by a gilded cupola.

Under the dome will be the large entrance hall, intended during the day time to serve as a covered playground for the children, and in the evening as a species of common room, in which the workmen may sit and chat. Opening out from this will be "The Queen's Hall," where the concerts will be held, and of this the Prince laid the foundation stone on June 28. Beyond will be the library, reading-rooms, schools, etc. The Palace is to form a center for the

formation of cricket, football, cycling, and other clubs, and the trustees hope to secure a suitable ground for the use of such clubs.—*The Graphic.*

Professional Statistics.

The number of men in the three professions—divinity, law, and medicine—was, in 1880, 254,520, of whom

Fig. 3

64,698 were ministers, 64,137 lawyers, and 85,671 physicians and surgeons, 12,314 dentists, and 27,700 pharmacists. Hence the proportion in the learned professions (so-called) is about 1 to 200 of the population. The proportion of ministers and lawyers is very nearly equal, and is 1 to 782 of the population. The propor-

Fig. 4.

tion of physicians and surgeons is 1 to 584, and of dentists 1 to 4,000.—*Journal of Education.*

DESIGN FOR A RESIDENCE.

In our last number on page 28 we gave the perspective elevation of an excellent design for a country residence by C. H. Stilson, architect, New Haven, Conn., and promised to give the floor plans in our present number. We accordingly present them herewith. This house has a very pleasing exterior aspect, while the interior is conveniently arranged, and might, if required, comfortably accommodate two families

First Floor Plan

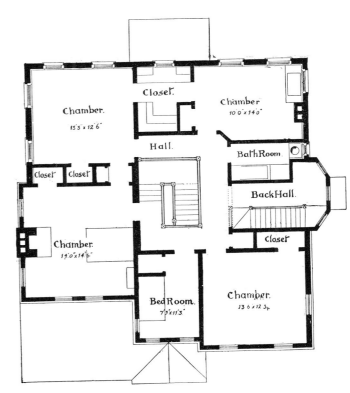

Second Floor Plan.

FLOOR PLANS FOR A RESIDENCE.

Hints for Builders.

The architects and builders of a thousand years or more seemed to recognize the peculiar construction of the eye and its ability to take in round objects better than square, and, no matter whether they understood this delusion or optical principle or not, it was apparently applied to all their public buildings and rooms of state. Though some of their specimens of architecture baffle the best engineering skill of the present age, these secrets were not buried beneath the ruins of Baalbec, Herculaneum, or Pompeii.

It may be that the massive stones in some of their large temples were put in place by some mechanical contrivances unknown in modern times; or it may be that large hills once occupied their temple sites, and the stones placed one above another, as we build a cellar wall, and when the structure was completed underground, the hill was razed and the edifice appeared in all its architectural beauty and simplicity, appearing, as it were, in a single night, a masterpiece to excite the wonder and admiration of generations countless centuries afterward.

But the external appearances of their structures were by no means the only features that deceived the eye, and were intended to so deceive. The writer has stood in some rooms, in old temples, that the apparent size would stagger belief; and in others very small as measured with the eye would be small and still have so many outside walls, showing them to be very much larger than one would estimate. On the other hand, the large room would not be half so large as it looked to be, and the smaller twice its apparent size. These people disguised distances by curves, domes and alcoves; even a slope of but three inches of the floor toward the center, with a corresponding elevation of the ceiling center, made a difference of as many feet in the apparent height.

These principles are of easy application in modern buildings. To make a room appear higher, the plain surface of the ceiling should be decreased by the mouldings of the cornice, by panels, or, in the absence of these, by bands of color performing the same office. A vertical system of line should be adopted in mural decoration, and the mantel should be lower.

Then, to make a room appear lower, precisely the opposite treatment should be adopted; that is, to increase the plain ceiling, adopt a horizontal system of mural decoration, with a dado and a high mantel. To make a room appear wider may be accomplished by making it appear lower; but where this is undesirable, or where it is insufficient, the effect can be reached by adopting a mural decoration on a graduated scale of form, decreasing upward, so that two or more patterns at the top similar to those at the foot are found to occupy the same space as one at the foot, and this effect can be much increased by a gradation of color upward from dark to light.

To make a room appear narrower is accomplished by making it appear higher; but in case enough deception cannot be produced in this way, the same effect can be obtained by adopting a strongly drawn, large pattern in strong color for mural decoration. To make a room appear longer is accomplished by making it appear lower and narrower, and the effect is increased by decreasing the scale and strength of color of the mural decorations adopted at the ends. To make a room appear shorter is accomplished by making it appear wider and higher, and the same effect can be reached by increasing the scale and strength of color of the mural decorations adopted at the ends.

Any of the foregoing can be modified or increased by treatment of the floor surface, whether by carpets, rugs, painted boards, or the parquet flooring; lines running across a room, or rugs laid down at intervals, having the effect of shortening, and to an extent of heightening and widening a room, consequently lines running in the length increase this dimension, and to an extent reduce the height and width. A floor polished increases the apparent height of an apartment by reflecting all vertical lines and prolonging them.—*J. F. E., St. Louis Miller.*

THE CULTURE OF FUCHSIAS.

Lovers of flowers will perhaps be interested in the accompanying engravings, reproduced from photographs representing some fuchsias of unusual forms and dimensions raised by an amateur florist at Evreux. These fuchsias are the ornament of the garden, and are admired by connoisseurs as much for the vigor of their growth as for the abundance and beauty of their flowers. Fig. 1 represents one of these shrubs in its fourth year, and one whose flat, dome-shaped head, two yards in diameter, is large enough to allow several persons to take advantage of its shade. Seated under this plant, one can converse or refresh himself, as is shown by the objects reproduced in the cut, which serve at the same time to well establish the dimensions of this exceptional specimen.

In Fig. 2, three other fuchsias are grouped, the tallest of which is 14 ft. in height. This plant is six years old, and the others four.

It is extremely rare to obtain such specimens of a plant which scarcely exceeds three feet in height in ordinary cultivation. The arrangements represented herewith are very pleasing and decorative, and might be oftener adopted by amateurs in horticulture.

The fuchsia is admirably adapted for the decoration of gardens. The elegance of its form, the lovely aspect of its flowers and their duration, and the little care that its culture requires should contribute to recommend it still further to the attention of landscape gardeners. In 1845, Mr. G. Porcher, president of the Orleans Horticultural Society, published a learned monograph upon fuchsias in an interesting volume which was soon out of print. A second edition of the work appeared in 1848, and to this the author added an enumeration of 738 species and varieties of the plant. We should add that since that period the list has considerably increased, thanks to the science of our horticulturists and to the zeal of amateurs, who are much more numerous than is usually thought.—*La Nature.*

Ivy in Hanging Baskets.

Among the very best plants for filling wire baskets that are hung up in corridors, verandas, and other exposed places all the year round are some of the many beautiful varieties of ivy, especially those with very small foliage and graceful trailing shoots. Some years ago I was very much pleased with the excellent effect produced by means of the common English ivy alone, that an amateur friend used to employ in a great variety of ways, for decoration, and especially for filling hanging baskets both indoors and out, the windows being draped with elegant shoots from plants growing in the smallest possible root space. Since that time I have employed ivies for baskets, for brackets, and balconies, and with excellent effect. Any one who has not tried them can have little idea of the variety of form and color to be found among these common hardy plants, and the smaller the root space the better do they display their variegation. The golden blotched variety, that only produces a few golden leaves at wide intervals apart when planted in rich soil, becomes beautifully variegated when starved at the root, and some of the silver variegated sorts are equally interesting. The large leaved kind called Hedera maculata, that in rich soil assumes a dull white variegation, is very much improved by basket culture, and the best of such hardy subjects is that they impart a cheerful look to a dwelling house at a time when other less hardy plants need the shelter of heated glass structures. For lining the base of hanging baskets nothing is equal to the stonecrops. They look fresh and green at all times of the year, except when covered with white or yellow flowers.—*J. G., Hants, in The Garden.*

To copper small pieces of sheet iron: Clean the article thoroughly by treatment in a bath of muriatic acid 1 part, water 4 parts, to remove all scale. Wash in hot water and tumble in sawdust wet with a solution of sulphate of copper in water, to which add as much sulphuric acid as is equal to the weight of the dry sulphate of copper. Use about 2 ounces of each to a gallon of water. You may also copper work that cannot be easily tumbled by dipping in the above solution hot. The work must be clean and free from grease.

CURIOUS DESIGN FOR WALL PAPER OR PANEL FOR A NURSERY.

Fig. 1.

Fig. 2.

SHRUBBY FUCHSIAS.

SCIENTIFIC AMERICAN

ARCHITECTS AND BUILDERS EDITION

Entered at the Post Office of

New York as Second Class Matter.

NEW YORK, MARCH, 1887.

Vol. III.   Subscription, $1.50 a Year.   Single Copies, 15 Cents.   No. 3.

A WINDMILL TOWER AND WATER TANK AT NARRAGANSETT PIER, R. I.

CONSTABLE BROTHERS ARCHITECTS.

STARRETT'S PATENT COMBINATION SQUARE.

With the adjustable scale this forms one of the most convenient and useful tools devised for the use of carpenters and mechanics. One is a complete substitute for a whole set of common try squares, and is one of the best gauges for transferring exact measurement or laying out work. It is also convenient for a depth gauge or to square in a mortise. For a miter it is perfect, while with the auxiliary center-head it forms a centering square, both inside and outside, which is unequaled for convenience and accuracy. L S. Starrett,

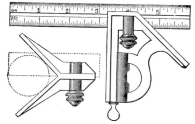

of Athol, Mass., is the manufacturer, and will be pleased to send his catalogue and price list of fine tools for carpenters and machinists on application.

WOMEN OUT OF DOORS.

It is thirty years and more since Thomas Wentworth Higginson wrote his famous essay on "Saints and their Bodies." It struck a new note. Before that time, the intellect and the soul had been cultivated. Learning, philanthropy, and religion were of consequence. To cultivate the body might be well enough for pugilists and circus riders, but was unworthy the serious thought of refined men and women.

Colonel Higginson's essay is to-day the keynote of a grand chorus in which men and women throughout the civilized world unite with ever-growing enthusiasm. Health is now the fashion. To cultivate the body is counted as essential to the best development as to fill the mind with learning. Every college has its gymnasium, every girls' school its regular system of exercise. Colonel Higginson is himself the president of the greatest 'cycle club in America, and in Boston a noble building for a ladies' gymnasium has just been dedicated under the auspices of the best society.

During the past five years a great advance has been made by the women of this country in the direction of physical culture. It is no longer counted unwomanly to use the same care in promoting health and vigor by intelligent exercise that one would use in developing literary taste or artistic skill by appropriate culture. The effect of this change is already seen in the growing strength of young women and their satisfaction in the ability to do things that would have crushed the belle of twenty years ago. Lawn tennis, rowing, horseback riding, tricycling, walking, and regular gymnastic training are in varying degrees popular among the women of to-day. They are found to be not only delightful in themselves, but of direct value in promoting health, strength, beauty, and happiness.

Among these, the tricycle is already recognized as the most useful and enjoyable means of bringing women into the open air and into contact with the attractions of nature. It is safe to say that five years ago there were not a score of lady 'cyclers in this country. Even in Europe there were few. To-day they are numbered by thousands, and hundreds of refined and cultured ladies are joining the ranks of riders every season.

The invention of the tricycle, and its rapid advance to the present state of mechanical perfection, is, I am firmly persuaded, the greatest boon to American women that the century has brought. Coming simultaneously with the conviction that "bodily exercise

profiteth" much for womankind, it provides a way to take that exercise which is at once fascinating, graceful, invigorating, and healthful.

The tricycle is in the first place an economical vehicle. Its original cost is about the same as that of a very ordinary horse; but once bought and paid for, its expense of operation and keeping in order is almost nothing. Its diet is oil, its shoeing needs to be done say once in every twenty thousand miles, its repairs—if the machine is a good one—are trifling, and its daily care is not so great as that of a pet poodle. The machine may be kept in a front hall, a cellar, or a barn. It is always ready, by night or day. A chain and padlock will securely fasten it at the house of a friend, the market, or the church.

In the second place, it is mechanically adapted to afford the best possible exercise at the smallest expenditure of fatigue and nervous energy. The lady who mounts a tricycle with pedals and handles properly adjusted will be nearly erect on the pedals, and will use feet and legs very much as in rapid walking. At the same time the shoulders are thrown back, the lungs expanded, and through the action of the arms and the muscles of the back, the whole system receives constant but not exhausting exercise. The deep breathing that is a necessity for the tricycler is of great value to women in developing the strength of their lungs and the faculty of continued exertion. The whole body is more thoroughly exercised in riding a tricycle than in any form of exercise which I have ever tried, and yet so perfectly adapted to human needs is it that the fatigue of a ten mile ride is less than one would experience in walking a tenth of the distance.

There is a fragile woman in a neighboring city, who could not bear a carriage drive of half an hour without being prostrated with weariness. Her husband rode home one day a tricycle, in the faint hope that it might be of use to her. She rode a mile at the first trial, and came home refreshed. The machine was purchased, and I have known her to ride a dozen miles in a hot July day, with pleasure and advantage, when a walk of forty rods would formerly have exhausted her strength. She has been riding now for two seasons, is greatly benefited by it, and is making extensive plans for using a tandem tricycle with her husband, next summer.

The tricyle is unique, as far as I am aware, in that it affords the most thorough and pervasive exercise of all parts of the body, at the same time that the mind is so fully occupied with the care of managing the machine and enjoying the feast which nature spreads on every side, that one is conscious only of the pleasure, and gets the exercise as it were gratuitously. A ride over a pleasant country road in the early morning hours of a June day is an experience of rare delight. With a congenial companion the enjoyment is doubled. The fragrance of the woods and fields, the music of the birds, the exhilarating sense of rapid motion through the soft air, the free bodily movements, in which the tricycle seems only an added physical faculty, all go to make up an experience that, having once enjoyed, one is eager for a thousand times again.

The practicality of the tricycle as a vehicle for the daily use of women is undoubted. There is scarcely a large town in the land where there are not some ladies who use the tricycle as others do their horse and carriage. It is always ready at the door for an errand to the market, a call on a friend, a spin for pleasure, or a journey to the next town. And where is the horse that, driven by his mistress, can be counted on for a uniform speed of eight miles an hour, with possibilities of ten or twelve on fine roads? The absolute independence which the woman with a tricycle has of mankind in every form, from the stable boy to her husband, is peculiarly gratifying to those who have always been compelled to wait the pleasure or convenience of the sterner sex.

The last two years has greatly developed the tandem tricycle in this country. which until that time was almost

wholly used in England and on the Continent. Very good machines are now made on this side of the water, and their use is rapidly increasing here. The special advantage of the tandem is that it affords pleasant conveyance for a gentleman and lady, or two gentlemen, giving each equal use of the strength of both in propelling the machine. A husband whose wife is fragile and delicate may ride with her on a tandem, using his own superior strength to supplement her weakness in imparting an enjoyable rate of speed, which would be impossible for her on a single machine. The tandem is a social vehicle, and for touring is used with great pleasure and advantage. An easy rate of speed for a well made tandem tricycle is eight miles an hour, and it is not uncommon for a gentleman and his wife who live near my home to take an evening spin of two or three hours at the rate of twelve miles an hour. The touring in Italy and England of Mr. and Mrs. Joseph Pennell, on a tandem tricycle, has borne fruit in two of the most delightfully written and illustrated books of travel which have lately been published.

I have avoided in this brief paper giving figures, dates, and statistics concerning the use of the tricycle by women. They are accessible by every one who cares to know exactly what has been done. Any 'cycle maker or dealer will gladly supply such information on application. I have only amplified and illustrated the undoubted facts of the wonderful growth of the belief in physical culture among American women, and the unique adaptation of the tricycle, in its single or double form, for the promotion of that end in a manner at once pleasant, practical, and popular.—*William B. Howland.*

STANLEY'S ADJUSTABLE CLAPBOARD MARKER.

A very considerable part of an ordinary carpenter's work, is the laying of clapboards or siding. A difficult

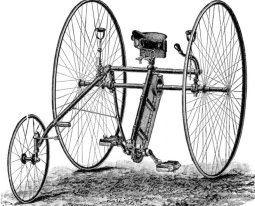

feature in this work has been the fitting of clapboards closely where they end, at the corner board or at window casings. The usual methods employed by workmen for marking and sawing off the boards, by use of a try-square and scrach-awl, or by aid of a clapboard-hook and scratch-awl, have demanded about one more hand than the average man has been supplied with by nature.

We illustrate on this page a tool which can be used with one hand, while the other is employed in holding a clapboard in position. The sharp edge of the teeth on the marking blade are just parallel with the outer edges of the legs when placed against the corner-board; and by moving the tool half an inch, it will mark a full line across the clapboard, exactly over and conformed to the edge of the corner-board or casing. There is then no difficulty in sawing for a perfectly close joint. The Stanley Rule and Level Company, of New Britain, Conn., are just now supplying hardware dealers with this excellent tool.

Impermeable Boxes.

Excellent water, air, and grease proof boxes can be easily made by immersing either paper, willow, or turned wood boxes in hot melted hard paraffin. Such boxes are very handy and useful for sending out ointments, pastes, pills, or anything of a hygroscopic or deliquescent character. They can be hermetically sealed by placing the lid on the box while warm. Mr. A. W. Gerrard, F.C.S., of University College Hospital, who communicates this note to the *Chemist and Druggist*, sends a specimen impermeable box. The appearance of the wood is little altered by the paraffin coating, and the box is perfectly water tight. Paraffin of high melting point should be used.

LADY'S AND GENTLEMAN'S TANDEM.

THE LADY'S TRICYCLE.

FRINK'S PATENT REFLECTOR.

The various reflectors manufactured by I. P. Frink, of 561 Pearl St., New York City, under his patents are now used to a considerable extent throughout the country. They are formed in various shapes, patterns, and sizes for numberless purposes, from a highly polished silver plate which is corrugated on the surface. The effect is to reflect the light in a manner free from an objectionable glare, and to well diffuse it throughout a room.

One of the purposes for which the plate is found eminently useful is for application to the outside of a window which, owing to the construction of the building or from local causes, admits but little light. The reflector is formed in an attractive frame, and being placed at a proper angle, reflects the daylight into a

FRINK'S PATENT REFLECTOR.

room. The advantage in saving gas and preventing injury to the eyesight is very great, and it is astonishing how much light may be obtained by these means.

Then the reflectors have been made in an immense variety of kinds for different uses, such as for lamps, gas, oil, and electricity; in fact, from the smallest reflector, costing only a few cents, for a kerosene lamp, up to the magnificent chandeliers used in the principal of our theaters, this reflector has been employed with excellent results. The annexed engraving shows its application to a gas chandelier.

An illustrated catalogue giving full particulars of the material, prices, etc., will be forwarded on request.

PENBERTHY INJECTOR.

At last a mechanical combination and device has been produced, and a man's labor and study crowned with success, in the production, for the convenience of engineers, of a simple and compact device known as the Penberthy injector or boiler feeder.

Its mechanical construction is very simple, but perfect. All its parts are movable and convenient of access (not being screwed in), its working so complete that an inexperienced person can operate it with success and perfectness. Its adaptability to all classes of boilers, such as stationary, portable, traction, marine, and locomotive, and its working on each, makes it very desirable, and recommends it to all classes of engineers. The automatic working of this injector is of very great advantage, as by this mechanical construction it works under all conditions of shakes, jars, and concussions. In

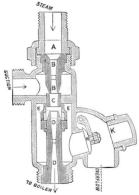

PENBERTHY INJECTOR.

case of a break, or the suction is to be removed and then returned. it picks up or begins working without any aid, assistance, or attention from the engineer, thereby relieving of much care and annoyance. Its convenience of access is of very great consideration and importance, owing to the advantage of cleaning and examining its interior parts.

The working parts of this injector are stationary in their work, thereby causing comparatively no wear in its mechanical parts. The inventor seems to have combined common sense with mechanical science, by leaving out all complications, and combining in the injector every convenience of operating, getting at, and putting it on the boiler.

The body is of a single cylinder or barrel, with two jets inside, "steam and combining," and governed by an automatic swinging overflow. The injector is operated by the opening or closing of the globe valves. It is connected to the boiler and pipes with uniform and interchangeable square centered unions, and can be put on or taken off very quickly without any annoyance or injury, and the only tool required being an ordinary wrench.

Another great point gained in this injector is its great range of working capacity. It will lift water twenty-five feet perpendicular, or take it a hydraulic pressure and force it into the boiler at a temperature of from 140° to 180° Fah. It will work under a steam pressure of from 20 to 140 lb. It will also lift and force water at a very warm temperature (say 120° Fah.) in tank or well, and under all circumstances and at all points it works automatically. The inventor and manufacturers of the Penberthy injector have great confidence in its working qualities, and to satisfy engineers of its merits and perfectness of work, solicit a trial. From observation, a brilliant future is in store for this little wonder of simplicity and compactness, which is a model of mechanism in appearance and finish.

For prices, etc., address Jenkins Bros., 71 John St., New York, 13 So. 4th St., Philadelphia, and 105 Milk St., Boston, agents for this injector.

DECORATIONS FOR A HALL.

We give a design for decorations for a hall and stair-

HALL DECORATIONS FOR A COUNTRY DWELLING.—DESIGNED BY C. J. KRUMBEINE, ARGYLE PARK, ILL.

way, of moderate cost, for a country dwelling. Part of the glass of the windows is painted and part treated with beveled plate. The whole effect is rich and pleasing. Designed by C. J. Krumbeine, Argyle Park, Ill.

OLYMPIA, THE NEW AGRICULTURAL HALL, LONDON—EXTERIOR VIEW.

OLYMPIA, THE NEW AGRICULTURAL HALL, LONDON—INTERIOR VIEW.

Redwood Logging in California.

The whole world concedes to America pre-eminence in the size of her trees available for timber. In no part of the world are trees to be found equaling in size the forest monarchs of California, save in certain parts of Australia and Tasmania, where the eucalyptus trees grow, perhaps, to equal dimensions, but the wood of the eucalyptus is gnarled and worthless, twisting and warping if used. California's big trees are of two varieties, the Sequoia gigantea, the most celebrated examples of which are found in the vicinity of the Yosemite, and the Sequoia sempervirens, or redwood, which, through extending from the vicinity of Santa Barbara on the south to Oregon on the north, are found in greatest size in Humboldt County. In the early English works on phytography, it was sought to link the name of their great Wellington to the trees of the Yosemite, but now it is agreed that to the father of the American nation this honor appropriately belongs, and the name of Washingtonia gigantea is now coming into favor in popular and scientific usage.

In the forests of Norway, Sweden, and Finland, the great timber-producing countries of northern Europe, the standard width of boards is 6 inches, and trees larger than 8 to 10 in. diameter are unusual. Several years ago a large American locomotive establishment shipped a cargo of locomotives to Hangho, the terminus of one of the Finnish railways. They were packed in boxes of Michigan two inch pine plank, many of them 15 in. to 18 in. or more in width. Boards of this extraordinary width attracted much attention, and an employe of the railway obtained sufficient of the empty boxes and fashioned them into a house—the best in the place—and people came in considerable numbers to marvel at trees which could produce boards like those. The thrifty housewives greatly prized pieces of the same boards for making moulding boards, and many were distributed for this purpose. If our ordinary lumber of commerce could excite such surprise, how much greater the astonishment and admiration of the same people at California's wonders!

An American gentleman was once waiting at a Russian custom house to have his effects examined and passed. As he opened his trunk a photograph of one of the great trees was lying on top exposed to view. The inspector examined it, eagerly. "Ah," said he, "that is from California. I have a brother there who has written us at home much about them, but we could not credit it. I have never seen a photograph of them."

The picture was presented to him, whereupon work was suspended until it had been handed about and discussed by all, up to the chief of the custom house. The photograph showed a great tree partially cut for felling, with twelve persons sitting uncrowded in the V shaped cutting. This calls to mind a bon mot of the late George Whitney, of Philadelphia, who, on seeing the same photograph, exclaimed, "Why, it is a photograph, but it really looks like a wood-cut!"

A peculiarity of the redwood forests is the absence of undergrowth. It is, therefore, difficult to realize their magnitude without a familiar object near by with which to compare them. Until one begins to make such a comparison the trees do not appear of extraordinary size. Like the cataract of Niagara, the first view is frequently disappointing, and familiarity, far from breeding contempt, serves to increase the feeling of awe inspired by overpowering magnitude.

In consequence of the great size of the redwood, the process of getting the logs to the mills has been a slow and expensive one. Floating has been impracticable, owing both to the size and the weight of the logs, even where there are streams. Hence, logging railroads are in California a necessity, instead of an economic convenience, as in the pine forests east of the mountains. Many of the readers of the Lumberman are familiar, by pictures and otherwise, with the old methods in use on the coast. In some cases long lines of oxen laboriously drag the logs through the woods,

and in other cases tackling, operated by cattle or mule power, or sometimes by donkey engines, is employed to load the logs. But those methods are too slow, and are being superseded by steam power conveniently applied.

The necessity for some special means of handling these great logs led Mr. John Dolbeer, a large lumber operator of San Francisco, to think of attaching a steam windlass to an ordinary locomotive. A patent was granted him for a device by which the steam windlass could be thrown into gear with the driving wheels of the locomotive for the purpose of propelling it, or could be used separately for its legitimate work of lifting and handling logs. Since then the Baldwin Locomotive Works, of Philadelphia, have built, for logging railroads on the Pacific coast and elsewhere, a special type of double-end logging locomotives, equally adapted for running in either direction, and equipped with a powerful steam windlass at the forward end. Unlike Dolbeer's locomotive, however, the windlass is entirely disconnected from the driving gear of the locomotive, and the locomotive can be built either with or without it. The locomotives referred to have two pairs of driving wheels coupled and a two-wheeled or pony truck at each end. A saddle tank carries the water, and the rear truck carries a large

DESIGN FOR AN ORNAMENTAL GATE.

wood box. The forward truck is center bearing, the rear truck side bearing. The wheel base is extended sufficiently to distribute the weight of the engine over a good length of track, while at the same time it is perfectly flexible, allowing the locomotive to run on the roughest track and pass the shortest curves with ease and without injury to itself or the track. A powerful steam brake acting on both pairs of driving wheels controls the motion of the engine on steep grades, and serves to lock it firmly while the windlass is in operation. The windlass is a Copeland & Bacon six inch double cylinder, with single or double gearing, as the weight of the logs to be handled requires

Some of the green redwood timber is very heavy, and will sink when put into water. The logs handled frequently weigh from twenty to thirty tons.

Redwood is the common lumber of the Pacific coast, taking the place of the pine and hemlock of the Eastern States and the deals of England. It is used for clapboards, siding, shingles, in fact for every purpose where it is not subject to wear. When dried, it is quite soft, and wears rapidly by attrition; it is, therefore, unsuitable for flooring, or stair purposes. It is used to some extent for railroad ties, though not so well adapted to this service as harder woods. Particularly on curves, the spikes become loosened by the lateral pressure against the rails. Redwood is remarkable in that its shrinkage is mainly in the direction of its length. Though its grain is usually straight, it can be found with grain curled, bird's eye, and other fantastic shapes, rivaling in this respect the most beautiful

bird's eye and curly maple. Its rich color, much resembling red cedar, its beautiful grain, when carefully selected, and its great durability, when not subject to wear, make it most desirable for interior decoration. With the low transcontinental freights now ruling and likely to continue, it must become recognized in the Eastern States as a wood rich in economic and ornamental possibilities.—Lumberman.

Grano-Metallic Stone.

The grano-metallic stone, the invention of Mr. J. H. Bryant, of London, is composed of blast furnace slag and granite, which are crushed, chemically treated, dried, and mixed with Portland cement. For use these ingredients are brought to a pasty consistency with an alkaline solution, and laid. It possesses the important property of always having a rough surface, which is due to the atoms of the vitreous slag always presenting themselves just above the other ingredients, which are more readily worn. This stone has undergone a special trial in one of the metropolitan gas works, where a section was laid at the request of the engineer. It was there successfully subjected to tests which natural and artificial stones have, it is stated, been unable to withstand. It is found to stand not only the wear and tear of heavy horse and van traffic, but the sudden and extreme alternations of temperature incident to the slaking of coke upon it. Valuable as this material has proved itself for paving and road making purposes, however, it has now been proved to possess the additional important feature of being highly refractory. A cement kiln lined with this stone has stood a number of burnings without any repairs having to be done. Even where the lining happened to be torn away by a portion of adhering clinker, there is not the least sign of the stone having been injuriously acted upon by the heat. This is certainly a most crucial test, and the satisfactory manner in which the stone has passed through it stamps it at once as an absolutely fire proof material, and, therefore, of special value for constructive purposes.—Iron.

ORNAMENTAL IRON GATE.

I send you a design of the gate belonging to the railing which was illustrated in your building edition for August, 1886, and which shows the crossed bars in the upper part.

In designing this gate, my endeavor has been to adhere as closely as possible to the outlines of the posts. All the cornered work (posts, etc.) is octagonal. In carrying out the design, the cast iron scroll work shown as of a circular or oval section in the drawing was made grooved and with edges rounded. The groove following all the contortions brings well out the intersections.   ED. C. MAGNUS.

Crefeld, 1887.

PATENTS.

Messrs. Munn & Co., in connection with the publication of the Scientific American, continue to examine improvements and to act as Solicitors of Patents for Inventors.

In this line of business they have had forty years' experience, and now have unequaled facilities for the preparation of Patent Drawings, Specifications, and the prosecution of Applications for Patents in the United States, Canada, and Foreign Countries. Messrs. Munn & Co. also attend to the preparation of Caveats, Copyrights for Books, Labels, Reissues, Assignments, and Reports on Infringements of Patents. All business intrusted to them is done with special care and promptness, on very reasonable terms.

A pamphlet sent free of charge, on application, containing full information about Patents and how to procure them ; directions concerning Labels, Copyrights, Designs, Patents, Appeals, Reissues, Infringements, Assignments, Rejected Cases, Hints on the Sale of Patents, etc.

We also send, free of charge, a synopsis of Foreign Patent Laws, showing the cost and method of securing patents in all the principal countries of the world.

MUNN & CO., Solicitors of Patents, 361 Broadway, New York.

BRANCH OFFICE.—622 F Street, Washington, D. C.

ROSE COVERED PORCHES.

T. W. GIRDLESTONE.

How is it that plants are often seen flourishing in cottage gardens with a luxuriance which seems unattainable in gardens where all conditions appear to be so much more favorable? The great masses of hepaticas, for instance, in the cottagers' gardens in some of the western shires are unsurpassed, while the clumps (sometimes almost forests) of madonna lilies are the envy of passers-by, and the climbers by which the cottage is often half hidden seem to grow with more enjoyment than anywhere else. Perhaps the reason may not be further to seek than in the employment of materials well suited to the climate and conditions, for there is no doubt that common plants well grown are more decorative than half starved specimens of more brilliant things, for whose proper cultivation the requisite means are not attainable; and a cottage porch smothered with honeysuckles and some old fashioned rose is about as pleasant a sight as can be seen, in spite of the climbers being neither rare nor costly. But the supposition that the denizens of cottage gardens are so fine because they are indigenous or exceptionally hardy plants is not sufficient to account for the handsome subjects there so often met with. The finest Catherine Mermet I ever saw was climbing on the chimney of a cottage by the roadside in Surrey, and in a similar position in another part of the same county I have seen blooms of Gloire de Dijon such as I have never seen elsewhere, even in celebrated rose gardens. Every one will doubtless recall Canon Reynolds Hole's description of the noble specimens upon the walls of a cottage of the glorious but hardly-to-be-flowered Noisette, Cloth of Gold, which so rarely gets sun enough to ripen its shoots in this climate, and even more rarely succeeds in preserving them uninjured until the flowering time. I myself have experienced the pangs of jealousy when passing a house masked with a climbing devoniensis in full bloom, the cultural attention to which consisted in its being occasionally gone over with a long handled bill hook, such as is used in trimming hedges, "just to keep the shoots from rattlin' on the windows."

In spite of these seemingly anomalous instances, however, the real reason of the presence of striking specimens in cottage gardens will probably be found in the fact that, not being too numerous, each plant is tended and looked after with the greatest care. The precious and carefully collected road scrapings, not having to be spread over too wide an area, are heaped round special favorites to provide at once food and protection, and thus is encouraged that luxuriance of growth which renders possible the rose covered porches of our Surrey cottages, whereby a pleasant feast of brightness is afforded to weary travelers passing by.

It is remarkable how seldom the white rose (double or garden variety of Rosa alba) is to be seen in any but cottage gardens, and the same may be said of its near relation, the maiden's blush. Such good roses, capable as they are of highly ornamental treatment and so individually charming, certainly deserve more general culture than they receive. The white rose does equally well as a bush five feet to six feet high, or as a low climber. The cottage porch we engrave shows it in the latter form, trained to meet a honeysuckle in the front, the training not overdone, but with that happy knack of supporting and guiding without apparently constraining, that best shows the beauty and natural growth of rambling plants.

ROSE ARCHES.

The mode of decorating our gardens with arches of roses carried over paths seems of late years to have gone very much out of fashion, although roses so grown may be made to constitute a very attractive feature, a fact to which an engraving in a recent *Garden* abundantly testifies. It has been urged that rose arches are always ineffective or inconvenient, and generally both; but if so, the reason is probably to be found in a want of skill in the cultivator or constructor, or both. For there is no design that is safe from being made to appear ridiculous through its attempted execution in ill chosen materials. A house built of bricks and stucco from designs intended to be carried out in stone would not be more grotesque than the gaunt iron arch one sometimes sees with a stunted rose bush growing half way up each of its pillars. Such an arrangement certainly is ineffective, but then it is not a rose arch. Where there has been a want of success in making rose arches decorative, the failure may usually be attributed to one of two causes—either an attempt to furnish them with roses entirely unfitted for the purpose, or the employment of too many varieties. The number of available sorts is not large, and perhaps a dozen names would exhaust the list of first rate kinds, but the employment of these or any twelve different roses upon some half a dozen arches would effectually preclude the possibility of anything like a fine display. On the other hand, what could be more striking than such a series of arches, each arch densely wreathed with the evergreen Felicite perpetuelle, probably the best of all varieties for the purpose, with its rampant growth, its dark green persistent foliage, and its myriad pure white flowers, each one a perfect rosette? If numerous varieties are employed, the result is seldom satisfactory from a decorative point of view, because the different sorts will not flower at the same time; but this difficulty is obviated by using only one variety at a time, whereby the striking effect obtainable by having a number of arches of roses simultaneously sheeted with bloom is insured.

In case of the employment of several varieties on a series of arches, each arch, at any rate, should be covered with one rose, and not have two different kinds planted beside its two pillars, so that at the flowering time each arch, at least, may be complete, rather than have one half blossoming while the other half is green or bare. Even if they can be induced to bloom at the same time, unless they are of the same class and habit, the effect of two different roses mixed up together is generally somewhat incongruous and unpleasing.

In the selection of varieties, the qualities to look for, in addition to the obvious essentials of rampant growth and profusion of bloom, are hardiness, pliability, persistence of foliage—which foliage should be handsome, but only of moderate size, as the very large leaved roses, when grown on arches, get their leaves so lacerated by the wind and soon look untidy—and comparative freedom from the more disfiguring of rose pests, such as mildew, etc. In addition to Felicite perpetuelle, which is unsurpassed as an arch rose, there may also be mentioned as fulfilling the above conditions the Ayrshire splendens, whose white flowers, less regular in outline than those of the last-named, are relieved by a slight pink edge. These two varieties are the pick of their respective classes, but if a pink variety in the same section be desired, there is no fault to be found with the hybrid Laure Davoust, whose charming pink flowers are produced in immense clusters, except that in the north it is not quite hardy enough to avoid some disfigurement in a severe winter, unless it be somewhat protected with bracken, or such covering. In the southern counties, however, both this and the climbing Aimee Vibert, or Aimee Vibert scandens, as it is sometimes pedantically called, make good arch roses, and the two are sufficiently near in character to make a good pair, the one pink and the other white, where several sorts are desired. But when it comes to the noisettes, there are two varieties of which use should be made whenever possible; for if not perfectly hardy they are well worth the slight protection of fern, which renders them so. The first of these is Reve d'Or, an exceedingly vigorous rose and the hardiest of its class—a rose which could not be considered otherwise than a highly ornamental plant, even if it never flowered, for its young shoots are brilliant red, and the handsome foliage is rarely without some bright tint; but its character does not belie its name, and the wealth of golden and tawny blossoms displayed constitutes truly enough a vision of gold, and not a fleeting vision like an every-day dream either, for the flowering only ends when the frosts begin.

The second variety is the now well known and deservedly popular William Allen Richardson, not so rampant as Reve d'Or, but quite sturdily vigorous enough for all practical purposes, and very nearly, if not quite, as hardy as the latter. At any rate numerous plants of William Allen Richardson of various forms passed uninjured through the trying winter of 1885-86 with only the slight protection of a few fronds of bracken twisted among them, which all teas and noisettes deserve, and are the better for in hard weather; and, as far as can be seen at present, the long spell of cold now coming (it is to be hoped) to an end, although the thermometer twice registered upward of 25° of frost, has not inflicted appreciable injury on plants of this delightful noisette, whose decorative value is enhanced by the fact that the bright orange color of its flowers is unique among roses, while the plant is almost evergreen and thoroughly autumnal.

Red roses that are available for training over arches are few and far between, but the hybrid tea Reine Marie Henriette is a first rate variety for the purpose, and, growing with immense vigor, produces its bright, clear red flowers in abundance throughout the season. The attractive semi-double red hybrid tea or hybrid noisette Reine Olga de Wurtemburg, which was figured in the *Garden* early last year, would make an admirable arch rose, but for the solitary objection that its magnificent foliage is liable soon to become "tattered and torn" by the action of the wind when this rose giant is grown anywhere away from a wall. But a lack of good hardy red climbing roses is no reason for ignoring good hardy climbers that are ready to hand, even though they be not bright colored; and there are two single roses which are both better worth growing to cover arches than all the hybrid perpetuals so often recommended put together. One is Rosa brunonis, often called the Himalayan brier, which makes incredibly long shoots, enough to furnish an arch in a single season, and of which the pretty bluish green foliage is almost hidden at the flowering time by the mass of snowy single blossoms. The other, last, but not least in value at any rate, is Rosa polyantha, a Japanese sub species of R. multiflora, and one of the most attractive roses in cultivation. It has all the recommendations enumerated above. It grows with the utmost luxuriance, and regularly becomes smothered with blossom. M. Jean Sisley, of Lyons, declares his belief that it is the hardiest rose in existence. It may be easily trained in any direction. The foliage hangs on late, and though composed of many leaflets, the leaflet is not large, and the plant appears almost exempt from mildew. Moreover, it will grow in any soil or situation, it roots as a cutting with the greatest readiness, and its white flowers, though individually small, are produced in such immense trusses as to be highly decorative, while their delicious fragrance scents the air for yards round a large plant in blossom. Under these circumstances, the only wonder is that this plant is not abundant in all gardens where roses are appreciated; but the fact probably is, that too many gardeners still consider single flowers a reproach to a rose, which no other merits can compensate.

CLIMBING ROSE ON PORCH OF COTTAGE.

There are many other roses which are often included in lists of kinds said to be desirable as arch roses, such as the Boursaults, which, however, cannot conscientiously be recommended on account of their dreary coloring. Again, the charming rose which goes under the name of Fortune's yellow is too tender to be grown in this country anywhere but against a wall—a position which it thoroughly deserves; and the same may be said of the banksias. None of the mosses are of real value for the purpose. Lanei is the only one of sufficient vigor, and that is too stiff and rigid to be ornamental. One or two hybrid chinas, such as Blairi No. 2, may be employed, but all the hybrid perpetuals practically involve an outlay of time and trouble by no means repaid by the effect produced; while the few gallicas, etc., that might possibly be available are such victims to mildew as to be hardly ever otherwise than an eyesore.

In arranging rose arches it must, of course, be borne in mind that it is essential that things intended for use be eminently usable; and if arches are made across a path, care must be taken that they do not make such path inconvenient for traffic. Thus, the pillars of an arch should be at least three feet from each margin of the walk spanned, in order that the dresses of passers-by may be safe from the thorny shoots; and if the walk be six feet wide, this will give a base of twelve feet wide, for which a central height of ten feet will be found to give an effective and practical arch. Where there is to be a series of arches, they should be at least three yards or four yards apart, and each arch should be composed entirely of iron, for if the uprights be made of wood they soon give way at the ground line, especially when the plants trained upon them become vigorous and offer considerable resistance to the wind. The only objection to iron uprights is that from their smaller diameter they are less convenient to train plants to than wooden posts; but any difficulty arising from this may be obviated by fixing a few horizontal cross bars on to the iron uprights, and to these the rose shoots can be tied so as to avoid undue crowding in the earlier stages of growth. The best way of planting is to put in two trees of the same kind, one at the foot of each upright, and then by liberal culture to encourage the most vigorous growth possible; but if a variety is used which does not furnish well, there is no reason why two or three plants of it should not be planted at either pillar in order to get the arch more completely wreathed. Then, if varieties well adapted to the purpose be employed, the shoots from the two sides will soon meet across the center, and, interlacing, form a triumphal arch or series of arches.—*The Garden.*

A $3,500 DWELLING.

We give herewith elevations and plans for a $3,500 house, by H. C. Palmer, architect, to be erected at Jersey City Heights, N. J. The estimate includes the "modern conveniences." The house presents a pleasing appearance, and the plans are considered satisfactory.

Women as Architects.

C. Harrison Townsend, a London architect of some note, writes in the *Pall Mall Gazette* on this subject. His remarks refer to the girl and young woman of the middle class, and he asks, "What really valid objection is there to asking her to become a 'draughtswoman,' and in due course an architect?"

The requisites for the preparation of architectural drawings are neatness and delicacy of touch, attention to detail, patience, and care, which women ought to possess more than men.

The present course of architectural training in England is as follows:

A youth on leaving school with an aptitude, more or less, for the profession, is articled as pupil for four or five years to an architect, to whom he pays a premium. This is, of course, in proportion to the position and repute of the architect in question, but may be stated at from a hundred pounds to four or five times that amount. As with solicitors, so among architects, the pupil is supposed by having "the run of the office," to acquire an intimate knowledge of its work—design, draughtsmanship, knowledge of materials, official routine, and so on. If a young fellow of parts, he soon begins "to feel his legs" and to understand his work, and, if wise, supplements his office instruction by attendance at the admirable classes of the architectural association and elsewhere. At the end of his articles he is qualified to dub himself a "junior draughtsman," in which capacity he claims salary from a pound to two

pounds a week. A couple of years should then see him a draughtsman proper, and in a position to obtain three, three and a half, or four guineas a week. In many cases, of course, thanks to such "backing" of his friends as he may be fortunate enough to get, the lucky pupil can set up on his own account immediately his articles are completed.

In this training Mr. Townsend finds but two objections. The first one is the "commingling of the sexes" which would result from their introduction to an office. This objection is proved to be invalid by the American experience in using females in all kinds of office work without trouble. But a "women clerks' room" would remove that conservative objection. The other objection is that attached to the inspection of buildings under construction. To those not wishing to encounter this objection. the way to drawing board work and competition in plans, interior decoration, etc., is open.

FRONT   SIDE

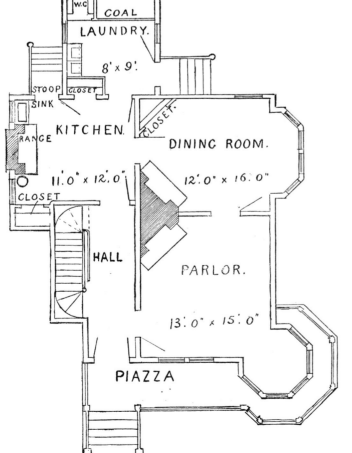

FIRST FLOOR.

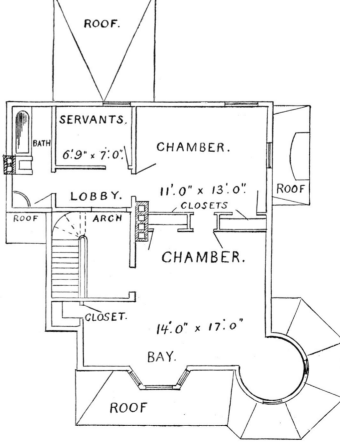

SECOND FLOOR.

A $3,500 DWELLING.

SCIENTIFIC AMERICAN

ARCHITECTS AND BUILDERS EDITION.

Entered at the Post Office of

New York as Second Class Matter.

Vol. IV.   Subscription, $2.50 a Year.   NEW YORK, AUGUST, 1887.   Single Copies, 25 Cents.   No. 2.

RESIDENCE, CORNER OF EIGHTH AVENUE AND BERKELEY STREET, BROOKLYN.

This house was designed for Mr. H E. Beguelin by F. Carles Merry, architect, of New York.

It is built mainly of brick with terra cotta trimmings, except the first story front on Eighth Ave., which is of Euclid stone.

Seven-foot-four Circulars.

It takes perfection to bar out improvement, and it is often taken for granted that an article of manufacture is perfect when it is not. The circular saw is a thing of slow growth. Various trade papers insist in keeping on deck an item to the effect that a man named Cummings, whose remains rest near Kalamazoo, Mich., was

making is a circular eighty-eight inches in diameter—the largest ever made—and of eleven gauge. It was manufactured by E. C. Atkins & Co., Indianapolis, Ind., and is in use in the mill of Hurd & Co., at, or near, Xenia, Ind. One may properly ask, What next? Will the time come when circulars will be made so large that no double or three saw rigs will be necessary

RESIDENCE CORNER EIGHTH AVENUE AND BERKELEY STREET, BROOKLYN.
F. CARLES MERRY, ARCHITECT.

The entrance doorway has been treated in Romanesque.

The entrance hall and staircase are designed in a very original manner, in "Old Colonial," of cherry.

The parlor is finished in mahogany. The dining room is of oak, while the library walls and ceiling are entirely wainscoted in oak of very pleasing effect. The upper stories are finished in cherry and ash.

The building, which is elaborately decorated throughout, has a frontage of 40 ft. on Eighth Ave. and of 47 ft. 6 in. on Berkeley Place, and was erected at a total cost of $35,000.

the inventor of the circular, notwithstanding it was invented before Cummings was born, and possibly before Cummings' father was born. It is within forty years, however, that the circular has become a success in the saw mill. Within that period circulars placed in Michigan mills were not satisfactory, and were made to give place to the straight saw. At first the thicker the saw, the better. It had never entered the mind of man that a thin saw would answer the requirements. Gradually saws of larger diameter and thinner gauge were made. It was discovered that speed gave backbone to a saw. The latest achievement in saw

for converting the monstrous redwood logs into lumber?—*N. W. Lumberman.*

MARBLE may be stained or dyed of various colors by applying the solutions mentioned below to the stone, made sufficiently hot so that the liquid will just simmer on the surface. Blue, tincture of litmus; brown, tincture of logwood: crimson, a solution of alkanet root in oil of turpentine; green, tincture of sap green; red, tincture of dragon's blood or cochineal; yellow, tincture of gamboge or turmeric. Success in the application of the colors requires considerable experience.

SCIENTIFIC AMERICAN

ARCHITECTS AND BUILDERS EDITION

Entered at the Post Office of · New York as Second Class Matter.

NEW YORK, OCTOBER, 1887.

Vol. IV. Subscription, $2.50 a Year. Single Copies, 25 Cents. No. 4.

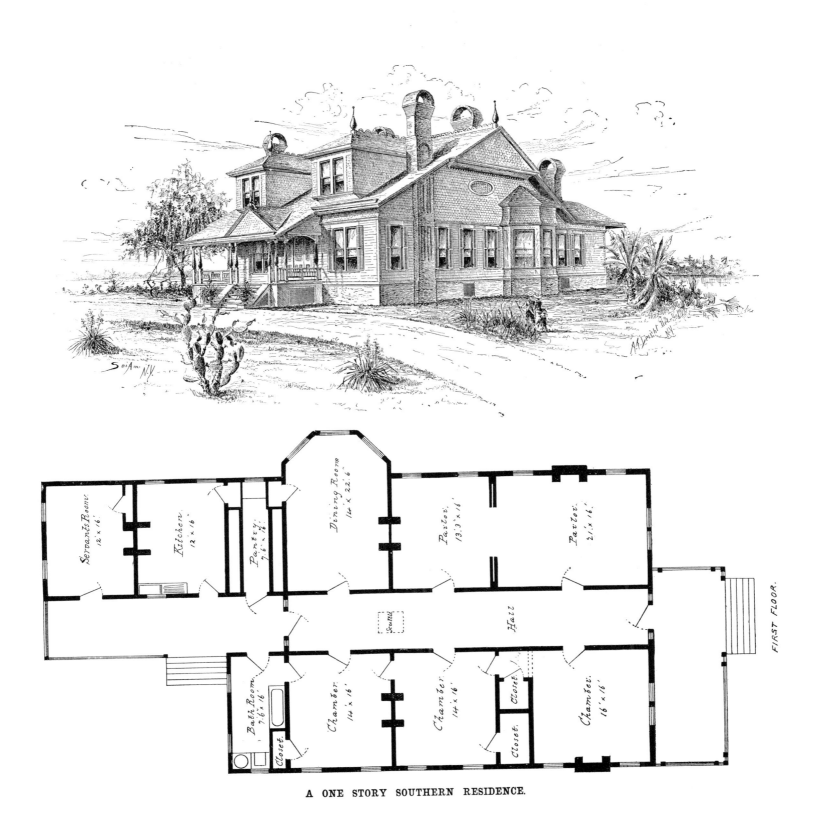

A ONE STORY SOUTHERN RESIDENCE.

A $2,500 CALIFORNIA HOUSE.

California can justly boast of a larger number of pretty places and picturesque localities in which to erect residences of moderate cost than can be found in any other State in the Union. The beautiful town of Alameda, covering, as it does, a large extent of ground, embracing several square miles, may be regarded as a paradise for those who wish a quiet retreat, away from the din and confusion of the city, and yet be in close connection with the great mart. Nearly every portion of the town is covered with a natural growth of oak trees. Nor does this growth stop at this point. For a long distance to the north the ground is covered by the beautiful trees from which the neighboring city of Oakland derives its name.

Extremes meet in architecture as well as other matters. Some æsthetic persons have sought to copy the humble abode of the laborer in the external view of a dwelling, while the internal arrangements and fittings rival those of Aladdin's palace. Others seek to have the outside present to the eye a conglomeration of whimsical ideas, while they have not deigned to cover the floors with a carpet, nor have a door between any of the rooms or halls, excepting those connecting with the outer world.

Much benefit has been derived from these whimsical erections, and it is only by much study and close application to the fancies of their clients that architects have been enabled to prepare the beautiful bijou plans, a good representation of which is given in this issue. In justice to the architectural profession, we must say that no portion of their practice has been so usefully bestowed as that which has been bestowed upon the production of plans for such homes, a full plan of which accompanies this article.

The elevation, as shown, is a model of neatness and economy. At once attractive in appearance and substantial in all its surroundings, it does away with all those horrible idiosyncrasies and bugbears of the Elizabethan and Queen Anne styles. There are no small windows to cause the one who cleans them to utter a whole vocabulary of cuss words at the architect who made so many corners to dig out. There is no part of California but what needs all the sunshine that was intended to enter a room, and the large windows shown allow the heat and light to make glad the hearts of the dwellers therein. Even with the thermometer at 100 degrees and over in the shade at noontime, still, when evening comes, the cool winds that invariably bless the sleep of those who are tired from their daily toil has easy ingress from these same large windows. And in winter, from the absence of snow in all of our beautiful valleys, the same windows are a source of joy and comfort for the occupants to observe the driving rains, or admit the blessed sunshine as it pierces through the wintry clouds.

Great care should be exercised in painting the exterior. The colors selected should be a happy blending of light and dark shades. They should be graded from rich, heavy grades at the bottom to the lighter tones at the gable peaks, preserving, through the intermediate section, a consistent harmony. The roof may be of dark slate color. The trimmings may be colored with a combination of blue, black, and Indian red. The body of the house may be varied to suit the above. It must be distinctly borne in mind that all buildings of the same class cannot be treated alike. Trees have a wonderful effect on colors used, and the main study of the painter and owner should be that the salient points of form and detail be enhanced by the proper selection of the various colors. By all means, if you are building a home for yourself, take the good wife into your confidence, and let her judgment be given on the various colors to be used.

The arrangement of the rooms, as shown by the plan, is very desirable for any one with a small family. A feature is made of the entrance way. From the hall, one can pass either to the parlor or dining room, the latter being the general sitting room. The parlor is large—13×17 feet in size. It has a fireplace, as shown. A cornice is also designated. Sliding doors connect this room with the dining room, the size of the lat-

A CALIFORNIA HOUSE FOR $2,500.

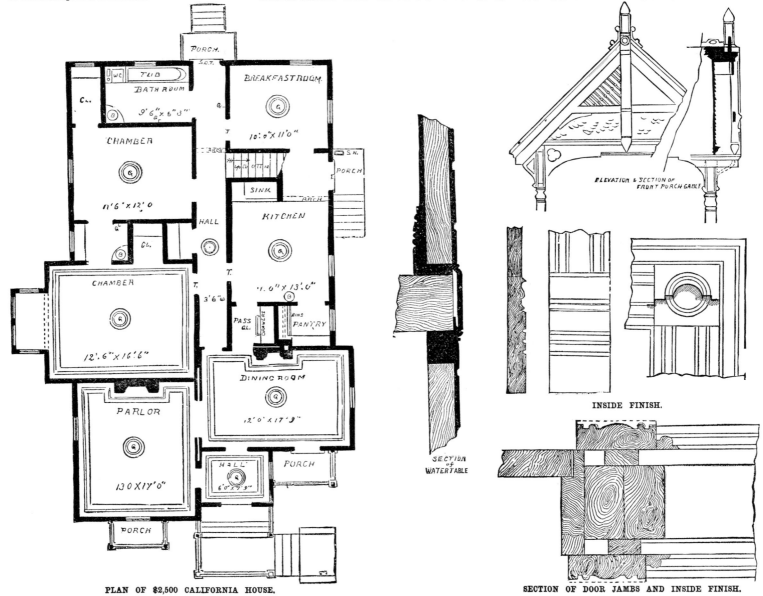

PLAN OF $2,500 CALIFORNIA HOUSE.

SECTION OF DOOR JAMBS AND INSIDE FINISH.

ter being 12×17¾ feet. A cornice and fireplace are also shown. In case of company or family gathering, the two rooms will be practically one. The porch shown in front will be very handy for the gentlemen who smoke, or, on warm days the ladies can use the same for sewing purposes, sheltered, as the plans show, by the roof overhead.

You pass from this room into a hall, from which you can enter all the rest of the rooms. The main chamber is 12 feet 6 inches by 16 feet 6 inches, besides a large bay window, having four windows for light and air. There is also a cornice in this room, and a place for a stove to connect with parlor chimney. There is a very large closet, and also wash room, which is well lighted and ventilated. Passing along the hall, we next come to a large linen closet. This will be found very serviceable for the storage of the linen in daily use. Then comes a large chamber, 11 feet 6 inches by 12 feet. No cornice is shown. Should a fire be needed in this room, a patent flue could be placed therein, starting from near the ceiling. A large closet is also connected with this room. At the end of the hall is the bath room, 6 feet 3 inches by 9 feet 6 inches. A wash bowl and water closet are shown. The window, being directly over the tub, assures perfect ventilation.

On opposite side of hall from bath room is a room designated as breakfast room, in size 10×11 feet, with two windows. This can be used as a bed room, should the dining room suffice for the needs of the occupants of the house. This room is very convenient, as it can be reached by three different ways. The next room is the kitchen, in size 10×13 feet, with plenty of light and ample means of ventilation. The place for the stovepipe is indicated by the dotted lines leading to the dining room chimney. Should it be found more desirable to have the stove in a different position from that indicated, a patent flue can be put in, starting near the ceiling. A large pass closet, amply fitted with drawers and shelves, connects with the dining room. There is also a large pantry fitted up with bins, etc.

A stairway is shown, near breakfast room, leading to the attic. No plan is given of the latter, as the space can be divided according to the individual tastes of the parties building. The rear hall is 3 feet 6 inches wide.

The whole plan is very compact, and will bear careful study. The detail drawings, as shown, will give an adequate idea of the various finishes. Each one is distinctly marked.

We append a general set of specifications to aid those who may see fit to adopt the design. Should any one want a complete set, we can forward them a printed copy.

SPECIFICATIONS.

Excavations.—All rock, dirt, etc., to be cleared away from site of the building. Trenches for walls and piers

to be extended down to firm and solid ground. The bank to be dug well away from the walls, and the same to be left open until the walls are well set and dry.

Drains.—To be of ironstone pipe, with cemented joints. The fall to be not less than one-fourth inch to one foot. No drains to be less than sixteen inches from surface of ground.

Brick Work.—Hard, well burned brick to be used throughout. All brick walls to be made level and straight to the proper and exact height, and to a true line from one end to the other, even to the splitting of a brick where necessary. Piers 12×12 inches. Turn trimmer arches for the support of all hearths at the time chimneys are built. All sills to be set in mortar after walls are proper height.

Size of Timbers, etc.—Main sills, 6×8 inches; plates, 2×4; studs, 2×4; underpinning, 4×6; joists, 2×10; ceiling joists 2×4; rafters, 2×4; bridging, 2×3 and 2×4. Studs and joists spaced 16 inches from center; rafters, 2 feet 8 inches from center; underpinning 2 feet 8 inches from center. All timber below main sills to be of redwood.

Roof to be sheathed with 1×6 Oregon pine, well nailed to every rafter. Gutters arranged so as to carry off water wherever directed.

Rustic.—All laps and butt joints to be painted before being nailed in position. Butt joints to have a 3×11 inch piece of tin to keep out water.

Outside Steps to be built upon strong stringers, inch risers of redwood, and two inch treads of Oregon pine, with nosing and scotia. The recess to front hall will be floored six inches below main floor, with three inch Oregon pine, put together with white lead.

Floors.—Oregon pine, tongued and grooved, 4 inches wide, to be used throughout the house. One tongue nail and one through nail to be driven in each piece at each nailing.

Grounds to be of ¾ in. Oregon pine at all openings. *No inside finish to be put on until the last coat of plastering is on.*

Face casings to be 6 inches wide and 1¼ inches thick, with suitable plinths.

Sash beads to be fastened on with raised head screws.

All interior work to be hand-smoothed and sand-papered.

All carved or planted-on work to be primed before putting up.

Bases in all rooms to be 10 inches wide, with 2 inch moulding.

Wainscoting.—Rear hall, kitchen, and breakfast room to be wainscoted 3 feet high, and capped with nosing and scotia. Bath room, 6 feet high all around.

Pantry and Pass Closet to be fitted up with shelves and hooks complete, and bins and drawers as shown.

Lathing.—Good sound lath to be used, laid on not less than ⅜ of an inch apart. Joints broken over 8 laths. No lath to be put on vertically, to finish out to corners or angles; neither must there be any lath run through angles and behind studding from one room to another. All angles to be formed and nailed solid by carpenter before laths are put on.

Plastering.—All walls, partitions, and ceilings to be plastered one coat of well haired mortar, made of best lime and clean, sharp sand, free from loam and salt, using best cattle hair. To be made at least eight days before using.

Brown coat to be covered with a good coat of best white hard finish. All plastering to extend to the floor. Center pieces where designated on plans.

Painting.—All interior wood work to have three coats of best white lead, in such tints as may be approved by the owner. Kitchen floor to be oiled two coats.

Gas Pipes to be introduced so as to give the number of lights shown on plans.

Plumbing.—Water pipes to be of galvanized iron ¾ inch diameter. No ½ inch pipe to be used. A 40 gallon galvanized iron boiler, with necessary connections,

to be placed in the kitchen. Sink to be of size shown by drawing, to have 2 inch iron water pipe and a Garland trap; 3½ inch brass strainer; back of sink to be lined with zinc. Slop hoppers to be placed as shown. Wash basins to be located as per plan, and to have all necessary hot and cold water connections. Water from all basins to discharge into an open slop hopper outside. Bath tub to be lined with No. 12 zinc, to have a 1¼ inch waste, with Garland trap. All necessary fixtures for bath tub to be placed in proper position. The water closet to be Budde's patent. Place safe trays under all sinks, bath tub, wash basins, water closets, etc., with 2 inch turned-up edges, well nailed to wood work. Three fourths inch wastes. All waste or soil pipes to be connected with the sewer, and extend the same above basins, sinks, bath tub, water closets, etc., out through the roof.

Generally.—Drawings and specifications are intended to correspond, and to be illustrative the one of the other. All drawings to be furnished by the architect. Details to be given from time to time as the work progresses. Should the necessity arise that any change or changes be made from the original design, the owner shall have the right so to do without invalidating the contract, adding to or deducting from the contract price the agreed sum of any change made.

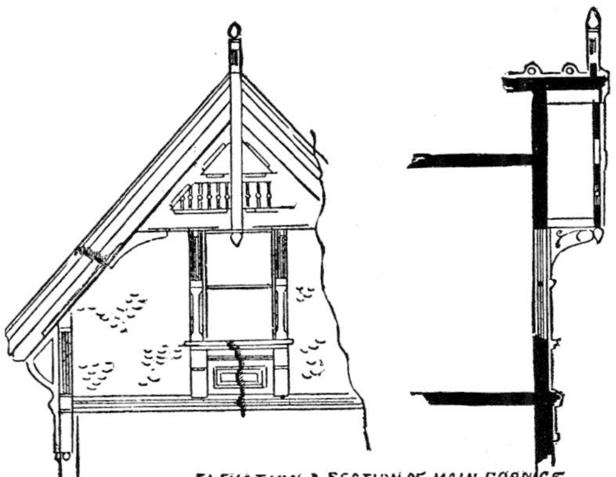

COST.

The above specifications are given as a general index of the work. No accurate estimate can be given from them of the cost of the house. Quality and price of hardware, etc., have been omitted, leaving same to the pocket books of intending builders. As shown, with finishes indicated by the details given, the house can be erected at a cost of about $2,500. Of course this figure can be changed considerably. Using the best of materials, etc., the price should be given at $3,000, at which sum a truly cozy home can be obtained by those seeking a permanent dwelling place.—*California Architect.*

The Architectural Era.

This is the title of a new monthly published at Syracuse, N. Y. It is finely printed, handsomely illustrated, and full of interesting reading matter. It forms a valuable addition to the architectural literature of the day. The elegant style in which it is produced does honor

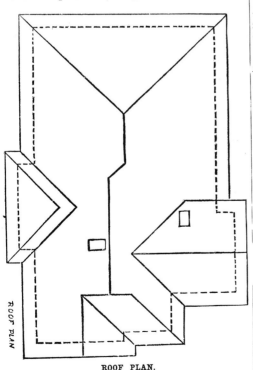

ROOF PLAN.

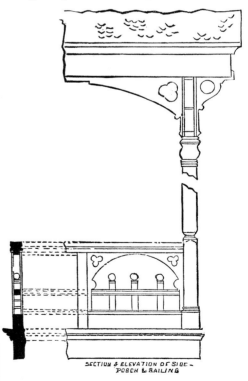

SECTION & ELEVATION OF SIDE PORCH & RAILING

to its enterprising publishers, Messrs. D. Mason & Co. Three dollars a year, twenty-five cents per number.

Blue Marking Ink for Boxes, Bales, etc.

Mix a sufficient quantity of ultramarine with barytes (sulphate of barium, blanc fix) and water to produce the desired tint. It may be rendered more permanent by adding some liquid glue (solution of glue in acetic acid) or some starch paste, prepared with the addition of a little wax.—*Chem. and Drug.*

A CALIFORNIA HOUSE FOR $2,500.

ELEVATION & SECTION OF MAIN CORNICE GABLE, ½ C.T.

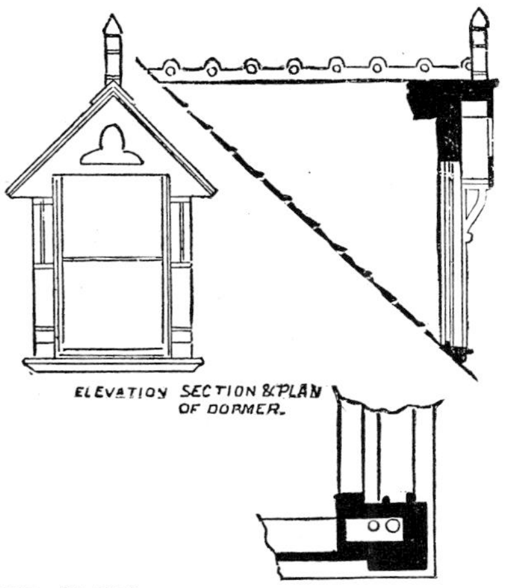

ELEVATION SECTION & PLAN OF DORMER.

THE NEW MASONIC TEMPLE AT NEWPORT, KY.

We present an engraving of the new Masonic Temple at Newport, Ky., lately erected from the designs of Samuel D. Peacock, architect, Cincinnati, O., who gives us the following particulars :

The building is built of common brick and white mortar. The front is tinted where there is freestone and black brick. The caps and sills on the sides are all freestone, and also all chimney caps. The cornices and front gable ornaments are made of galvanized iron.

floors. The building, when completed, will have American plate glass in front and on the side of the first story.

The cost complete, with freestone sidewalk and all, was $23,000.

Clay Roofing Tile.

In a recent number of the *Brick, Tile, and Metal Review*, we find the following account of the manufacture of roofing tile as carried on at Akron, Ohio. Or-

shape, and then to press it into the required shape. The pressed tiles are removed and set in piles to dry. Drying takes about two weeks in a steam heated chamber, as the oil used in the pressing of the clay hinders the escape of the water.

"They are finally piled in loose order in a kiln to a depth of about 6 ft., and subjected to a light burn. The kilns employed are circular down draughts. The ware is of several classes. Shingle tile, which are more like shingles than anything else, are slabs of burnt clay

THE NEW MASONIC TEMPLE AT NEWPORT, KY.

The roof is best Virginia black slate. The fourth floor, over the main hall, is carried by two iron box girders, weighing 8½ tons each, and manufactured by the Keystone Bridge Co., of Pittsburg, Pa.

The second floor will be occupied as offices. The third and fourth floors will be occupied by the Masonic fraternity of Newport, Ky. The building is finished in Southern yellow pine and black walnut, oiled, varnished, and rubbed down with pumice stone and oil.

The floors are all double and deadened. The top floor is tongued and grooved yellow pine, and no board is over three inches wide. The joists are all poplar. There is a cornice around the ceilings of the third and fourth

dinary brick clay is used. "The grinding and tempering is done in tracers, such as used for sewer pipe. When tempered, whatever is put into the cylinder is forced out at the end of the stroke in a series of parallel plates, about 6 in. wide by ⅜ in. thick, and extending along until cut up in lengths. Considerable oil is used to keep the clay smooth and to keep the freshly pressed plates from sticking. These plates are adjusted, one after another, on a series of disks arranged on the circumference of a circular revolving disk. This disk moves through one-sixth of its circumference at a stroke, boring in succession each plate of clay spread out on its table under a compound piston. This piston is arranged to cut off the edge of the plate in a symmetrical

12×6 in. × ⅜ in., with holes in proper places for nailing them to the roof. Their uses are as nearly like those of a real shingle as well can be. About 5 in. of each tile are exposed to the weather. The so-called diamond tile ' are made to hook into each other, but are also supplemented by nails. They are more ornamental than the shingle tiles, but as they are more dependent on each other for support, they are not so durable or strong. One of the chief objections to a tile roof is its weight ; a 10 ft. square of plain shingle tile weighs about 1,100 pounds, and the same area of diamond tile weighs from 650 to 850 pounds. The advantages claimed for them are durability, beauty, and immunity from danger by fire or lightning."

SCIENTIFIC AMERICAN

ARCHITECTS AND BUILDERS EDITION.

Entered at the Post Office of New York as Second Class Matter.

Vol. V. Subscription, $2.50 a Year. NEW YORK, FEBRUARY, 1888. Single Copies, 25 Cents. No. 2.

AN APARTMENT HOUSE—GEORGE H. GRIEBEL, ARCHITECT, NEW YORK.

SCIENTIFIC AMERICAN

ARCHITECTS AND BUILDERS EDITION

Entered at the Post Office of   New York as Second Class Matter.

NEW YORK, APRIL, 1888.

Vol. V.   Subscription, $2.50 a Year.   Single Copies, 25 Cents.   No. 4.

THE CALDWELL HOTEL AT BIRMINGHAM, ALA.—EDOUARD SIDEL, ARCHITECT.

69

A COUNTRY HOUSE IN CONNECTICUT.

We give from *Building* a sketch of a country residence designed for an elevation. Architects, Rossiter & Wright, New York. The house presents a substan-

increase. Their roots and leaves do not thrive well, and the plant is soon reduced to living upon its own substance. We here have a phenomenon of autophagy, which is shown first by the yellowing and then by the

the fact that they do, for these plants are admirably adapted to the ornamenting of apartments. The number of these flowers of so simple culture is quite large. Yet all do not succeed with the same ease.

A COUNTRY HOUSE IN CONNECTICUT.

tial appearance, and the design is in many respects desirable.

BULBOUS PLANTS FOR APARTMENTS.

Whoever occupies himself with plants likes to see them grow and prosper before his eyes. Yet every one knows that it is often difficult to cultivate flowers in our dwellings, close to us, and usually it is necessary to limit one's ambition to seeing them preserved in the room and to prolonging their existence in the surroundings in which one is placed. The reason is that the majority of the elements necessary for their development are totally wanting, and that other agents, on the contrary, act upon them unfavorably. What they especially need is light, and what injures them most is the dryness of the air and the action of the dust.

There are, however, certain plants that will grow and thrive in rooms, and these have the inappreciable advantage of allowing us to witness their development; and they afford us the pleasure of following step by step the progress that is made each day.

It may be of interest to know to what cause this peculiar manner of behaving is due. The ordinary plants that we have in our rooms do not find in their surroundings the elements necessary for the formation of the materials that must make provision for their

withering of the basal leaves, that is to say, those that are the oldest.

Mr. Deherain has shown that most plants, at the time of the maturing of their seeds, utilize the useful

Fig. 3.—HYACINTHS IN PORCELAIN BASKET.

principles stored up in their organs by a phenomenon of migration. He has shown that in wheat, for example, the leaves gradually become exhausted of the useful elements that they contain in order to concur in the formation of the seed. What occurs in the plant that has reached a normal state at the end of its development operates in every vegetable which, placed in unfavorable surroundings, can no longer manufacture in sufficient quantity the materials necessary for its increase. It therefore draws upon the provision made by the old leaves, which soon become yellow and drop off. But such provision is not sufficient to permit the plant to grow indefinitely, and the latter is soon exhausted and dies.

Bulbous plants have the advantage over all others of containing a supply of food in the bulb that permits them to provide for the development of leaves. This is not a simple hypothesis; experiment on the one hand and direct observation on the other decide in favor of this view. In fact, if we preserve the bulbs that have been cultivated in a room, and plant them in a garden the next year, it will be found, not without surprise perhaps, that they will produce scarcely any leaves, and that, at all events, no flowers will be obtained. The reason of this is that the plant, at the time it was cultivated in a room, became exhausted of all the useful elements contained in its bulb, and that the leaves and roots have not been able to form a new supply of food again.

Whatever be the cause that allows bulbous plants to develop easily in our dwellings, it is interesting to know

For certain of them, it suffices to put the bulb in contact with water to see it soon produce roots that will rapidly elongate and live in the liquid element. For this sort of culture, special vases have been devised that are provided at the top with a wide mouth in which the bulb may be placed (Fig. 1).

Of all bulbous plants, the hyacinth—that charming plant with racemes of bells of all shades, so elegant and with so penetrating a perfume—is the one best adapted to this sort of culture. The production of its bulb in Holland, where it is specially cultivated, has given rise to a very large business. All varieties of it, however, are not equally adapted to culture in vases. Those with simple flowers and strong roots give the best results. The varieties with double flowers have the disadvantage that they often expand imperfectly.

Now is the time of the year when the culture succeeds best. It is well to select large and healthy bulbs, and to so place them in the vase previously filled with water that the latter shall touch their lower part. These vases may, for a time, be placed in a closet. It is important that the place in which they are put shall be only middlingly warm, for too great a heat would make the leaves develop before the roots, and the flowers would be stunted. As soon as the roots are numer-

Fig. 2.—POTTED CROCUSES.

Fig. 1.—HYACINTHS IN VASES.

ous and the leaves begin to appear, the moment has arrived for placing the plants in the light. On a table near a window is the place best suited to them, although they are capable of growing far away from the direct light. In most cases, it is well to support the racemes of flowers with a prop in order to prevent them from lopping over.

This prop should be a slender stick, which, sharp at one end, may be stuck into the bulb and be tied to the raceme, the number of flowers in which often renders it so heavy that it cannot preserve its rigidity. Then we shall soon see the flowers opening one by one, and the elegant raceme of bells will send its penetrating perfume throughout the entire room, and we shall enjoy them for a long time.

Sometimes, by way of amusement, the hyacinth is made to flower abnormally. Two bulbs are placed in a glass vase having a large aperture at each extremity. One of the bulbs is placed in the bottom, upside down, the vase is filled with earth, and the second bulb is placed in the top, right side up. This vase is set upon another one filled with water. In a short time the two bulbs will develop, one growing normally, and the other throwing its leaves and flowers down into the vase filled with water (Fig. 1).

The culture of bulbous plants in apartments allows of very varied combinations. Very good success is obtained by planting the bulbs in earth simply. For some years past, quite an extensive series of models of earthen vases, especially adapted for this culture, have been sold in Parisian stores. One of those best adapted to the happiest combinations is shown in Fig. 2. It consists of a spherical earthen vessel containing numerous apertures in its sides. In front of each of these holes is placed a flowering bulb, and the vessel is then filled with earth, or with chopped-up moss rammed down so that the bulbs may be regularly supported. The operation is finished by planting in the upper part of the vase several bulbs that will furnish an abundant growth of leaves and flowers.

In parlor cultures, these earthen vessels are advantageously replaced by Chinese or Japanese faiences, or by vessels of colored porcelain (Fig. 3). In this combination, chopped moss should always be used instead of earth, which would soil the vessel and might even injure it. In this way, we may obtain the most charming effects, and, at slight expense, provide for a continuous succession of flowers during the long winter months, and precisely at the moment in which, deprived of the sight of all vegetation, we best appreciate the pleasure of having a few beautiful fresh flowers about us.

Hyacinths, however, are not the only bulbous plants that can be cultivated in apartments. They are the ones that succeed best in vases, but narcissuses, jonquils, and amaryllises may be cultivated in the same way. All bulbous plants flower well in chopped moss, and the crocus and tulip, likewise, can therefore be employed for this purpose. On combining these different plants, we may obtain excellent effects and a continuous succession of flowers for the entire extent of the inclement season.—La Nature.

DRAWINGS FROM THE ARCHITECTURAL LEAGUE.

We give a page of drawings representing some of the exhibits of the late display of the Architectural League of New York.

The row of New York houses gives an idea of the growing tendency to return to the old colonial style of dwellings.

The Spanish grille is from a famous Spanish house, called the House of Pilate, in Seville. The house was designed in the style of the Alhambra, and the feature of it is the large patio off which the rooms are ar-

ranged. The floors and walls are tiled in the curious Moorish tiles, and the hall is completely tiled, walls, sides of stairs, etc., making a peculiarly rich effect. The grille is taken from a window looking out into the superb garden, and facing groves of palm, orange, and

A SPANISH GRILLE.

lemon trees. This is reproduced from a sketch by Charles A. Rich, architect, of New York City.

French Farm House.—Taken from an old place midway between Dieppe and Paris, and shows the beautiful arrangement of interior courtyard. The window spaces are few, it will be noticed, on the court, but abundant on the outer side. There are many examples of this

A FRENCH FARM HOUSE.

planning in France, another noted one being the Chateau d'Anjou, at Dieppe, built in flint stones laid like mosaic. They are both examples showing the beauty of simplicity of design. This, also, was sketched by Charles A. Rich.

Color in Greek Temples.

The discovery of Greek temples colored on the exterior is doubtless a very remarkable fact in archæology, for if any monuments seemed to reject the application of colors to their external decoration, it was assuredly those of the Greeks. At this day it is impossible not to admit that it was among these people that the alliance of colors with architecture was made, not in the declining epoch, but at a period when monuments were erected in the best style; in fact, the ruins of colored temples discovered by the excavations made in Greece, Italy, and Sicily, in places where many Greek colonies prospered, have this characteristic in a remarkable degree. If we seek the cause which determined the Greek architect to seize upon one of the most powerful means that the painter has of addressing the eye, we shall find it especially, I think, in a taste for colors rather than in the intention of rendering the various parts of an edifice more distinct from each other, and of substituting painted ornaments; indeed, the communication of the Greeks with the Egyptians may have induced them to imitate the latter in this application of colors to ornaments. In the colored drawings of Greek monuments which I have been able to procure, I have remarked not only the number of colors employed in these monuments—white, black, red, yellow, green, and blue—but also the use which has been made of them under the relation of variety and purity of tint, of distinct view of the parts, and of the harmony of the whole. For instance, the principal lines, as the fillets of the architrave and of the cornice, are red; the mutules blue and their guttæ white; the triglyphs blue, the channels black, and their guttæ white; and the more extended parts of the frieze and the cornice, as well as the architrave, are of light yellow. We see that red, a brilliant color, indicated the greater part of principal lines; that blue, associated with black, in the triglyphs and their channels, formed an harmonious and distinct union of the neighboring parts; also that the dominant color, light yellow, produced a much better effect than it would if the most intense or the most somber colors had predominated.—E. Chevreul.

Fever from Sewer Gas.

An epidemic of typhoid fever has been prevailing at the Michigan State prison at Jackson. A committee from the State board of health was invited to make an investigation of the causes of the epidemic. The water supply and milk supply were first ruled out as possible vehicles by negative evidence. It was then thought that the defective condition of the sewers, combined with the insufficient suppy of fresh air, was the most probable cause of the epidemic. The cases nearly all were from a distinct portion of the prison, and investigation proved that the soil pipe running from the hospital and the house drain into which it entered were defective. Professor Vaughan took to his laboratory a sample of the air from within the soil pipe, and has found within it the specific germ of typhoid fever. This fact explains the epidemic. The first case may have been introduced into the prison in a new prisoner, but once the germs of the disease were introduced into the soil pipe with the undisinfected fecal discharges of the patient, the infected soil pipe and sewer spread it freely throughout the prison. The committee from the State board of health recommended that before there is any digging into the sewers or drains, there should be thorough disinfection by pouring into the drainage system half a barrel of solution of bichloride of mercury, one part of chloride to four hundred of water; that, after such disinfection, the soil pipe leading from the hospital be taken up and reconstructed under the direction of a competent sanitary engineer.—Sanitary News.

A ROW OF NEW HOUSES, NEW YORK—J. H. DUNCAN, ARCHITECT.

71

SCIENTIFIC AMERICAN

ARCHITECTS AND BUILDERS EDITION

Entered at the Post Office of   New York as Second Class Matter.

NEW YORK, MAY, 1888.

Vol. V.   Subscription, $2.50 a Year.   Single Copies, 25 Cents.   No. 5.

1. End view of hotel resting on cars. 2. View beneath the hotel. 3. Front, showing tracks after moving. 4. Original position. 5. The start.

MOVING THE BRIGHTON BEACH HOTEL—GENERAL VIEW OF THE OPERATIONS.

MOVING THE BRIGHTON BEACH HOTEL.

We illustrate in our present issue the moving of the Brighton Beach Hotel, one of the great buildings of Coney Island, near this city. For many months there has been a marked tendency on the part of the water to wear away the sandy beach upon which the building was erected. During the past winter this tendency increased, and assumed alarming proportions. It is possible that the erection of protecting bulkheads on the neighboring property had the effect of creating a scouring action on the part of the waves and currents. Whatever the cause, during the past fall and winter months the sea advanced. The music stand, once safely on the beach between the ocean and the hotel, was surrounded by water, and remained supported by piling a few feet above the tide. The water still encroached, and soon made its way under the hotel, and it was evident that unless some preventive measures were taken, the house would be undermined, and carried away.

An adjoining building, of much smaller size, called the pavilion, had already been moved several times as the waters advanced. Small as it was, compared with the hotel, it had been moved in three pieces, having been cut into sections for the purpose. After this experience the most natural idea was to attack the problem of dealing with the great hotel upon a similar basis. It was proposed to saw it into a number of sections, and to move it back piecemeal. The cost of the operation deterred the managers from attempting it.

The hotel is owned by the Brooklyn, Flatbush, and Coney Island Railroad Company. The superintendent of the road, Mr. J. L. Morrow, and the secretary, Mr. E. L. Langford, in discussing the matter, originated the highly ingenious and novel plan which was adopted. Its execution was confided to Mr. Morrow. The plan was to place the hotel upon a number of freight cars, resting on parallel tracks, and to draw it where wanted by locomotives. The nearest approach to such a method is to be found in the Eads ship railroad, and the moving of the gigantic hotel is a happy augury for the success of the other project.

The building is a wooden structure four hundred and sixty-five feet long, one hundred and fifty feet deep, and three stories high, as regards its main portions. Five towers rise from the roof. Its longer front faces the sea. It had to be moved backward in the direction of its shorter axis. The estimated weight of the structure was five thousand tons. From one hundred to one hundred and fifty tons of plaster were contained within it. It rested upon a series of short posts which, in their turn, were supported by piling.

The first operation was to lay a series of parallel tracks from underneath the building. Longitudinal planks two inches in thickness were placed in the lines where the rails were to run. Upon these the cross ties, or sleepers, were placed, and sand was eventually rammed under the planks and sleepers alike. This gave the sleepers a double support, directly from the earth and also from the stringer planks. The rails were of the ordinary type, weighing fifty-six and sixty pounds to the yard. They were laid with a four foot nine inch gauge rod, and rather freely, so that their gauge was probably five-eighths of an inch more than the normal. The idea of this was to provide for any lateral play that might be necessary. Twenty-four lines of track were laid, and were carried under the building and out from it about three hundred feet landward. To lay track for moving the building its own depth, a mile and a half of rails were required. Ten thousand ties were used.

One hundred and twelve platform cars were hired for carrying the building. They were supplied by the Iron Car Co. Their brake wheels were removed and stowed, each pair under their own car. The building

was next attacked in twenty foot sections, and jacked up.

One 90 ton, three 60 ton, five 30 ton, and four 10 ton hydraulic jacks were used. The sills were raised from the supporting posts and the cars were rolled under, carrying with them transverse timbers of 12×14 yellow pine. Each piece rested upon two cars on adjacent tracks, the longest timber being only forty-one feet long. One hundred and ten thousand feet of this timber was required. As far as possible the timbers were made to bear upon the central axis of the car, and over the trucks. The house was raised enough to permit the cars and timbers to go under it, but one or two inches clearance being allowed for. In one place the building had settled nearly a foot. This was straightened up. The cars on each track were coupled together, and then were jacked apart so as to pull out the drawheads to their fullest extent. The weight of the building lowered upon the cars kept them in this position. In some cases this jacking apart was omitted. Such cars were connected by rope slings twisted so as to rigidly hold them together. The idea was to prevent any separation or alteration of the longitudinal distance between cars. No system of diagonal bracing was used, the utmost simplicity characterizing the arrangement.

In sections of twenty feet the whole building was gradually placed upon the cars. It is believed that the strain upon some of them cannot have been less than seventy-five tons, yet nothing has given away, although the springs were strongly compressed, so that the bolsters were nearly in contact.

A number of heavy blocks and falls were now connected to the front ends of the twenty-four lines of cars. As abutment the forward blocks were attached by chain slings directly to the rails. The tackles were arranged so that there were twelve falls, the end of each of which was carried to the motors. A number of thirty-five ton locomotives were on the ground. They were placed upon two tracks, and six ropes leading from the falls were attached to the coupling at the rear of each set of engines. Some of the tackles crossed each other, so that each set of engines had its pulling strain distributed over more than half the face of the building. The strain was taken up on each fall before it was attached. Three tons of rope were used in making these connections. The handling of falls, etc., incidental to their final arrangement was executed partly by a small engine. A man was sent around under the hotel with a steel wire to work the oil and waste well around the journals of the wheels. This was no small affair, as there were nearly nine hundred to be attended to.

When all was ready, the signal to start was given. For the first pull, April 3, the orders were to start the building and then immediately stop. Six locomotives were used. The ropes gradually tightened, and the building without a shake or tremor moved back majestically, and stopped after a short distance had been traversed. A careful examination showed that all had worked perfectly. On the afternoon of the same day a longer pull was given. Then on April 4, with only four engines, the hotel was again moved, and was left two hundred and thirty-nine feet back of its original posi-

tion. The work now had to stop as far as moving the building was concerned, because the rails were not laid any further and because the piling for the new foundation was not all driven. The rails, sleepers, and stringers left between the house and the water were transferred to the front, and a way provided for the hotel to move the rest of its journey to its new resting place, four hundred and ninety-five feet from its original location.

No difficulty of any kind was encountered. Want of power had been the principal thing that was feared, but four locomotives proved enough to carry the house along at the rate of a fast walk. The engines were found to work admirably in producing an absolute and definite pull. Windlasses or capstans might have been used, but Mr. Morrow felt that they were inferior to the engines, because of the tendency of the rope to slip upon the drum. The total weight moved was placed at one thousand tons for the cars and five thousand for the building. This represents the weight of about one and a half miles of loaded coal cars, or of a large ocean steamer.

Reference has already been made to the Eads ship railroad. In the moving of the great hotel, a far more difficult task than that called for in the operation of the ship railway was accomplished. Instead of a ship, compact and strongly built to resist every kind of strain, a large house, of relatively little intrinsic strength, was dealt with. A little settling or inequality of movement would have wrecked it. As regards power, light locomotives only were used. Compared with an iron, or even wooden, ship, the hotel might be pronounced a house of cards. The confidence in the Eads scheme cannot but be largely increased by this feat in engineering.

Boston Hot Water.

A system of hot water distribution is being introduced in Boston. Thirteen thousand feet of mains have been laid, and lateral connections are in progress. Hot water under a pressure of about 300 pounds to the square inch and heated to 350° to 400° is used. The supply pipes are 4 inches in diameter and the returns 8 inches. These pipes are thoroughly covered by non-conductors of mineral wool and asbestos paper, and rest upon rollers, and also have suitable stuffing boxes at frequent distances to allow for expansion and contraction. The tunnel or subway containing the pipes is surrounded by a double row of brickwork with an air space between, and frequent manholes lead to the surface.

It is proposed to use this system for steam heating, making use of reducing valves to diminish the pressure from the water pressure of 300 pounds to the square inch to some convenient amount, allowing it to expand into steam. The portion of the water which is not converted into steam will be able to return to the system through the large return pipes before referred to. In addition to ordinary purposes for which steam is used, it is the intention of applying it for protection against fire. It is estimated that there are 1,000 buildings within the area selected for the work of the company, and containing 130,000,000 cubic feet of space requiring artificial heat in cold weather. This, in addition to the amount of steam power required for elevators and some minor manufactures, will represent an aggregate of 10,000 horse power from the station.

MOVING THE BRIGHTON BEACH HOTEL, CONEY ISLAND.

Naval Carrier Pigeons.

The French authorities are attempting to make use of carrier pigeons for conveying information from war ships at sea to certain stations on land, and with this object have fitted up on the St. Louis a dovecote, painted the most gorgeous colors, in order to permit the birds to recognize their home from a great distance.

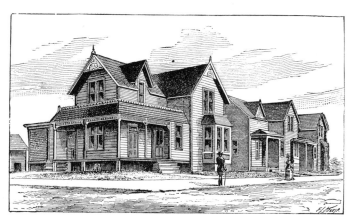

Fig. 1.—MODEL COTTAGES OF LOW COST.

Fig. 2.—RESIDENCES, NORTH ST. PAUL.

Fig. 3.—ST. PAUL KENNEL CLUB, SILVER LAKE.

Fig. 4.—RESIDENCE OF C. R. McKENNY.

Fig. 5.—PUBLIC SCHOOL.

Fig. 6.—RESIDENCE OF E. S. OSBORN.

ILLUSTRATIONS OF NORTH ST. PAUL, MINNESOTA.

RESIDENCE OF JOS. T. ELLIOT,
MIDDLETOWN, CONN.

RESIDENCE OF J. RICHARD SMITH, WATERBURY, CONN.

RESIDENCE OF SETH H. BUTLER,
MIDDLETOWN, CONN.

RESIDENCE OF EDWARD S. DAVIS,
MIDDLETOWN, CONN.

RESIDENCE OF W. S. WHITNEY,
MIDDLETOWN, CONN.

RESIDENCE OF JEFFERY O. PHELPS,
SIMSBURY CONN.

RESIDENCE OF THEODORE COLSTON,
HARTFORD, CONN.

RESIDENCE OF A. A. OLDS, HARTFORD, CONN.

RESIDENCE OF L. B. PLIMPTON,
HARTFORD, CONN.

RESIDENCE OF W. H. RISLEY, HOCKANUM, CONN.

RESIDENCE OF GEO. TRACEY, WATERBURY, CONN.

RESIDENCE OF J. B. WILLIAMS, GLASTONBURY CONN.

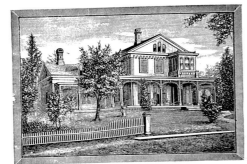

RESIDENCE OF DWIGHT LOOMIS, ROCKVILLE, CONN.

Some Residences
in Connecticut.

RESIDENCE OF R. O. CHENEY, S. MANCHESTER, CONN.

RESIDENCE OF D. W. BOND, FLORENCE, MASS.

RESIDENCE OF CHAS. KEITH,
GREENFIELD, MASS.

RESIDENCE OF A. B. WALLACE,
SPRINGFIELD, MASS.

RESIDENCE OF WILLIAM ARNOLD,
WEST SPRINGFIELD, MASS.

RESIDENCE OF N. H. WHITTEN, HOLYOKE, MASS.

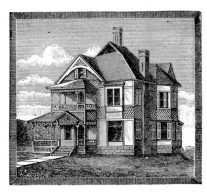

RESIDENCE OF E. C. SHELDON,
SPRINGFIELD MASS.

RESIDENCE OF W. C. POMEROY,
NORTHAMPTON, MASS.

RESIDENCE OF JOS. L. MERRICK,
HOLYOKE, MASS.

RESIDENCE OF W. M. MERRILL,
SPRINGFIELD, MASS.

RESIDENCE OF MRS. ALMIRA COOK,
WOONSOCKET, R. I.

CITY ASYLUM, NEWPORT, R. I.

RESIDENCE OF H. D. SCOTT, NEWPORT, R. I.

RESIDENCE OF GALEN DAVIS,
NEWPORT, R. I.

RESIDENCE OF MARK HOUGH, WOONSOCKET, R. I.

RESIDENCE OF C. W. COOK,
WOONSOCKET, R. I.

SOME NEW ENGLAND RESIDENCES.

ELM HOTEL, GREENFIELD, MASS.

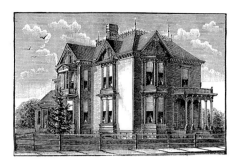

RESIDENCE OF A. MESSER, ST. PAUL.

RESIDENCE OF F. H. POWNALL,
JAMESBURG, N. J.

RESIDENCE OF THOS. J. WALKER,
HAGERSTOWN, MD.

RESIDENCE OF O. D. BROWN, ST. PAUL.

RESIDENCE OF FRANK W. DRUMMOND,
BANGOR, ME.

RESIDENCE OF A. F. BEHNKE,
ST. PAUL.

RESIDENCE OF J. ROSS NICOLS, ST. PAUL.

RESIDENCE OF C. J. HAZARD,
HIGHTSTOWN, N. J.

RESIDENCE OF J. G. CLARK,
BANGOR, ME.

SOLDIERS' HOME, BENNINGTON, VT.

RESIDENCE OF DR. J. L. SUYDAM,
JAMESBURG, N. J.

HOTEL, HAYDENVILLE, MASS.

"THE PARSONAGE," HAGERSTOWN, MD.

RESIDENCES AND HOTELS.

RESIDENCE OF J. WINTER,
HAGERSTOWN, MD.

77

A COTTAGE FOR $2,500.

Our photographic illustration shows a cottage built on Sherwood Avenue, Bridgeport, Conn., at a cost of $2,500.

The house contains all the modern improvements and conveniences, the plan is nicely arranged and has a very pretty elevation.

There is a cellar under whole of the house, which is cemented. The foundation is of stone, with under pinning of brick.

The first story is 9' 6" and second story 9'.

The exterior is covered with clapboarding and shingles, giving a pleasing effect.

On the first floor there is a square hall, a parlor, sitting room, dining room, and kitchen; four good-sized bedrooms and bath room on second floor.

The bedrooms are amply provided with closets, fitted up in the usual way.

There is a very nice attic, and additional rooms can be done off if desired.

The kitchen is wainscoted, and contains a sink, provided with hot and cold water, a pantry fitted up with counter shelf, with closets under and shelves.

Back stairs from cellar to attic.

The dining room has two closets, fitted up in the usual way.

The bath room is provided with bath tub, wash bowl, and water closet, all supplied with hot and cold water, and fitted up in the best manner. Wash trays are provided in cellar.

The front stairs are easy and have neatly turned newels, balusters, and rail.

The parlor and sitting room are separated by sliding doors. Neat wood mantel in each.

The trim throughout is of white pine, and the door and window casings are hand moulded.

Our engraving was made direct from a photograph of the house, specially taken for the SCIENTIFIC AMERICAN.

In connection with the publication of the BUILDING EDITION of the SCIENTIFIC AMERICAN, Messrs. Munn & Co. furnish plans and specifications for buildings of every kind, including Stores, Dwellings, Carriage Houses, Barns, etc. In this work they are assisted by able and experienced architects. Full plans, details, and specifications for the various buildings illustrated in this paper can be supplied.

Those who contemplate building, or who wish to alter, improve, extend, or add to existing buildings, whether wings, porches, bay windows, or attic rooms, are invited to communicate with the undersigned. Our work extends to all parts of the country. Estimates, plans, and drawings promptly prepared. Terms moderate. Address Munn & Co., 361 Broadway, New York.

A YOUNG French officer is said to have invented a microphone which will record and announce the approach of a body of soldiers and give some idea as to their numbers.

FIRST FLOOR.   A COTTAGE FOR $2,500.   SECOND FLOOR.

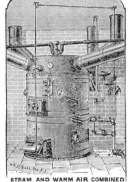

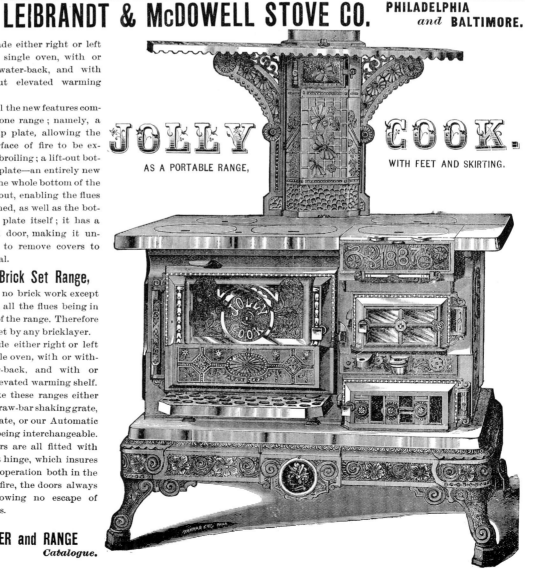
79

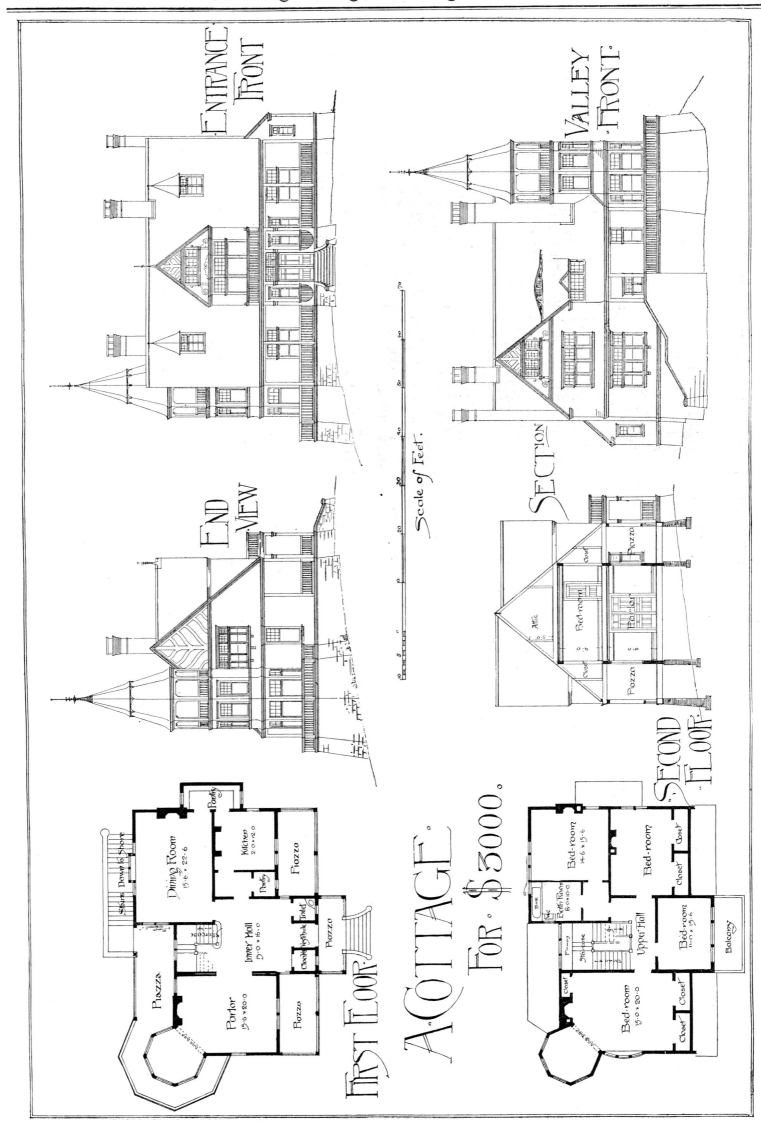

ENTRANCE FRONT

VALLEY "FRONT.

Scale of Feet.

END VIEW

SECTION

A COTTAGE. FOR $3000.

FIRST FLOOR.

SECOND FLOOR.

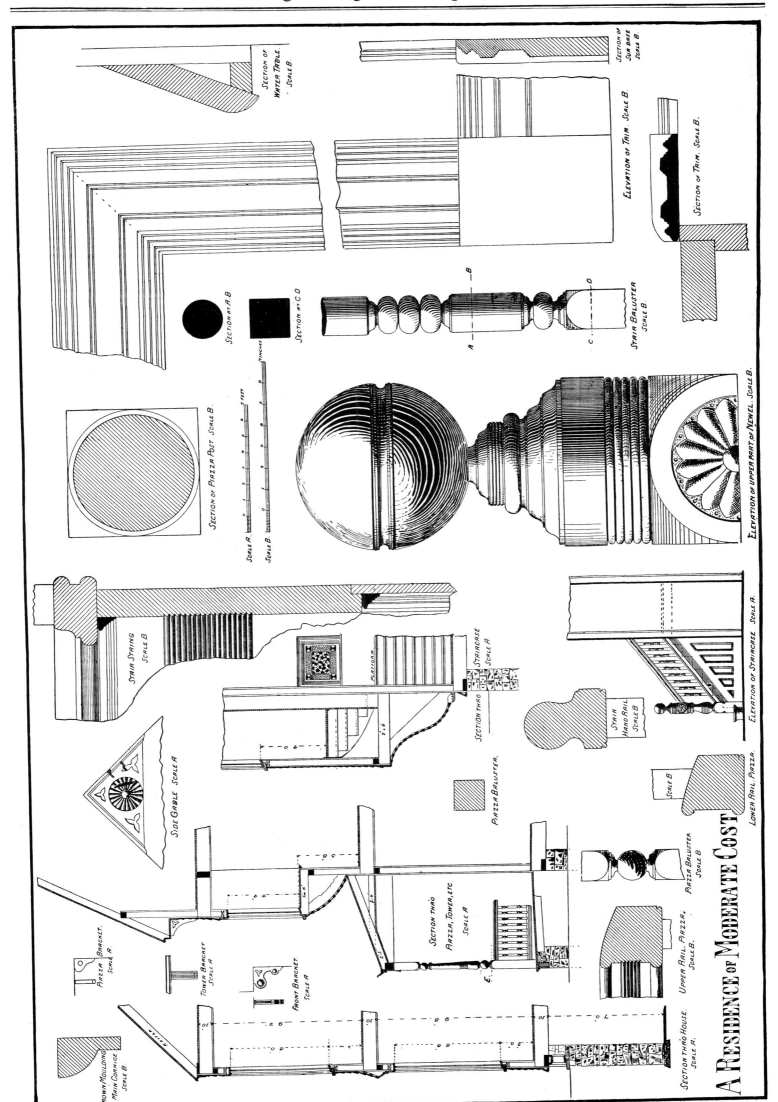

A RESIDENCE OF MODERATE COST

Mahogany.

Mahogany is a prince among woods! And why? Not alone for its beauty (that would make it a princess), for its durability, its freedom from atmospheric influence, the permanence of its brilliancy, and the unequaled grace of its grain. I cannot understand how any rich man, with the desire to have his house artistic as well as elaborate, can lose sight of the enormous advantages possessed by mahogany, if only in its decorative phase.

Let me, briefly, revert to the process of preparing this wood for practical use in the construction of wainscotings, furniture, and the numerous other purposes to which it is applied. My excuse for this is that the comprehension, even superficial, of how and why certain things are done often gives them a much brighter complexion and an entirely different aspect.

When the enormous logs are landed from the numerous points whence mahogany originates, they are carefully examined by an expert, and those promising the showiest and most elaborate grain are marked with a cross upon either end. I say an "expert," for it requires an experienced eye to distinguish a difference, and especially an advantage, in the forbidding exterior of the ill-shaped masses lying about the yard. The ordinary observer would find it difficult to muster sufficient imaginations to discover in this raw condition the beautiful results that follow the lead of a saw and chisel.

The popular application of any wood is in the form of veneer, and to produce veneer is very different in mahogany than in the multitude of other lumber. It is brought forth by a delicate circular saw or by a gigantic razor. The first rips off the thin slices, the latter shaves it off. With the saw the life of the wood is preserved, its vitality is retained, it has a freshness when it comes from the crisp cut that makes it appear rich and bright without further manipulation. The slicing or shaving, however, has a somewhat different effect. In order to soften the tough wood, that the knife may plunge into it without producing the ragged edge of a rough, uncouth incision, a volume of steam is thrown upon the log, and the shaving comes forth from the keen edge, curled and smoking. This unavoidably kills, or at least wounds, the freshness of the veneer's beauty, as it requires no preternaturally quick eye to discover.

In its natural condition, as the wood comes from the saw, whether it be in the delicate veneer or in cumbersome planks, it is light in color, and has a richness that nature invariably bestows in some measure to the most ordinary of her products, and defies the keenest effort of art to successfully imitate. Finished in this condition, varnished in the shade and tone of its growth, mahogany can have no competitor in the taste and fancy of men, for it is infinitely above and unapproachably beyond any other decorative material extant.

And right here is where the unsuspicious householder has been deceived. Instead of resting satisfied with the innate beauty of the wood, injudicious manufacturers have stained it, darkened it, muddied it; in other words, robbed it of its sparkle, and given it a heavy, funereal semblance that is foreign to it, and therefore disfiguring. And why has that been done? Solely so as to make it possible for whitewood, maple, birch, and anything that may come that way to be dyed and painted to the same color that mahogany has been artificially brought; where both are stained, the false is not so readily discovered.—*A. Curtis, Decorator and Furnisher.*

Flexible Foundations.

The ordinary conception of a foundation is that its virtue is in exact proportion to its rigidity, and that the more unyielding it is, the better it serves its purpose. And while this assumption may be true in supporting a heavy load, yet where questions of impact enter, the "soft answer will turn away wrath," as well in dynamics as in polemics. At a factory in the United States some beveled gears which were used to change the direction of main shafting from one mill to another were at the end of very heavy shafts, which ran in pillow blocks, simply bolted to an outcropping ledge, which was dressed to a level for the purpose of sustaining the foundations. Some of the teeth of these beveled gears would break from time to time, and in a most unaccountable manner. The accident might be deferred for three months, or it might occur at any moment. Various expedients were tried, and finally that of taking up the pillow blocks and placing them on seats of raw hide which had been soaked in oil; these gave the bearings enough elasticity to prevent a concentration of shocks upon the teeth of the gear, and in that way acted as a buffer preventing the gears from committing a mechanical suicide. A steam engine used to operate the dynamos for lighting an insurance building in New York gave a great deal of annoyance to the occupants by the jar which was transmitted throughout the building. It is supposed that the motion of the engine was in rhythm with the key note of the building. The makers of several engines tried to solve the problem, which was at last achieved by one firm, who bolted the bed of their engine to a timber raft which rested upon a layer of hair felt such as is used for non-conducting coverings for steam pipes and boilers, but 14 in. thick. This felt was placed upon the masonry foundation recently prepared for the engine, and surrounded by a heavy timber box which prevented its spreading. An engine used to operate the electric light plant in one of the principal hotels in New York City gave annoyance to the guests because, when it was in operation, beats could be heard all over the building, notwithstanding that the engine was situated in a tightly closed room in the basement. After various other expedients had failed, the doors to this room were taken down and replaced by double thicknesses of carpet fixed upon the framework. This served to break up the rhythm in such a way that the sound was not heard throughout the building. Sawdust has been used for foundations in many instances, and there are numerous towns in the United States which have been built up from small villages originally around a sawmill, and the sawdust from the mill has been used to fill up low places which have afterward served as building lots. In course of time such filling becomes very compact, and does not appear to waste by decay.—*Engineering.*

WALL PAPER DECORATIONS.

Messrs. Jeffrey & Co. have just published an exceedingly novel folio in illustration of what they term "The Victorian series" of designs. In this publication the various patterns are arranged after the fashion of a folding screen, which shuts like a book, and reads both ways, so that room is obtained for a double number of examples. These have been reduced by photo-lithography from the actual papers, and are shown to scale, giving at a glance the general effect of the design illustrated. Of course without actual specimens of the papers to be used, reduced copies like these before us may possibly be misused; but, anyway, they give a complete idea of how the pattern groups itself over a surface, and whether the repeats supply tiresome combinations or not. A small piece of a pattern may be extremely nice, but when multiplied an endless number of times over a wall, its restlessness may assert an overpowering effect, and be simply unbearable. Another advantage of these reduced copies is the comprehensive idea they afford of large patterns, enabling the intending purchaser to judge how they fill spaces and will cut up for friezes or staircases; and experience has taught us that large, broadly treated patterns, even for small apartments, if well chosen, are by far the most effective, and certainly do not make little rooms look smaller, as some have contended. We now illustrate one such pattern by Mr. Lewis F. Day, called the "Arabesque Panel Decoration." Mr. A. F. Brophy's "Flower Scroll" paper, of which we give an illustration, makes one of the most successful wall patterns for staircases that we know of; and having used it, we can say how well it fills almost any space, without tiresome effects.

FLOWER SCROLL—DESIGNED BY A. F. BROPHY.

STRAP CEILING—DESIGNED BY G. A. AUDSLEY.

DRUGSTORE ARCHITECTURE AND DECORATIONS.

Notable as has been the progress made by druggists in the last few years in the way of handling their material, from the useful as well as the ornamental standpoints, it can scarcely be realized without a personal inspection of some of the stores recently opened at New York. The new study of necessity, as one of the elements of good art, has led to the discovery of the fact that space and time have hitherto been much wasted in drugstores. One of the latest ideas in arrangement is that of using numbers on drawers and shelves instead of names, catalogues being kept to correspond. Thus the druggist can find anything he wants at a moment's notice. Another good idea is to make the colored globes answer the purpose of illumination as well as of advertisement, by placing an electric light inside of them. The retail department of a store in which these two ideas are illustrated is long and rather broad than narrow. The dispensing department is at right angles with it, extending to the left. This department has one show window, which looks on the side street, and is decorated in an original and appropriate manner. In the middle of the window space is a glass case which forms a pedestal for a tall block of crystallized alum, beautifully pure in its different whites There are small colorless glass instruments surrounding it. In front of the case, extending across the window, are tall percolators graduated in height from the middle one. On a colored oak pedestal, at either end of the window, is a large colorless glass globe containing an electric light. Behind the window is a small oaken table, with a yellow globe upon it, surrounded by medical pamphlets. Just behind the table, facing the store, is placed the druggist's private desk, also of fine carved dark oak. The dispensing department has a beautiful arrangement of color. Either side of the large, full-length mirror which faces the store are wall casings of oak, with bottles and jars filled with deep-toned yellow, red, and brown liquids, relieved against a backing of gold cathedral glass which gleams and shimmers most beautifully with the changing light from the side windows. This idea is carried out throughout the department. The gold leaf is placed behind the glass instead of in front, and thus a smooth, solid, united surface is presented to the eye. A cabinet between the mirror and the window has yellow silk curtains. The chairs throughout the store are of oak with leather seats.

The dispensing department is divided into two sections by the drug clerk's desk. Back of this desk, filling a large rectangular space, is an enormous two-sided prescription counter, with various attachments, among others an apparatus for distilling water. At the desk end, on the side, are numbered sections forming cupboards, opening from the top, but made to look like drawers. Other drawers on the walls are made with open sides, especially those for the pills and elixirs. These sides are graduated according to the size of the bottle, and thus the contents are at once secure and easily accessible. In the front division of the dispensing department are small, square numbered drawers for herbs. Each holds exactly one pound. At the end of the compounding department is a fume closet in which prescriptions or mixtures having disagreeable odors are put up, in order that the odors may escape into the open air through the ventilating shaft. The ceiling is treated with stamped paper of a pale terra cotta tint, in geometrical designs, and has a border of green in a beaded pattern.

The low flight of steps which separates the retail department of this store from the prescription department has a handsome oaken post at each side. On one is a large crimson globe, on the other a dark red, the color being, as is usual in drugstores, produced by chemically treated water. In the middle of each globe is an electric light, which, when turned on, produces quite a theatrical effect. The cashier's desk is an elaborate and well-treated piece of furniture, forming an admirable decoration. It is designed partly in twisted and interlaced ropes, and the front presents a fan-like effect of lines. This is probably the most ornamental desk of the kind to be found in any New York drugstore. The soda water fountain, which is placed against the wall, is unusually handsome with its deep-set mirrors, black wooden framing effectively carved, and its green and white marbles.

By the side of these drugstores, fitted up according to modern ideas of beauty and convenience, the older interiors have rather a *passe* look, but hints may be gleaned from them in the way of adapting old decorations to the present methods of treatment. One New York drugstore has Pompeiian red and terra cotta in the frieze above a light wall. The wall cupboards and casings are in whitewood with gilt mouldings. They continue along the back, forming curves at the corners. The prescription desk extends across the back of the store, which is unusually large. It has glass windows hung with cream-colored glass, with a tall red and blue bottle at one corner and a green and yellow one at the other. The carved oak chairs, with their tawny plush seats, belong to a more modern school of drugstore decoration.

Another drugstore presents an example of pleasing window decoration, produced by a skillful arrangement of stock. A large, squat, colored jar is supported

DRUGSTORE ARCHITECTURE.

in the middle of each window by solid brass rods, one starting from each of the four corners. In one window is seen a tasteful grouping of brushes. In another, sponges fill a case, upon the top of which stand large bottles of lavender water, which, with their clear emerald green bodies and white kid tops, look like a company of soldiers mounting guard over a heap of delicate painted, satin perfume sachets. A feature of the interior is the presence of three tall white jars, with rich-colored coats-of-arms on them and gold tops, on a slab at the foot of a long mirror. A large white jar of mineral water standing on a brass pedestal is the decorative feature of the soda water counter, which is in brownish marble. Tiles are effectively introduced into the decoration of the soda water fountain, which is

DRUGSTORE ARCHITECTURE.

composed of green and salmon-colored marble. There is one soda water fountain in a New York drugstore which is made entirely of tiles in shaded light greens, with heads in relief and bright silver finishings. This is a great improvement on the old-fashioned, heavy marble fountains, which were the very reverse of suggestive of coolness and freshness. It is by such details as this that the advance of art, as applied to the daily exigences of American life, may be gauged. The ceiling of another drugstore is covered with a velvety paper in which there are stars of pale green formed by geometrical ribbon interlacings of a greenish white. The wall casings are of white-painted wood with gold trimmings. Pale green tiling might be effectively used throughout this store. The tile idea is worth considering by druggists who meditate refitting their stores, for its decorative possibilities. Many hints may be gleaned from other stores for the arrangement of drug establishments. A New York liquor store has its window space floored with figured and shaded tiles in greens and mahoganies The pillars supporting the roof of the windows are carved in Moorish designs and painted in delicate colors. A loose, hanging screen of long beads and bits of bamboo, such as can be purchased at a Japanese shop or made at home, is used to conceal the interior of the store, and large palms in jars form the decorations. There is, besides, an enormous champagne bottle, which in the case of a drugstore might be changed to a colored glass jar.—*American Druggist.*

The First American Marble Quarry.

There is considerable doubt as to when and where the first marble quarry was opened in the country. There has been much time spent in researches in regard to the early history of marble quarrying in New England, but nothing definite as to who is entitled to the honor of the first quarry has been obtained. Perhaps one opened in Pittsford, Vt., was the oldest. It was being worked in 1795 by Jeremiah Sheldon This quarry is now known as the Owen quarry. There were many quarries in operation throughout New England in the early part of this century. In 1800 Philo Tomlinson was at work quarrying marble in New Milford, Conn. Many headstones bearing a date early in the century are still to be found in the graveyard at New Milford. He invented machinery for working marble which is in use to this day. Remnants of his machinery are still to be found where his first mill was located. In Alford, Mass., in 1803, Johnson & Stevens concluded a contract for furnishing marble for the city hall of New York. For this they received $1.06 per foot. Five years later they contracted for more marble for $3 per foot. The value of this marble may be estimated when it is known that after an exposure of three-quarters of a century it shows no sign of crumbling or decay. The extension of the capitol at Washington is from the same region, though not the same quarries. In the early part of the century much marble was produced in West Stockbridge, Mass.; in fact, the demand was greater than the supply. The mills were run night and day. Water power was used in sawing, though for a time steam was employed. Its use was discontinued on account of the increase in expense, and water was again used. Quarrying stopped here in 1855, it having declined for some years previous to this. Competition from other quarries, principally from Vermont, caused the extinction of this industry. Vermont marble is better in quality, and could be quarried cheaper. Hence the competition.—*Stone.*

Wood Carving and Furniture.

The art of carving in wood is carried to great perfection in Florence. It is applied to decorative furniture, such as mantel pieces, sideboards, bookcases, bedsteads, chairs, chandeliers, etc., to wall panels and balustrades, and to frames, caskets, brackets, and smaller ornamental articles. Some of the original work, executed by artists in the true sense of the word, merits special attention. Tuscan carving is softer in tone than the work of Northern Italy. It is distinguished by delicacy of feeling and accuracy of design, found even among the humbler artisans, whose natural artistic taste is now promoted by an excellent school of design. Many fine works have, of late years, been sent abroad, principally to Great Britain, the United States, Germany, Russia, and France, by Barbetti, Frullini, Scarselli, and Romanelli, among other excellent carvers in wood.

The average day's work is ten hours for cabinet makers and nine hours for wood carvers. Men on piece work, however, often work after hours, and on fete days up to 2 P.M. The hours of work in a frame maker's shop in Florence are thus distributed: Work begins at 6.30 A.M. to 9, when half an hour is allowed for breakfast, then from 9.30 to 1 P.M. Two hours' rest till 3 P.M., when work continues until 8 P.M. The above day of eleven hours is the rule for summer; in winter the day's work is ten hours.

The native woods principally used in wood carving and furniture making are "giuggiolo" (*Zizyphus vulgaris*) for fine work, walnut from the province of Modena, pear, alder, poplar of different qualities, maple, cypress, and fir. The chief foreign woods employed are ebony, rosewood, and manogany. Ivory is used for inlays. The iron fittings employed appear in certain cases, at all events, to be imported from Germany. The bronze and gilt ornaments are now generally made in Italy.

RESIDENCF AT SURBITON, SURREY.

This house is now in course of erection within ten minutes' walk of Surbiton Station. It is built of red bricks, with Broseley tile roof, the upper floor being finished rough cast. The exterior woodwork is principally of teak, merely oiled, while shutters are appended to the bedroom windows in front, which face due south. There are eight bedrooms, bathroom, housemaids' and linen closets, etc., on the upper floors, and the trimmings of staircase and best rooms are being executed from special designs prepared by the architect, Mr. J. Nixon Horsfield, Market Place, Kingston-on-Thames.—*Building News.*

European Health Resorts.

At the recent meeting in Paris of the International Congress on Climatology and Hydrology, Mr. Adolphe Smith opened a discussion on the necessity of improved sanitation at various health and winter resorts. He trusted the congress would not misunderstand the object he had in view; his interests were not connected with those of any locality or nationality. This was an international congress; its sole object was to guide, in a scientific manner, those who suffered so that they might soon be cured; and this must be done on purely scientific grounds, without stopping to consider for a moment the interests of any particular district. He was willing to assent to the asserted inferiority of the English climate; but unfortunately a great number of English patients would not repair to the Continent, because they feared to encounter the bad sanitation, especially of the French, Spanish, and Italian so-called health resorts. It was only necessary to compare the death rates to show the appalling difference that existed.

In England, at seaside and health resorts, and in spite of the presence of numerous patients, there were death rates of 12, 13, and 14 per 1,000. A small town in a healthy position, where there were no factories, no accumulations of poor people, but for the most part lodging house keepers and people fairly well off, should have a death rate below 15 per 1,000 per annum. But he had found in France and elsewhere that the death rate in such places amounted to 22 and in one case to 28 per 1,000. This was all the more remarkable as there were fewer children in France. With the same proportion of children as in England, the mortality in France would be still higher. The reason for this distressful state of affairs was not far to seek. Even today new houses were in course of construction with cesspools placed under the front sitting room, so that they could be easily emptied from the street. The closets were constructed with soil pipes so large that it was impossible to cleanse them; there were no traps, and practically nothing to prevent cesspool gases entering the house. In the kitchens the leaden pipes went straight to the sewers, without trap and interception. The houses were simultaneously permeated with sewer air and the emanations from the cesspool. The patient while he was out of doors enjoyed a much better climate than in England. But what was the good of a pleasant walk in the sun for three or four hours if, during the remaining twenty hours, the patient was condemned to breathe sewer air? He could understand that municipalities should hesitate to build large sewers and adopt vast expensive schemes of drainage; but domestic drainage could be very much better managed, and at little or no expense.

In England, in some health resorts, it was proposed to examine lodging houses and hotels, and give diplomas as to their sanitary condition, so that visitors might have the option of selecting for residence only such places as were certified to be in a healthy condition. The *Lancet* had taken an active and successful part in this campaign, and it served to arouse public opinion. Could not something similar be done on the Continent? Then there was nothing to prevent the letting of rooms where there had been cases of small pox or scarlet fever, and where no measures of disinfection were applied. Finally, in towns where a good public water supply existed, he found the inhabitants still supplying their lodgers with contaminated water taken from private wells. In conclusion, he felt convinced that in many health resorts of France, Italy, and Spain the death rate might be reduced to the extent of 40 or even 50 per cent., if a proper system of public and domestic drainage were introduced, if a supply of pure water were rendered obligatory and all private wells closed and, finally, if all persons suffering from infectious diseases were isolated and their rooms rigorously disinfected.

Fireproof Paint.

It is said an effective composition for fireproofing exterior surfaces may be formed by slaking a sufficient quantity of freshly burned quicklime of the best grade, and when the slaking is complete there is added such an amount of skim milk, or water in its absence, as will make a liquid of the consistency of cream. To every ten gallons of this liquid are added, separately and in powder, stirring constantly, the following ingredients, in the order named: Two pounds of alum, twenty-four ounces subcarbonate of potassium or commercial potash, and one pound of common salt. Whatever tint is used, it is incorporated at this stage, and the whole, after being strained through a sieve, is run through a paint mill. When ready to apply, the paint is heated nearly to the boiling point of water, and is put on in its hot condition.

Testing Well Water for Sewage.

Professor Blake, of the University of Kansas, makes a valuable suggestion for testing well water for sewage contamination. The ordinary way, where contamination from a given cesspool, vault, or sewer is feared, is to pour salt water into the suspected source of contamination, and, after a time, to test the well water for salt, by means of nitrate of silver. In fact, as salt is always present in considerable quantity in sewage and house wastes, the presence of salt in well water is presumptive evidence of contamination. It is not, however, positive evidence, as many innocent soils contain chlorides, and Professor Blake proposes that a lithium compound should be used instead of common salt. Lithium is a substance so rare that it would hardly be found in any natural soil, and a very small quantity can be detected by means of the bright red line which its spectrum shows in the spectroscope. According to the best authorities, one forty-millionth of a grain of lithium will give the red line clearly. Professor Blake proposes to make a test by dissolving one ounce of carbonate or chloride of lithium in a quart of water, and pouring the solution into the suspected cesspool or vault. After a week or more, the well water is examined, by evaporating a little of it, dipping a platinum wire in the concentrated liquid, and holding the wire in a Bunsen gas flame. If, on looking at the flame with a spectroscope, the lithium line is seen, the contamination is proved.—*Amer. Architect.*

A RESIDENCE AT SURBITON.

PATENTS.

Messrs. Munn & Co., in connection with the publication of the **Scientific American,** continue to examine improvements and to act as Solicitors of Patents for Inventors.

In this line of business they have had *forty years' experience*, and now have *unequaled facilities* for the preparation of Patent Drawings, Specifications, and the prosecution of Applications for Patents in the United States, Canada, and Foreign Countries. **Messrs. Munn & Co.** also attend to the preparation of Caveats, Copyrights for Books, Labels, Reissues, Assignments, and Reports on Infringements of Patents. All business intrusted to them is done with special care and promptness, on very reasonable terms.

A pamphlet sent free of charge, on application, containing full information about Patents and how to procure them; directions concerning Labels, Copyrights, Designs, Patents, Appeals, Reissues, Infringements, Assignments, Rejected Cases, Hints on the Sale of Patents, etc.

We also send, *free of charge*, a synopsis of Foreign Patent Laws, showing the cost and method of securing patents in all the principal countries of the world.

MUNN & CO., Solicitors of Patents, 361 Broadway, New York.
BRANCH OFFICE.—622 F Street, Washington, D. C.

The Carpenter.

Probably there is no one of the building trades in which the opportunities for advancement are so many and so certain as in carpentry. The prominence and importance of the wood-worker's art has made the carpenter the leading mechanic upon modern buildings. The carpenter is ordinarily the virtual, if not the nominal, superintendent of the building upon which he is engaged. Accordingly, he is required to know all the peculiarities of the various trades which enter into the construction of a building. He must be familiar not only with his own trade, but he must likewise know very much about that of the mason the bricklayer, the iron worker, the cornice maker, the plumber, etc.

If a building is to be erected without the assistance of an architect, the carpenter is the first mechanic consulted, and to him is given the general direction of the undertaking. Therefore, the carpenter in reality becomes the builder, and so well recognized is this that the two terms, carpenter and builder, are used almost synonymously. The carpenter's general and special knowledge is made use of at every stage in the progress of a building.

He is very frequently called upon to lay off the ground upon which a building is to be erected. It is often the carpenter who pronounces the foundation satisfactory or otherwise before the superstructure is commenced. It is the carpenter who sees that the iron floor beams are placed exactly right. It is the carpenter who prepares the centers for the bricklayer and the mason, and sees that their respective parts of the building are left in proper condition. It is the carpenter, in the wording of many specifications, who must supply whatever is necessary for the completion of the building, and which has not been included in any of the other trades.

If any new feature of work is introduced in a building for which there is not a special contractor, it ordinarily falls to the carpenter's lot. Whatever shortcomings there may be in the plans, whatever errors have been made by the architect, it becomes the duty of the carpenter to overcome and make compensation for. It is necessary for the carpenter to know everything about the building from beginning to end, and the more thorough and practical his knowledge, the more rapid his advancement and the wider his field of operations always becomes.

There are several distinct stages in the carpenter's career. First, the apprentice and helper; then the common mechanic, working under a foreman; next he becomes foreman, directing workmen under him, and has the superintendency of the building upon which he is engaged. From this he easily steps into business on his own account, and takes contracts for the erection of buildings.

Not infrequently he combines a theoretical knowledge of architecture with his practical experience as a builder, and enters upon a professional career with decided chances of success. The rate of his advancement from stage to stage depends largely upon the natural ability of the man, his care in studying the various parts of his trade, and close attention to business. Of course, something is attributable to opportunities, but, all things being equal, the man who is the most earnest in acquiring knowledge concerning his trade, who secures a fund of information from which he can answer almost any question that may come up in his daily work, and who provides ready means for overcoming any unusual difficulties that may arise, is likely to make the most rapid advancement.

Carpentry pure and simple may be defined as the art of combining pieces of timber for the support of any considerable weight or pressure. The theory of carpentry depends upon two distinct branches of mechanical science. The carpenter gives his timbers their form by the principles of geometry, and he adjusts the stress and strain so as to preserve them in their original shape by the laws of mechanics. In the wide range of application of these branches of science the carpenter finds ample field for exercise of his best powers; his familiarity with them forms the foundation of his usefulness, and in a measure, aside from the relative importance attaching to his trade, gives him an advantage over other mechanics.—*Southern Lumberman.*

PAINT FOR SHINGLE ROOFS.—One bbl coal tar, 10 lb. asphaltum, 10 lb. ground slate, 2 gals. dead oil Add the dead oil after the others have been mixed by aid of heat.

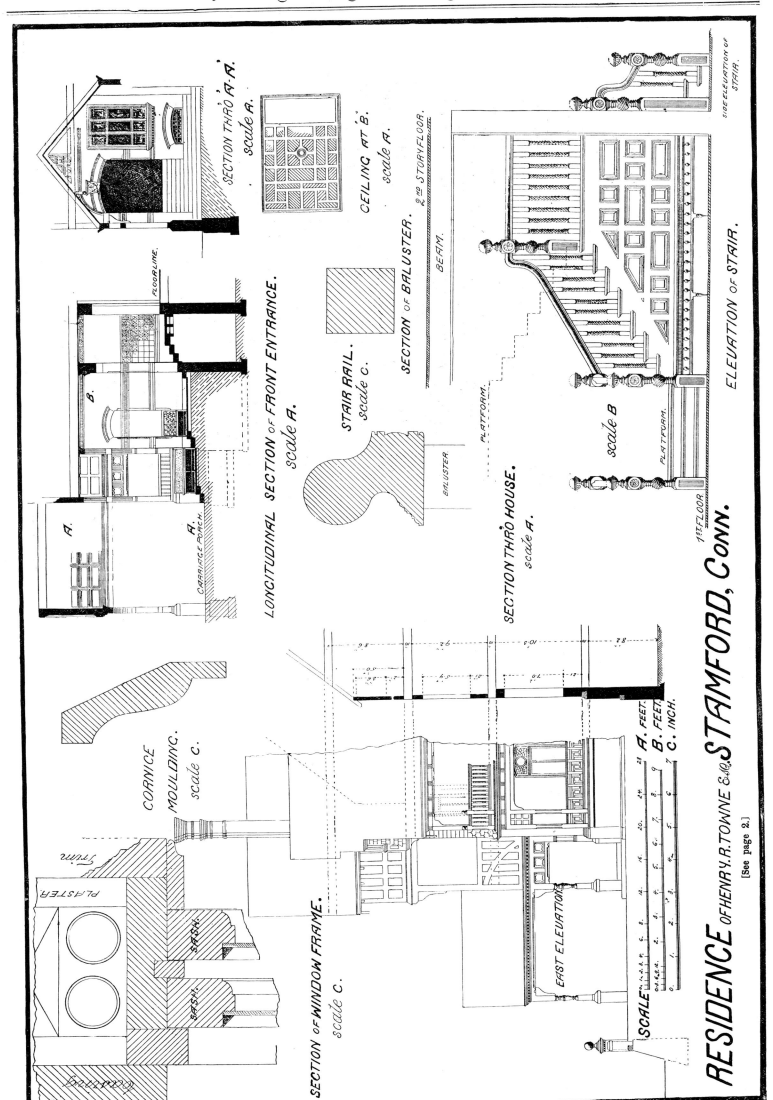

SECTION THRO' A-A. *scale A.*

CEILING AT B. *scale A.*

SIDE ELEVATION OF STAIR.

FLOORLINE.

LONGITUDINAL SECTION OF FRONT ENTRANCE. *scale A.*

STAIR RAIL. *scale C.*

SECTION OF BALUSTER.

BEAM.

2ND STORYFLOOR.

B.

A.

A. CARRIAGE PORCH.

BALUSTER.

PLATFORM.

SECTION THRO' HOUSE. *scale A.*

PLATFORM.

PLATFORM.

scale B

1ST FLOOR.

ELEVATION OF STAIR.

CORNICE MOULDING. *scale C.*

TRIM.

PLASTER.

SASH.

SASH.

SECTION OF WINDOW FRAME. *scale C.*

EAST ELEVATION.

SCALE

A. FEET.
B. FEET.
C. INCH.

RESIDENCE OF HENRY R. TOWNE ESQ., **STAMFORD, CONN.**

[See page 2.]

85

A RESIDENCE AT STOCKTON, CAL.

We give a sketch and floor plans of a residence at Stockton, Cal., for which we are indebted to the *California Architect and Building News.* C. R. & J. M. Wilson, architects, San Francisco. It is a compact, comfortable, and well-arranged dwelling. The dimensions of the several rooms are given on the floor plans. It will be seen they are liberal and well proportioned. The estimated cost of this house, finished in first class style, is $10,000. But it might be built for less money by reducing the nicety of finish, also by lessening the various dimensions.

Staining Floors.

For the benefit of those who desire to stain their own floors, the New York *Tribune* thus goes into details: In the first place, as to brushes, you can purchase at any paint shop what is necessary. Do not get them too heavy, as they will tire you; a medium round brush, a flat brush about six inches wide, a small "liner" to mark the edges and go into corners, and you have enough. After you have bought them soak them in water for half a day to swell the wood and prevent the falling out of the bristles, and they are then ready for use. Lard cans are most useful for mixing your stains, but if you buy that article in a more economical fashion tin vegetable cans will do if the top is cut entirely out.

To begin with the hall, I should recommend, if you are undecided about the color, raw sienna, rather than a darker stain, as it does not show dust or foot marks, and it harmonizes with any rug. The half of a pound can of prepared paint mixed with a gill of turpentine will give you all the color you require for quite a large room.

Now take your small brush and paint a line around the edge of your floor to prevent your large brush from smirching the walls. Then with the round paint brush paint the lengths of board with the grain of the wood. When stopping your work always complete the board on which you are working; thus the stain will look equal and even. Take a low chair by all means, as you can then paint your lengths of board with very little fatigue, merely moving the chair when desired. This is certainly not professional, but it has been tested and found most satisfactory.

The flat brush is for the hard oil finish, which you can apply as soon as the stain is dry to the touch. Then leave it for twenty-four hours at least, before placing any furniture upon it. Wax is recommended as the neatest, cleanest and most attractive way to keep a floor after it has been varnished.

Now for the floors of the drawing and dining rooms. For the first, if you do not mind a little trouble, try a border; it has a very pretty effect and is not much work. With a piece of chalk draw a straight line about a foot and a half from the wall; then with the small brush paint over it a broad flat line and another line of equal width against the wall. Now draw a geometrical figure—any figure will do—on brown paper nearly as large as the width of your border. Cut it out, and with your chalk draw lines around it at equal distances from each other and connect your figures with lines curved or straight as you like—the geometrical figures to be filled in solidly with stain. This border may be put on after the entire floor has

been stained. Of course the border may be made as elaborate as one wishes. One floor which was done in this way was very successful. The parquet itself was stained with raw sienna, and the figure on the border done in Prussian blue. If you like browns, try raw umber for your dining room. It will be sure to please you, but it must be well diluted—one gill of turpentine to a third of a pound can of the umber. If you wish it darker, add more of the color.

The Peruvian Temple of Pachacamac.

The Temple of Pachacamac, or Castle, as it is called by the Indians, is on the summit of a hill, with three terraces; the view of it from the north is somewhat like that of the pyramid of Cholula, given by Hum-

boldt, except that the flanks were perpendicular. The whole height of the hill is 250 feet, that of the masonwork 80 feet; the former is rectangular, the base being 500 feet by 400 feet. At the southeastern extremity the three distinct terraces are not so perceptible, and the declivity is more gentle. The walls, where great strength was required to support the earth, were built of unhewn square blocks of rock; these were cased with sun-dried bricks (adobes), which were covered with a coating of clay or plaster, and stained or painted of a reddish color. A range of square brick pilasters projected from the uppermost wall, facing the sea, evidently belonging originally to the interior of a large apartment. These pilasters give it the aspect of an Egyptian structure. In no other Peruvian antiquities have pilasters been seen by us. On one of

the northern terraces were also remains of apartments. Here the brick appeared more friable, owing to a greater proportion of sand. Where they retained their shape, their dimensions were 9 inches in width by 6 inches deep, varying in height from 9 inches to 2 feet, and they were laid so as to break joint, though not always in a workmanlike manner. The remains of the town occupy some undulating ground of less elevation, a quarter of a mile to the northward. This also forms a rectangle, one-fifth by one-third of a mile in size. Through the middle runs lengthwise a straight street, 20 feet in width. The walls of some of the ruins are 30 feet high, and cross each other at right angles. The buildings were apparently connected together, except where the streets intervened. The large areas were again divided by thinner partitions, and one of them was observed to contain four rectangular pits, the plastering of which appeared quite fresh.

No traces of doors or windows toward the streets could be discovered, nor indeed anywhere else. The walls were exclusively of sun-dried brick, and their direction, northeast and southwest, the same as those of the temple, which fronted the sea. Some graves were observed to the southward of the temple, but the principal burying ground was between the temple and the town. Some of the graves were rectangular pits, lined with a dry wall of stone, and covered with layers of reeds and canes, on which the earth was filled in to the depth of a foot or more, so as to be even with the surface. The skulls brought from this place were of various characters; the majority of them presented the vertical elevation, or raised occiput, the usual characteristic of the ancient Peruvians, while others had the forehead and top of the head depressed. Eight of these were obtained, and are now deposited at Washington. The bodies were found enveloped in cloth of various qualities, and a variety in its colors still existed. Various utensils and other articles were found, which seemed to denote the occupation of the individual: Wooden needles and weaving utensils, netting made in the usual style, a sling, cordage of different kinds, a sort of coarse basket, fragments of pottery and plated stirrups. They also found various vegetable substances: Husks of Indian corn with ears of two varieties, one with the grain slightly pointed, the other the short and black variety, which is still very commonly cultivated; cotton seeds, small bunches of wool, gourd shells, with a square hole cut out, precisely as is done at present. These furnished evidence of the style of the articles manufactured before the arrival of the Spaniards, and of the cultivation of the vegetable products. When to these we add the native tuberous roots (among them the potato) cultivated in the mountains, and the animals found domesticated, viz, the llama, dog and guinea pig, and the knowledge of at least one metal, we may judge what has since been acquired.— *C. Wilkes.*

THE DUNHAM MANUFACTURING COMPANY, of Chicago, engaged in the manufacture and sale of patent devices for railway construction and equipment, has established a widely extended business in several important specialties, which they have brought prominently before the leading railroads of the United States and Canada.

FIRST STORY PLAN.　　SECOND STORY PLAN.

A RESIDENCE AT STOCKTON, CAL.

SCIENTIFIC AMERICAN

ARCHITECTS AND BUILDERS EDITION.

Entered at the Post Office of   New York as Second Class Matter.

Vol. XL.   Subscription, $2.50 a Year.   NEW YORK, FEBRUARY, 1891.   Single Copies, 25 Cents.   No. 2.

A CORNER OF A BOUDOIR.

Our illustration is from a colored drawing which appeared in the Royal Academy Exhibition last year. The chimneypiece, arch, and paneling of the room were finished in ivory white, door and furniture of dark mahogany. The frieze was an embossed paper, cream with gold background. Draperies, pale steel blue, and carpet background a darker shade of same color. The design and drawing are by Mr. J. Armstrong Stenhouse.—*Building News.*

Non-Porous Walls.

The prevention of the saturation of ordinary brick walls is one of the many problems in modern buildings. Architects, with true conservative instincts, still cling to the solid brick walls, though sanitarians and hygienic builders have been preaching a crusade against them for many a year; and they still believe in solid walls, although it has been shown how easily all the beauty of solid moulded jambs and reveals can be produced in walls constructed with a cavity, and that the hollow wall has quite as much strength, if properly bonded by ties, as the solid wall, and can carry all the weight that is ever likely to be brought upon it. The preference for solid walls lies in the sentiment of the thing; the glory of ancient architecture has, in the popular mind, been associated with solidity and massiveness, and the thick stone wall, such as we see in the Tower of London, and in hundreds of our English castles and fortresses, has become a thing in the imagination that cannot be eradicated by any amount of scientific theory. The Englishman puts his faith in thick walls as symbolical of impregnable England. The Americans, and our colonists, who live in or have visited countries where timber abounds, are ready to assert the merits of wooden houses and log cabins, though they must have a liking for the old English wall of stone or brick. Their houses

and villas have a thin, tawdry look about them; the reveals to windows look meager; there is a lack of projection and shadow, which are such valuable features of English indigenous architecture. Even the half-timbered houses of the States cannot compare for picturesque qualities with those erected in England, where the original types of half-timber building are to be found. The timbers have a "skin deep" appearance; but the shingle wall of the States has merits which cannot be disputed. The shingle construction there adopted and perfected combines warmth and dryness in the colder and damp climates, and those who live in frame houses half built of brick and covered with clapboarding and shingles say they combine all the advantages of both systems. One reason of this is because there is a cavity—the walls are partially hollow. But there are advantages in the material; being a non-conductor of heat, it retains the warmth. Take for example the dwellings of this kind found in New York, Massachusetts and other States. The exteriors are shingled, and stained a bright sienna or painted red, with olive-green "trimmings;" the roof is also shingled and painted red. The interiors are finished in cherry or some hard wood like oak. There is considerable comfort in these well finished houses. Other dwellings are sheathed and papered exteriorly, perhaps the first story is clapboarded and painted colonial yellow, with bottle green trimmings; the second story is shingled and painted red. Sometimes the clapboarding is painted a gray, with trimmings of darker shade. Whatever are the artistic merits or otherwise of these wooden houses, they are certainly comfortable, while the ordinary brick villa is subjected to every discomfort in wet weather, owing to the porousness of the bricks that are generally used.

If hollow walls are objected to, there are remedial measures. Thus, Sylvester's processs of repelling moisture is an old and simple plan that might be followed by builders before houses are let. It consists of

using two washes alternately for the surface of the walls, one composed of Castile soap and water, and the other of alum and water. The proportions are three pounds of soap to one gallon of water, and half a pound of alum to four gallons of water, both substances to be well dissolved before applying. The first soap wash should be laid on while boiling hot, with a flat brush, and a frothy appearance be produced. After twenty-four hours, when it will become dry and hard, the alum wash is to be applied warm, and should also be allowed to dry before a second coat of the soap wash is put on. These coats can be repeated till the walls are rendered impervious to water. The combination of soap and alum forms an insoluble compound which fills the pores of the brick. The reason why so many houses are uninhabitable through dampness is because the remedy is applied too late, when the bricks have become begrimed with soot. The solution should be applied to newly built walls, and in the manner we have described, thoroughly, not merely a weak solution improperly applied in about two coats. If the provision were made in the contract and specified, there would be little of the trouble afterward experienced by the tenants.—*Building News.*

If any of our readers have made an invention for which they have thoughts of taking a patent, they are invited to communicate with Messrs. Munn & Co., the publishers of this paper, who for a period of forty-three years have conducted a most successful bureau in this line. A pamphlet of instructions will be sent free, containing full directions how to obtain a patent, costs, etc. In very many cases, owing to their long experience, they can tell at once whether a patent probably can be obtained; and advice of this kind they are always happy to furnish free of charge. Address Munn & Co., SCIENTIFIC AMERICAN office, New York.

A CORNER OF A BOUDOIR—DESIGNED BY J. ARMSTRONG STENHOUSE.

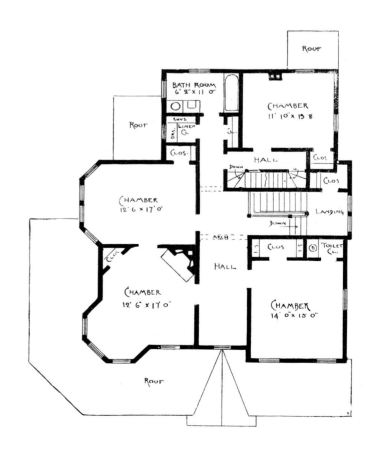

FIRST FLOOR PLAN

SECOND FLOOR PLAN

RESIDENCE OF E. B. BARTRAM, ESQ., BRIDGEPORT, CONN.

AN IMPROVED SANITARY EARTH CLOSET.

Where there are no water works or sewers, an earth closet such as is shown in the accompanying illustration is designed to serve as a convenience of the utmost importance. By its use dry earth or sifted ashes are made to absorb the offensive odors, and in a short time the resultant mass forms a rich garden soil, inoffensive to sight or smell. For its proper use three to five barrels of fine earth should be provided, in a place where it can be kept dry, and one empty barrel for changing. The case is of ash, and the receptacle, A,

LEONARD'S EARTH CLOSET COMMODE.

of galvanized iron, with bail and handle. The urine receptacle, B, is a common chamber vessel, and should be frequently emptied and kept clean. D is a swinging box containing the dry earth, suspended from a pivot, G, the spout, C, being held back out of the way. The flow of earth is regulated by a gate, E, and F is a bronze water closet pull attached by a rope to the swinging box, the earth being deposited on simply pulling the handle. These closets are made by the Grand Rapids Refrigerator Co., Grand Rapids, Mich.

STAMPED METAL CEILINGS.

Residence work in stamped ceilings requires the choicest designs, perfection in the seams, and a sufficient variety to meet the various sizes and purposes. The stamped ceiling invented by the manufacturer whose work is shown in the accompanying illustration meets these points, and makes a durable decoration, easily applied by decorators or carpenters.

The illustration is drawn to a scale of ⅜ inch per foot. The parlor shows the 14 by 14 inch plates with Greek border and leaf cove, with embossed mouldings. The hall shows the 24 by 32 inch plates. The rear hall, the leaf diaper pattern, made in large sheets. The library shows panels 18 by 18 inches and 18 by 27 inches with mouldings and cove cornice. The dining room, 30 by 30 inch panels. The kitchen and pantry, a plain panel, 24 by 28 inches. The large variety of panels, borders, mouldings, etc., made by Mr. Northrop enables him to furnish ceilings suitable for all classes of buildings, and his patented method of joining the panels makes the simplest and most perfect seams. Parties writing should send a diagram of the room to to be ceiled, and mention whether it is a new or an old building, and if old, whether plastered or not. Catalogues free, on application to Henry S. Northrop, manufacturer, 18 Rose Street, New York.

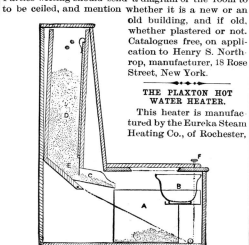

EARTH CLOSET COMMODE—SECTIONAL VIEW.

THE PLAXTON HOT WATER HEATER.

This heater is manufactured by the Eureka Steam Heating Co., of Rochester, N. Y. It is a Canadian invention, which was first used in the province of Ontario, and has been put to its most thorough test in the very severe climate of Winnipeg, Manitoba, in which city it has now been in use for four years, and where more than one hundred and fifty of these heaters are in successful operation.

They are there used for heating the largest commercial buildings. For such structures, where the space to be heated is too great for the capacity of a single heater, the largest sizes are set in pairs or even in groups of three, connected by headers and so arranged that in very cold weather the group of two or three heaters, as the case may be, may be fired all at the same time, and all act together as one heater, maintaining the circulation in the whole connected system of piping. In milder weather, only one heater need be fired. The economy of this arrangement and its adaptability to changes of temperature is apparent.

It is simple in construction and can therefore be furnished at a moderate price. There are no parts liable to give out or get out of order. The entire back and front, except the doors, are water spaces, while the body of the heater is composed of sections made in pairs, with intercalating fingers, as plainly shown in the cut. These fingers are not simple water spaces. A diaphragm is so placed in each that the finger, except near its extremity, is divided into two parts, one above the other. This device insures a positive circulation in

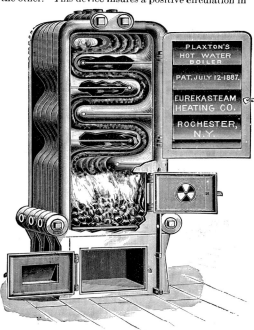

THE PLAXTON HOT WATER HEATER.

the general upward direction throughout the entire length of each section and its fingers. The pairs of sections and their fingers, when set up in the assembling of the heater, stand in close apposition with each other and so form the sinuous flue which is the most striking and unique feature of the apparatus. The large cleaning door gives an open view of all these fire surfaces and renders it easy to clean the fire. The heater when set up is covered with a smooth jacket of asbestos mortar, which prevents loss of heat by radiation into the cellar. The rocking grate, with its vertical shaking handle, is convenient and labor saving. The proportion of grate surface to fire surface is properly adjusted and is constant throughout different sizes. The Eureka Steam Heating Co. will furnish all correspondents with testimonials attesting its highly successful record.

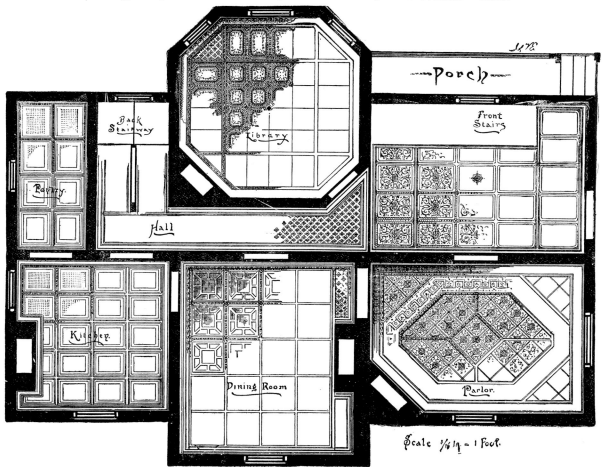

APPLICATION OF NORTHROP'S STAMPED METAL CEILINGS IN RESIDENCES.

SCIENTIFIC AMERICAN

Copyright by Munn & Co., 1891.

ARCHITECTS AND BUILDERS EDITION.

Entered at the Post Office of New York as Second Class Matter.

NEW YORK, JULY 1891.

Vol. XII. Subscription, $2.50 a Year.

Single Copies, 25 Cents.

No. 1.

THE NEW BUILDING OF THE HIBERNIA SAVINGS AND LOAN SOCIETY, SAN FRANCISCO.

A GARDENER'S LODGE.

The picturesque little dwelling shown below of colored pine, was built at X by O. André, of Neuilly, on private property. It is a gardener's lodge of modest pretensions, the projecting roof of which affords shelter to pedestrians from rain or from the burning rays of the sun. Its general appearance reminds one of Alsatian dwellings.

In its erection pains were taken to use only wood cut by machinery.

The little projection added to the roof in the rear is utilized for the storage of utensils, etc. Under the front roof is a shelf for bee hives.

Wall Paper.

Although wall paper has become an essential feature of interior decorations and is found in almost every house in the country, it would seem from general observation, says the *American Stationer*, that nothing which enters into our home life is selected with less thoughtful attention. The pattern is often chosen from a sample, with no reference whatever to the furniture, the carpets, the size or shape of a room, and it too often happens that after great outlay and no little trouble and inconvenience the effect is totally at variance with preconceived ideas of the effect. The fault, quite likely, is less in the paper than in the individual who selected it.

Of course there is a great deal of ignorance regarding decorations; few people understand the underlying principles, and, strange as it may seem, fewer still have grasped the first laws of color effect, of contrast and of harmonious scheme.

In no single feature of the decoration of a room is there more need of discriminating judgment and cultivation, for the very obvious reason that there is a character of permanency in the wall hangings which does not inhere in any other class of furnishings. If they are out of taste and harmony, it must be endured for a period of time, at least, while the movable articles can be changed about, grouped or replaced if they are not wholly satisfactory. Indeed, it is not difficult to believe that a poor and homely wall paper might seriously affect a nervously organized system sensitive to, although possibly ignorant of, the influence of color and forms, so that the story of the farmer's wife who committed suicide because she was so tired of looking at the ugly paper on the walls is not altogether improbable.

Paper hanging may not be an exact science, but it is something of an art. To be able by the use of paper to make a low-ceilinged room look higher and a too lofty one lower; to give a cozy aspect to an oversized room and enlarge the apparent area of a little one certainly requires a knowledge of cause and effect and taste and skill in making such knowledge obedient which are things the average man and woman do not possess.

Then, too, the effect of stability should not be wanting and the function of background for furniture and pictures should not be ignored. In the architecture of antiquity proportion played a conspicuous part in the arrangement of walls, in which there was a sort of upward striving which expressed itself in the heavy, solid-looking dado, the lighter middle wall, and the bright, airy, unconstrained frieze, thus conveying in the dado the idea of the strength and solidity needed to support the wall, a lighter decorative scheme for the middle portion, which suffers less strain, and a purely decorative frieze which requires little or no strength for the work it has to perform.

In observing these and many more details, and in carrying them out successfully, requires special acquirements and experience. The exercise of taste—its possession being a first necessity, of course—and familiarity with the laws of proportion and harmony are essential, so that on the whole it would seem best, in all situations requiring such technical skill, to employ a professional decorator, and trust to his taste to produce a scheme of wall covering which will bring all of the contents of the room into sympathetic and harmonious relation with it and to each other.

Many of the new styles of wall paper brought out within the year are singularly rich and effective. Some flat papers are marvels of tasteful and effective designing. While these are classed among the cheaper goods, they are in many other respects equal to any other made, especially where luster tints are used, which give a depth of tone to the coloring not seen in ordinary flat papers.

There are also extremely elegant papers known as "crystalline" and "opalescent," in which the effect is produced by mixing mica with the pulp. Pulverized mica is also mixed with the colors in the process of printing, by which brilliant results are secured. There are many charming designs produced in mica paper, the grounds generally being of a pale, soft tone, which throws up the flowers in the design clearly and sharply. On a pale sage green there are thrown irregular branches of cherry blossoms, and laurel blossoms in white mica shining upon a warm gray ground is another most charming design. Often the flowers have an iridescent glow, as though sparkling with dew under the beams of a morning sun. As may be supposed, the effect is quite wonderful.

Satin papers show trailing vines of arbutus, morning glories and trumpet flowers in deliciously soft tints. Cornflowers, bluebells and graceful grasses, falling in showers or gathered in loose clusters here and there on an ivory ground, are indescribably pretty. Then there are brocaded patterns showing details in soft, pleasing colors outlined with gold, and sometimes the stencil is used with fine effect with blended colors on a pale or creamy ground. A pattern of aster blossoms rendered in this way is very handsome. The borders for these papers are often very striking, the grounds being of bright colors at the base and shading away to a light neutral tint at the top, overlaid with garlands of flowers or upright, reedy growths mingled with bright-hued blossoms.

"Damasks" form another line of beautiful papers in which the designs are usually in floral effects of softly blended tints, there being sometimes several colors of harmonious shades thrown up in pretty groupings on gold grounds. In these, too, there are patterns in large leaves in pale colors running hither and thither over the paper, the veins and ribs being stenciled in with great precision and beauty.

Flock papers are showing raised effects which are marvelous. The contrasts are stronger than ever, too, and striking effects are secured by using different colors in the various layers of flock used to secure the relief effect. Crystalline grounds are used also, on which are raised patterns in light, pale colors. Palm leaves, iris, water lilies and immense flowers are used in designs for this paper. A design showing a flat arrangement of leaves and grasses, upon which is superimposed a flock palm leaf in three layers, the first a shell pink, the second a light tan shade, and the top a creamy white, is very elegant.

Leather papers are handsomer than ever, various effects, such as carved woods, bronze relief, old ivory carving, burnished copper and leather in illuminated designs being secured with beautiful exactness. In the patterns all sorts of floral conceits, landscapes, marines, Moorish scroll, birds, animals and insects, glowing with the sheen of gold, silver, copper, or in the metallic colors, give a sort of mediæval splendor to their appearance.

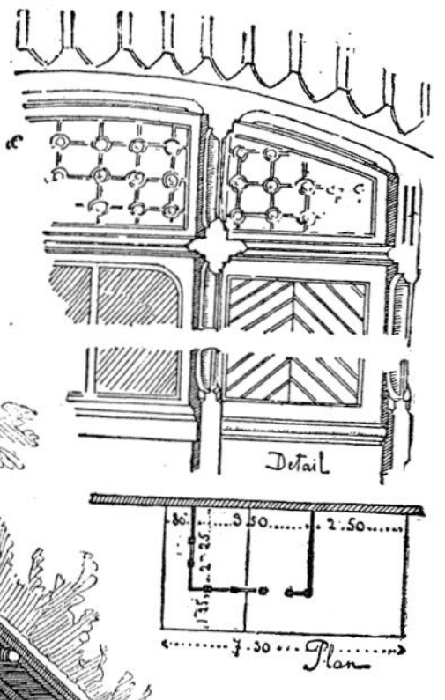

A GARDENER'S LODGE.

The Hall.

Mr. Palmer Henderson has been writing for a syndicate of daily papers his impressions of the modern house. His fancies are interesting, but not often of much value, for he talks about the homes of that wealthy class who make fads of furnishing their houses and have no limits as to cost put upon them; nevertheless, he makes some suggestions that may be of value to the designer of the humblest cottage. He says of the hall:

You remember when it was dark as Africa, four feet wide, with narrow stairs straight down to the door, leaving only space enough for a sewer pipe umbrella stand decorated with decalco—how do you spell that? —and a black walnut hat rack squeezed into the side, upon whose pegs you bid fair to be impaled, so dizzy did the six inches of wavy mirror make you. How fortunate there was never more, it would have been as bad as a sea voyage! I don't remember anything else either ornamental or useful, except the kerosene lamp with pendent glass prisms which used to hang just low enough to catch your silk hat. Look on that picture, and then on this.

The hall should be about the pleasantest room in the house, cheery, homelike, inviting. At its threshold a man should throw off the perplexities, cares, and work of the day with his overcoat; and after a seance with the world, the flesh, and the devil—otherwise society—a woman should glide into it as a ship into a quiet harbor, saying to herself the minute she enters the room:

> "Stay at home, my heart, and rest,
> Homekeeping hearts are happiest."

While the stranger within the gates should feel at once the gracious atmosphere of home, and be inclined to answer its "Abandon grief all ye who enter here," with the old Jewish salutation, "Peace be to this house."

What is an ideal hall? Well, if you are blessed with a sizable piece of the root, this: It should be wide, with all the other rooms opening from it by archways. The floor, of course, hard wood, parquetry best, even yellow pine in narrow strips, with here and there a rug. Have the ceiling beamed with wood corresponding to the floor and build a high wainscoting around and up the stairs. The walls? Here I'd defy tradition: brilliant scarlet and gold. Red is the color of warmth and hospitality; make it speak for you before you appear to offer your hand in the good old way. Have a fireplace by all means.

To resume, if your stairs are broad and turn, this fire nook might be under them. From the mantel may hang your ornate Chinese gong whereby the household are awakened for a new day. Hall trees and all kindred affairs, no matter how handsome, when hung with dejected coats, make a pretty hall look like an "ol' close" emporium. I think I have solved it: A tiled vestibule with seat built in at either side should precede your hall. This need not be so wide. Have two narrow closets taken off the sides, opening into the hall. The doors can be invisible, the wainscoting forming the bottom, beveled mirrors the top, and there you are, one for the masculine members of the family, one for the ladies.

Boxes with door fronts can be built at the end at a convenient height, for silk hats and bonnets. Inside the doors can be linen cane and umbrella cases, or you can put them with your driving gloves, rubbers—no, let us be swell, gums—and gossamers, into the handsome carved chest seat which should stand against the wall. If this chest is modern it means simply money; if 'tis a Florentine antique, for instance, it means travel; but if it's an actual heirloom, it's equivalent to an American patent of nobility.

PATENTS.

Messrs. Munn & Co., in connection with the publication of the **Scientific American**, continue to examine improvements and to act as Solicitors of Patents for Inventors.

In this line of business they have had *forty years' experience*, and now have *unequaled facilities* for the preparation of Patent Drawings, Specifications, and the prosecution of Applications for Patents in the United States, Canada, and Foreign Countries. **Messrs. Munn & Co.** also attend to the preparation of Caveats, Copyrights for Books, Labels, Reissues, Assignments, and Reports on Infringements of Patents. All business intrusted to them is done with special care and promptness, on very reasonable terms.

A pamphlet sent free of charge, on application, containing full information about Patents and how to procure them; directions concerning Labels, Copyrights, Designs, Patents, Appeals Reissues, Infringements, Assignments, Rejected Cases, Hints on the Sale of Patents, etc.

We also send, *free of charge*, a synopsis of Foreign Patent Laws, showing the cost and method of securing patents in all the principal countries of the world.

MUNN & CO., Solicitors of Patents, 361 Broadway, New York.
BRANCH OFFICE.—622 F Street, Washington, D. C.

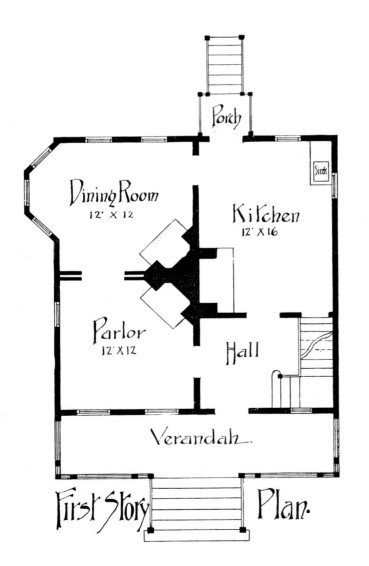

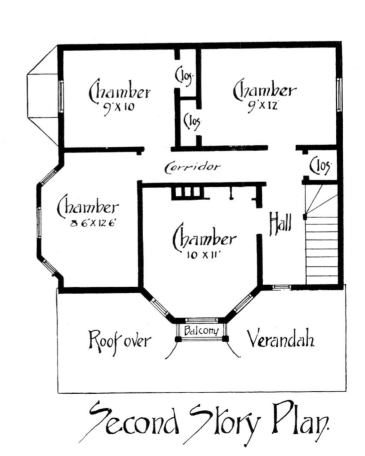

First Story Plan.   Second Story Plan.

A COTTAGE FOR ONE THOUSAND DOLLARS.

AN ARCHITECT'S HOME.

"Netherheys," Watford, the residence of W. Wallis Baldwin, architect. To design a house on a small scale which shall have the comfort and convenience of a large one is not an easy matter, or, if it be easy, it is not often done. In houses of little more than cottage dimensions there is generally a nip or a pinch somewhere; entrance, parlors, bedroom, or kitchen usually succumb to some hardship of size, aspect, or shape. But in "Netherheys" there has been a very critical adjustment of claims; in fact, so nice did it appear to me that I feel much indebted to the architect owner for his permission to publish the plan, which explains for the benefit of others how he has worked out the problem of making a small house thoroughly cozy, comfortable, and complete.

In an area of less than an acre, surrounded on two sides by broad roads, in the suburbs of Watford, "Netherheys" has advantages of position, aspect, and surroundings which are not usually devoted to so small a house. By the design of its exterior the cottage-like appearance is very marked, more especially on the entrance front. Passing through the quaintly designed gateway, the drive opens into a square gravel court bordered by square-cut yew hedges. It will be seen from the plan that the outbuilding to the left flanks and protects the entrance agreeably, and between this and the stair turret is a paved landing. The porch is nicely finished with marble step, mosaic floor, high dado of oak framing with serge panels, and leather paper wall filling and ceiling. A good feature, and one we seldom meet with, is the circular stair turret. The stairs are shut off from the porch by a doorway, and from the hall by a curtained archway. This semicircular arch repeats at the other end of the hall, and within it are arranged in a V-shape the doors to the drawing room and own room (see sketch). This little hall is a great feature of comfort in the house with its little corner fireplace (hooded over from marble jambs) and long five-light window with fixed seat under. Generally speaking the good points of the plan will be obvious to many of my readers. The dining room is conveniently served from the kitchen, as much out of sight and sound as is possible in a small house, and far more so than one usually finds in large houses. The fireplace recess is just deep enough to provide comfortable fixed seats at either side of the mantel jambs, and gives a very convenient breadth to the room. The garden porch forms a useful connection between the dining and drawing rooms. The drawing room is a pretty apartment, with a sort of orange-colored paper, specially printed for the architect. The third room is fitted as a sort of library and business room, with an arched fireplace recess. The bedrooms, bathroom, and upper corridor landing are all nicely treated. A long terrace and Dutch flower garden are good items in the surroundings which my sketches indicate. (See pages 28 and 29.)

As the proof of a pudding is in the eating, so we may say of a house that a proof of its comfort is found by living in it, and we can safely affirm that in all our wanderings we have never realized more fully the benefits of a well designed modern English home than at "Netherheys."—*T. Raffles Davison, The Brit. Arch.*

If any of our readers have made an invention for which they have thoughts of taking a patent, they are invited to communicate with Messrs. Munn & Co., the publishers of this paper, who for a period of forty-three years have conducted a most successful bureau in this line. A pamphlet of instructions will be sent free, containing full directions how to obtain a patent, costs, etc. In very many cases, owing to their long experience, they can tell at once whether a patent probably can be obtained; and advice of this kind they are always happy to furnish free of charge. Address Munn & Co., SCIENTIFIC AMERICAN office, New York.

The Planning and Construction of American Frame Houses.

Mr. C. H. Brodie recently read before the Architectural Association a paper on this subject, illustrated by some sketches, details, and tracings by the author, and also by numerous plans and perspectives from the United States professional journals, says *Building News.* Mr. Brodie mentioned that he was engaged on business in America during the winter of 1887 and the spring of 1888, during which period he spent considerable time in New York and Chicago, with flying visits to Boston, Baltimore, Philadelphia, Washington, Pittsburg, St. Louis, Kansas City, Milwaukee, St. Paul, and Minneapolis, and other cities. Such houses as were illustrated on the walls are, he remarked, the type of American homes, alike in the North, South, East, and West. In the actual town area, the erection of timber houses is now forbidden. Still, in the Southern States universally, and over the country and suburban districts generally, it is rarely that any but timber houses are erected. The average time for erecting a frame house is ninety days, but many have been built in sixty, and while the life of the structure may be averaged fifty years, there are very many in existence even one hundred and some two hundred years old and over.

Again, stone quarries as yet worked are few and far between, and brickworks are not by any means numerous. But the country abounds with the most beautiful timber, with which even the denuded Eastern States are kept plentifully supplied by means of immense rafts floated down the great rivers to convenient points for transport by rail or boat. A frame house may be very expeditiously erected. The drawings on the walls show a basement, arising only one foot or so out of the ground, built of either brick or undressed stone, and on this is a frame of quarter partitions, two stories high, forming inclosure and divisions. These and the joints being fixed in position, the roof can be immediately constructed and covered in, so that while the outside is being completed, the inside, too, is progressing, and during the time that we should be getting up a scaffold, the frame house is built. The plasterwork being then, if necessary, dried by artificial heat, the joinery and other fittings are placed, and the dwelling is ready for occupation in a very short time. Should the worthy owner's family increase, additions to the house are just as easily and expeditiously made. The plans show a basement and two upper stories, and the roofs being mostly of steep pitch, plenty of room for attics is obtained in them. The basement contains a laundry, beer and wine cellars, coal cellars for both house and furnace coal, larders, and the heating chamber, containing either a boiler for steam or a furnace for hot-air heating. The heat there generated is distributed by ducts quite evenly over the whole house, and most of the rooms have no fireplaces. This is a stage of civilization to which we have not yet generally attained. Where fireplaces do occur—and this is chiefly on the ground floor—an ash pit is provided under each, into which, when the hearth is swept up, the ashes, etc., are dropped by moving a dump or hopper. These ash pits are marked on the basement plans. The ducts serve in the hot weather to distribute cold air over the house, the air in the cellar, whence they start, being naturally cooler than that outside, while it can, if necessary, be cooled still further by artificial means.

Coming to the ground floor or first story, as their plans have it, we find a parlor and dining room, and also perhaps a library or a second parlor. The dining room is always in connection with the kitchen, through a lobby or pantry. You will note, also, that there is no scullery shown, although on some of the plans is a diminutive space marked "sink room." On this floor are also various store rooms and closets, water closets, lavatory, etc., depending as to size, number and variety on the general dimensions of the house. And here I would call special attention to the very complete way in which all classes of American houses are fitted with cupboards, shelves, drawers, sideboards, bookcases, etc., all conducting in so eminent a degree to the comfort and ease of the occupants. No bedroom that I occupied in any private house in the States was without a cupboard large enough to walk into and turn round in. The convenience of this is too obvious to need expression. The hall is always furnished, and used as a room; most of the American plans have it designated "reception hall," and some even "sitting room." The veranda is also a most important feature, and one never omitted. During the hot season it is inclosed with blinds, and becomes the most frequented part of the house. The first floor has the usual bed and bath rooms, linen closet, etc. You will observe that in most cases the water closet apparatus is kept away from, and not, as with us, next to the outside walls. This is to avoid fracture by freezing during the intensely cold weather. To return to our first floor plan.

You will note that all the chief bedrooms have a fixed lavatory fitted, generally, in a cupboard, so as to be out of sight. This adds, of course, very considerably to the plumber's bill, but in the long run it is a great saving, for labor of all kinds is terribly costly. Balconies are freely provided on this floor, and are delightful spots in the hot weather, while they always form a feature in the elevations. The attics are used for servants'

The Hall

AN ARCHITECT'S HOME.

from the Terrace End

The Planning and Construction of American Frame Houses.

rooms—each still with a good cupboard—box rooms, store rooms, etc., or the space is frequently just floored and then left to be cut up as the wants of the occupants may later on suggest. About the elevations, outside and in, or the artistic part, one need say nothing, except that, to our eyes, the calm and dignified treatment of the English example contrasts very favorably with the fussiness and over-picturesqueness and evident striving after "features" which spoils so many of the other designs. The construction you can study at your leisure by referring to a specification printed in black, which is in the Institute Library. It is indexed under the name of the publishers, Messrs. Palliser, of New York, to whom I am indebted for a good deal of the information this paper contains, and for a drawing and specification hung on the wall. I was struck with the very practical character of the specification. For instance, among the general clauses I read: "The carpenter will make all patterns, etc., and will provide suitable protections to all openings to keep out the cold, rain, etc., and will clear the building of all carpenter's waste materials before the plastering is commenced.

panded metal now coming into use in this country. The plastering is to consist of "a good coat of brown, well-haired mortar, made of pure unslaked lime and clean, sharp bank sand, free from loam and salt, and best cattle or goat hair, well mixed by continued working, and stacked in the rough for at least — weeks before putting on." The finish is to be "a coat of best soapstone finish, manufactured by the company, composed of finishing lime putty (two parts) and patent soapstone finishing (three parts), thoroughly mixed two days before using, and applied in the most careful manner, as per directions"—I suppose of the manufacturers. The order of the trades as they are placed in the specification differs considerably from our usual arrangement; and we next come to the carpenter and joiner. All the timber which will be exposed at the finish is required to be of a certain quality pine. The joists are to be placed, in all cases, with the "crowning" edge upward, and those over so many feet in length are to be "worked crowning" so many inches before being placed in the building. Describing the partitions—a most important item of a framed house—the specification directs that "all door and window studs are to be set double, and all openings over three

The Entrance Front

feet wide trussed overhead. All angles must be formed solid by blocking and spiking two studs together. No studs are to stand on the floor, nor on the joists, if there are partitions under, but all are to foot on top of the partition plate below."

The outside of the external partitions, and also the roof, is covered with seven-eighths inch matched boarding, called "sheathing," which has to be "nailed at each edge at every bearing with 10d. nails." Nails are throughout the specifications described as so many "penny" ones—a nomenclature common also in Ireland. The whole exterior is then covered with waterproof felt, the joints lapping two inches, and it is tarred under all architraves, friezes, cornices, brackets, etc., "so as to make a perfectly tight job." Outside this felt comes the finish which is actually seen, which on the partitions is weatherboarding, or, as it is called in the States, "clapboarding." This is to be of "clear, beveled white pine, five inches in width by one-half inch thick at the butt, and three-sixteenths inch at the thin edge, laid with not less than a lap of one and one-fourth inch, and nailed with 8d. box nails every sixteen inches. The nails are to be set in." The veranda floor is to be constructed with one and one-fourth inch by three and one-half inch white pine boards, laid with "paint joints." The roof is generally covered with

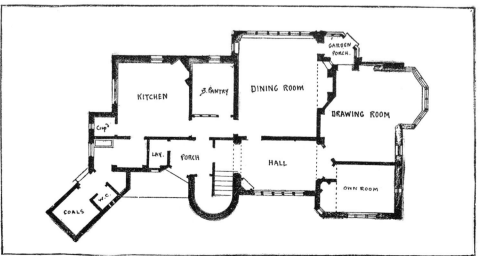

The Terrace Front

The mason must provide coal and stove in cold weather for heating the building while his work is going forward and until it is dry."

Continuing, we shall get particulars how this class of house is put together, and we naturally find after the general clauses the necessary directions as to the excavations. The only unusual point here is: "The bank is to be dug well away from the walls, and left open until the walls are set and dry." The damp course is to be either slate and cement or asphalt. The brick walls are required to be built to "a true line from one end to the other, even to the cutting of a brick where necessary, so that a carpenter can size the joints to an exact width, and place them directly upon the wall without blocking up with chips or pieces of wood." The facing of these brick walls is to be "neatly tucked and properly cleaned down with aquafortis, and oiled with raw linseed oil at completion," care being taken not to injure, in cleaning down with acid, any cut stone work.

The laths for lathing are to be "laid a full one-fourth inch apart, and joints broken every eighteen inches." Wood laths, however, are now rarely used. I never saw any at all. The plastering is put on wire netting, or one of the many forms of pierced or ex-

AN ARCHITECT'S HOME.

shingles, and so also are the gables and other features. The shingles are usually of cypress, which grows abundantly in the swamps of New Jersey and the more Southern States. The logs are floated down the river to the various mills, where the shingles are cut in enormous numbers. One mill cuts 300,000 daily. They are eighteen inches by six inches and are on battens, width on roofs five and one-half inches to the weather, and on vertical parts six inches, each nailed with two nails, and kept three inches from angle of valleys. Sometimes the roofs are of slate, and frequently they are flat, in which case they are mostly covered with tin, although asphaltum or gravel composition is sometimes used. In either case the roof is boarded on the joists with seven-eighths inch boarding.

Coming to the floors, pugging—or, as it is called, "deafening"—is used in all the best rooms, and these have also a double floor—a rough deal one and a hard wood finished one, with between them a layer of "all wool Pyramid brand, resin sized, deafening felt," fixed down by two inches to one-half inch slips, to which the hard wood floor is secret-nailed. The rough floor is described to be fitted carefully around all studs, etc., up to the sheathing, so as to prevent mice circulating. Here is a good clause: "All the plastering is to be finished, cellar cemented, and all mason work done and thoroughly dried through before any of the interior joinery is brought into the building or put in position." The materials used for doors are required to be thoroughly seasoned and kiln-dried, and on the plans the sizes for both width and height are figured. Sliding doors are much used, while many openings have no doors at all. These would be provided with curtains, which give the desired privacy. There is no question of "draughts" in an American house, which is warmed equally throughout. All the doors have a hard wood slip three-fourths inch thick, splayed each edge, fixed under them. This enables the door to open clear of carpets, etc. The windows are mostly double hung sashes, requiring no special description. All are directed to have a burglar-proof fastening. After a description of the stairs most minute directions follow for the fittings of the various pantries and closets upstairs and down. These include clothes closets, linen and china closets, and butler's and kitchen pantries, as well as the various store rooms. Then we get a full description of the refrigerator and ice safe, which consists of two thicknesses of boarding, two inches apart, filled with mineral wool, then an air space of one inch, and a layer of resin-sized waterproof paper, the actual inside being of clean, narrow matched spruce. The lower part is the ice safe or tank, and it is lined with sheet zinc, and the bottom covered with a wood grating to prevent the ice cutting the metal. The doors of these spaces are constructed in precisely the same way, and the joints between door and frame are double rabbeted.

The wood finish is described to be first a certain patent "mineral filling," and then another "patent transparent wood finish." The hard wood floors are to be done in the same way, but with a "vegetable" filler. The tinwork is to be painted two coats of metallic paint, and here I may say that this tin—or, to speak more correctly, tinned iron—is used wherever we use lead, and also for the rain water pipes and gutters. Lead is too expensive, and is also more affected by changes of temperature.

PAPER FROM CORN HUSKS.—Corn husks boiled in caustic soda are being utilized for the manufacture of paper. The cooking process results in the formation of a spongy, glutinous paste, which is subjected to heavy pressure so as to eliminate the gluten, the fiber remaining being made into paper in the ordinary way.

The Entrance

The Dining Room

AN ARCHITECT'S HOME.

THE WASHINGTON STREET TUNNEL, CHICAGO.

It is impossible to estimate how many people daily cross the branches of the Chicago River, which separate the business portions of the city from the great north and west sides and divide the city into three distinct sections, each having its particular characteristics. It is sufficient to state that the various bridges long ago proved inadequate, and tunnels were built under the river to accommodate the currents of traffic continually passing to and from the north and west divisions. It is stated that 22,000 vessels pass through the Chicago River in the seven months comprising the season of navigation, and the constant swinging of bridges is a hinderance and delay that even the tunnels cannot adequately relieve. The Washington Street tunnel, through which the West Chicago Street Railway Company has the right of way, well illustrates tunnel construction. This tunnel is a little more than 1,525 feet long, and was built in 1869, at a cost of nearly $600,000. The bed of the river and the top of the masonry of the river portion are the same, and as it allowed a depth of but 14 feet at low water in the river, the top of the masonry was continually being damaged by vessels, and proved an obstruction to the free navigation of the river at low water.

A few years ago the West Chicago Street Railway Company got permission from the City Council to operate its cars through the tunnel, on condition that the level under the river should be lowered so as to have at least 17 feet of water over it at the lowest stage, or 19 feet at mean water, and also that they build a masonry center and end piers over the tunnel to accommodate a swing bridge, the city supplying the superstructure. Mr. S. G. Artingstall, the well known Chicago engineer, was intrusted with the work, and it was completed in the spring of 1890. For the river section one-half of the stream was closed by a cofferdam, the timber crib which was to serve as the foundation for the masonry center pier being used as the head of the cofferdam; when this was pumped dry of water the arch of the old tunnel was taken up and a cover for the tunnel built with steel girders 20 inches deep and 2½ feet centers, with brick arches between the girders in four rings of brick, covered with a layer of asphalt and then with 12 inches in thickness of cement concrete. For the portion under the crib for the center pier, and also under the dock walls or end piers, a three-centered arch, built with five rings of bricks, was adopted. The part under the center pier was built by the usual methods of tunneling under the cofferdam. This part has not only to serve the purpose of a roof over the tunnel, but also is now supporting the masonry center pier and swing bridge. The approaches and all parts of the tunnel at the time were put in thorough repair, the grade of roadway under the river lowered to correspond with the lowering of the roof, and the grade of approach changed.

The West Division Street Railroad Company are now building under the Chicago River, about one-quarter mile south of Washington Street, a tunnel for the exclusive use of their street cable cars. This work is being done under the direction of Mr. Artingstall, who is now chief engineer of the sanitary district of Chicago, and it is expected will be finished in the fall of 1892. The dimensions of the tunnel are very large, as the company are sparing no expense to make it light, airy, and pleasant for their passengers. The tunnel is 30 feet clear width inside by 16 feet high, and besides passing under the river, goes 'under two seven-story buildings and one five-story building, and also under all the railroad tracks entering the Union Depot. A large portion of this tunnel is built, and the part under the tracks is in process of construction; the tracks have been undermined and supported without interfering with the passage of a single train. The cost of this tunnel will be about $2,225,000.—*The Graphic.*

Church Spires.

The origin of the spire, like that of the pointed arch, is merely matter of conjecture. The probability is that it arose out of the peaked roof usually given to campaniles and towers of a preceding period, which form was afterward gradually improved upon and refined, till it eventually grew up into the slender tapering spire. According to such supposition, we would refer to the tower of Thaon Church, in Normandy, as an example exhibiting the rudiments of the spire, it being no more than a steep peaked roof or low pyramid, whose height does not exceed three-fourths of its base. A peak of this kind differs also from the spire, both in being the same in plan as the tower on which it is placed and in being immediately set upon it, whereas the spire is almost invariably an octagon or other polygon, and is surrounded at its base with a parapet. In Italy, where campaniles are usually detached square towers of very slender or lofty proportions, the spire is almost unknown, for such towers have seldom more than a mere pyramidal roof or peak, which, though it may be considered as the germ from which the Gothic spire was afterward developed, is in itself of quite different character; yet, at the same time, that of each is best adapted to the respective style. There are some few instances of square spires,

THE WASHINGTON STREET TUNNEL CHICAGO.

among them a very singular one at Egeln, in Germany, where two such spires are set immediately together upon the same tower. But however slender in their proportions such spires may otherwise be, they have a certain heavy massiveness of form. When, therefore, greater loftiness and lightness were aimed at in this feature, the adoption of a polygonal plan for it became almost matter of course; for although, in a geometrical drawing, the general outline and proportions of a spire are the same, whether it be square or octangular in plan, the perspective or actual appearance is widely different; because, in the latter case, the diagonal breadth of the square tower below is cut off, and each side or plane of which the spire is composed becomes a much more pointed triangle. Besides which, the polygonal spire produces a degree of contrast and variety highly favorable to general effect in the pointed style.

Ownership of Plans.

The question of the ownership of plans, under French law, is brought up, and very clearly answered, in *La Semaine des Constructeurs* for Oct. 3, 1891. A correspondent asks the "Committee on Jurisprudence" of that journal, which is composed of persons thoroughly acquainted with the subject, whether an architect is bound to deliver the plans of a building to the

proprietor of the building, after the work is completed. The reply, which is certainly definite enough, is as follows: "The architect is obliged to deliver, to the proprietor who has employed him, the plans of the constructions which have been carried out under his direction, as soon as the work is completed, on the condition, however, that the architect's fees have been fully paid." This view of the law is supported by several decisions in France.—*Amer. Architect.*

Simplicity in Furnishing and Decorating.

If people could only be guided into simple habits and ideas as regards so-called comforts and ornaments, we should not only be more likely to develop nobler art, but also to secure less toil and trouble in the care and keeping of the useless gimcrackery with which the homes of all, from noble dukes to well-to-do tradespeople, at present abound. As a rule, it may be safely admitted that rooms are too much furnished and that the doors, windows, fireplace, floor, walls and ceiling have too little competent care bestowed upon them. Were the constructive features of a room properly looked after, much furniture and upholstery would be as needless as it is troublesome to keep in order and move about. And this brings up another important point in house furnishing too often forgotten—the question of dust. Dwellers in town are particularly subject to this all-prevailing evil, an evil arising not altogether from without.

Houses are more or less vibratory, especially where there is heavy street or train traffic in the vicinity, and we have not yet cleared out our stock of smoky flues. So that in addition to paying particular attention to the fitting of doors and windows, we would urge the selection of only such furniture as may be easily moved about, or so raised above the ground as to leave at least 9 inches clear space underneath. Avoid useless side tables and cabinets, which are so often dragged in for no other purpose in the world but to carry "art emporium" rubbish. Remember that all furniture beyond what is really necessary for comfort and convenience only provides so many more traps wherewith to catch the dust. Avoid all woolen and fluffy stuff in such upholstery as it may be deemed necessary to have. These two or three simple hints can be acted upon by nearly everybody. To those whose means admit it, we would suggest the use of thin parquet over old floors; upon such a floor only one or two rugs, in lieu of the usual carpet, would be needed, which should be of a close, hard texture. Then we would substitute the grand and semi-grand piano for the dust-attracting cottage instrument where possible, and abolish forever the hideous practice of covering our furniture with all kinds of drapery and frippery.

PATENTS.

Messrs. Munn & Co., in connection with the publication of the Scientific American, continue to examine improvements and to act as Solicitors of Patents for Inventors.

In this line of business they have had *forty-five years' experience*, and now have *unequaled facilities* for the preparation of Patent Drawings, Specifications, and the prosecution of Applications for Patents in the United States, Canada, and Foreign Countries. Messrs. Munn & Co. also attend to the preparation of Caveats, Copyrights for Books, Labels, Reissues, Assignments, and Reports on Infringements of Patents. All business intrusted to them is done with special care and promptness, on very reasonable terms.

A pamphlet sent free of charge, on application, containing full information about Patents and how to procure them; directions concerning Labels, Copyrights, Designs, Patents, Appeals Reissues, Infringements, Assignments, Rejected Cases, Hints on the Sale of Patents, etc.

We also send, *free of charge*, a synopsis of Foreign Patent Laws, showing the cost and method of securing patents in all the principal countries of the world.

MUNN & CO., Solicitors of Patents, 361 Broadway, New York.
BRANCH OFFICE.—622 F Street, Washington, D. C.

SCIENTIFIC AMERICAN

ARCHITECTS AND BUILDERS EDITION.

Copyright by Munn & Co., 1892.

Entered at the Post Office of New York as Second Class Matter.

NEW YORK, MAY, 1892.

Vol. XIII. Subscription, $2.50 a Year.

Single Copies, 25 Cents.

No. 5.

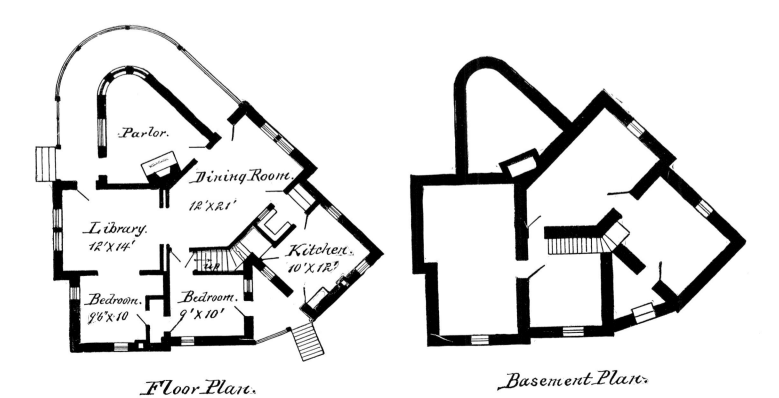

Floor Plan.

Basement Plan.

A ONE STORY BRICK COTTAGE

97

STAIR BUILDERS' GOODS.

The design for a stair finish, shown in the illustration, appears in the 1892 catalogue of Messrs. S. E. Smith & Brother, 197 W. Seventh Street, St. Paul, Minn. The company are constantly getting out new designs, of which their catalogue presents a large number, and have the highest class of special machines and machine tools for getting out such work. Their goods are sent to every State and Territory between

DESIGN FOR STAIR FINISH.

the Hudson River and the Pacific coast, including the Southern States, while they also have some trade in New England.

ORNAMENTAL HARD WOOD FLOORS.

The use of thin hard wood floors, made in a wide variety of ornamental designs and pleasing patterns, is undoubtedly becoming very popular. A portion of the rooms, at least, of every modern house, arranged in good taste to give the largest degree of comfort, should be provided with these hard wood floors, walls, wainscoting, or ceilings. Our illustration represents a few samples of this class of work, such as is produced in the finest grades by the Interior Hardwood Co., of Indianapolis, Ind. Such floors, when well laid, are permanent and improve with age, forming a part of the house decorations. They can be laid on old floors as well as new, the work being done by any good carpenter, and when down require less care than carpets, banishing moths and being decidedly more healthful. The strips and blocks are fastened together in slabs of convenient size, and nailed down with small-headed brads. They are finished with wax or shellac, heightening the natural beauty of the wood, which is well brought out by the contrasting colors of the different varieties employed, and the weaving effects produced by changing the direction of the grain in the perfectly made joints. Such floors are by no means new, having been in use for centuries in palaces and homes of the wealthy in Europe, but at no former period have they been so well made at so moderate cost as they can now be had for.

THE University of Paris was founded by King Philip II. about 1200.

Large Winding Partition Doors.

A pair of doors of unusual size and novel construction have recently been placed in a church in Paterson, N. J. Filling an opening 39 ft. in width by 11 ft. in height, they can be rolled back at either side and concealed in pilasters 22 ft. by 24 ft. square. This ingenious method of disposing of a door or partition was invented and is now manufactured in Worcester, Mass., a city noted for the variety of its inventions and products. The doors are constructed of narrow strips of wood, securely hinged together by a series of concealed "table leaf joints," and when pushed back, wind about a steel spindle in the pilaster or door casing. The entire width of a room is thus left free when the doors are open, and when they are closed, what was, apparently, one large hall is divided into two separate apartments by handsome, substantial doors, as close fitting and as sound-proof as any door can be. This would seem to be a feature greatly to be desired in the construction of large assembly rooms and double parlors. The same principle is applicable to small doors and to inside blinds, which can be concealed in the side casings, thus not interfering with draperies or curtains.

The "Alberene" Laundry Tub.

The value of a trade mark as a means of protecting not only the manufacturer, but the community at large, is well illustrated in the case of the Albemarle Soapstone Company (recently at 4 and 6 Peck Slip, New York) with their "Alberene" stone tub.

Their business was started at a time when there was in the minds of many a well founded prejudice against the use of soapstone for the manufacture of laundry tubs (well founded because of the poor grade of stone used and the lack of care in putting the tubs together). Recognizing the weakness of the soapstone then in use in the market, and confident of the real value of their own product, they introduced the most improved methods in the manufacture and handling of their goods, and by dint of energy and push have worked up a large trade in this one specialty.

At the start they adopted the trade mark "Alberene" which now appears plainly upon the face of every tub which leaves their hands, thus protecting not only the manufacturer, but the buying public. The company have recently found it necessary to move from their old quarters to a new and more commodious location at 393 Pearl Street, New York.

House Heating and Ventilation.

The Abram Cox Stove Company, Philadelphia, have recently issued a handsome quarto of 112 pages, in paper covers, on water and air circulation in heating and ventilating. Their special form of heating apparatus, known as the Novelty Circulator, is fully described, with illustrations, table of dimensions, prices, etc., and the book has an introductory chapter on circulation by John J. Hogan. The book also contains a large amount of technical information touching practical heating and ventilating which cannot fail to be of interest to the architect, builder, steam fitter and house owner.

NOLAN'S HOT WATER AND STEAM HEATER.

The accompanying engraving shows a novel hot water and steam heater, invented and manufactured by Wm. E. Nolan, of No. 94 Quay Street, Brooklyn, N. Y., which the manufacturer claims has established a record for economy and durability. It is very simple in construction, consisting of a series of hollow annular conical castings, arranged one within the other, leaving an intervening flue space and exposing a very large amount of surface to the direct action of the fire. The

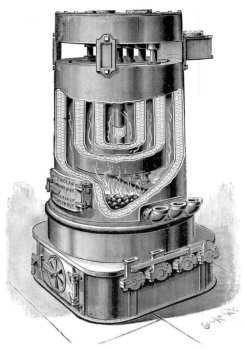

NOLAN'S HOT WATER AND STEAM HEATER.

outer annular section is longer than the other, forming a water leg and inclosing the fire pot from side to side. The grate is of the rocking and dumping pattern, and all the parts are arranged for simple and quick manipulation.

The Crushing Resistance of Bricks.

The Department of Experimental Engineering, Sibley College, recently received from an Ithaca manufacturer four samples of brick to be tested. All the brick were tested entire and on edge, as they would be used for the purpose of paving. The sides were dressed to parallel planes on an emery wheel, so that the bearing should be uniform over every part. A single layer of thick paper was placed between the surfaces of the brick and the testing machine.

The repressed brick exhibits the greatest crushing strength of any brick on record; it is also superior in strength to sandstone, and fully four-fifths as strong as granite. The tests of stone are usually made on cubes one or two inches on each edge, and such tests show a greater strength per square inch than would be the case if the form of the block was like that of the brick tested; so if the proper allowance for form should be made, there is little doubt but that the crushing strength of the best brick would compare favorably with the strongest granite. The best results from ordinary pressed brick usually show a strength from 6,000 to 10,000 pounds per square inch, so that the other bricks tested, considering the quality and method of manufacture, show an extraordinary strength. No test could be made for wearing qualities, but the brick exhibit, so far as can be determined by striking them with a hammer, sufficient toughness to make them a superior article of paving brick.

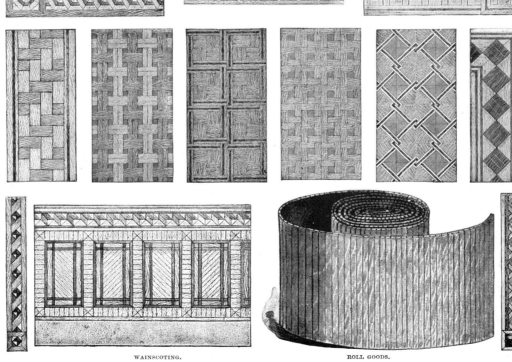

WAINSCOTING.   ROLL GOODS.

PATTERNS FOR PARQUETRY FLOORS AND BORDERS.

First Floor Plan.

Second Floor Plan.

RESIDENCE OF CHAS. E. DICKENSON, DENVER, COLO.

SCIENTIFIC AMERICAN

Copyright by Munn & Co., 1894.

Entered at the Post Office of New York as Second Class Matter.

ARCHITECTS AND BUILDERS EDITION

Vol. XVII.

Subscription, $2.50 a Year.

NEW YORK, FEBRUARY, 1894.

Single Copies, 25 Cents.

No. 2.

MOORISH DRAWING ROOM FURNITURE.

MOORISH BEDROOM FURNITURE.

MOORISH HALL WITH FRETTED ARCH.

MOORISH DIVAN ON HALF STAIR LANDING.

100

EXAMPLES OF INTERIOR DECORATION AND FURNITURE IN THE MOORISH STYLE.

INDEX

102